The Catholics in Caroline England

The Catholics
in
Caroline England

MARTIN J. HAVRAN

STANFORD UNIVERSITY PRESS

Stanford California

1962

Stanford University Press
Stanford, California
London: Oxford University Press

Library of Congress Catalog Card Number 62-9561

Printed in the United States of America

Published with the assistance of the
FORD FOUNDATION

For my Clara

PREFACE

THE ELIZABETHAN and Jacobean Catholics have had many historians, but the Caroline Catholics have been paid little attention, perhaps because it has been more or less commonly accepted that they enjoyed almost total relief from the deprivations imposed by the penal laws. Most historians of the early seventeenth century have accepted the thesis that Charles's marriage to the Catholic Henrietta Maria of France, the absence of an anti-Catholic Parliament for eleven years, and Charles's dislike of religious persecution, permitted Catholics to enjoy unusual religious freedom during the 1630's. The results of the research for this book, undertaken partly to test the validity of this thesis, suggest that it has been based primarily on the Catholic upper classes in the home counties, particularly around London. The generality of Catholics and their priests, about 360,000 in all, have been all but ignored. Moreover, scholars have heretofore stressed the official actions taken by the Government through statutes, orders by the Privy Council, and royal proclamations, even though the Crown's policy toward Catholics was not often fully implemented at the local government level. Whatever Parliament, the Council, or the King may have prescribed for the Catholics is not always an accurate barometer upon which to gauge their welfare.

It is very difficult to determine how the generality of Catholics fared. Most of them wrote little and preserved less because they were quite understandably wary of incriminating themselves. Some of the leading clergy carried on a lively correspondence among fellow missionaries and with colleagues abroad, but they often intimated more than they forthrightly asserted out of fear that their letters might fall into unsympathetic hands. Accordingly, one must piece together bits of information from a wide variety of sources, and even then the result is often the indeterminate rather than the positive conclusion.

My principal sources of information have been the letters of the Catholic clergy and laity in the A Series and the Roman Letters of the Westminster Archives, Archbishop's House, London. I have also relied on the Privy Council Registers, and the Roman and Paris Transcripts in the Public Record Office. Manuscripts and pamphlets in the British Museum, the Bodleian Library at Oxford, and the Berkshire Record Office at Reading proved invaluable, especially in determining Protestant attitudes toward the Catholics. Frequent use was made of the Calendars of Domestic State Papers, which are quite good for this period. The calendared dispatches of the Venetian ambassadors, and the Tuscan ambassador's reports, when used cautiously, contain information on the Catholics not to be found elsewhere. Other printed sources and secondary works that have been cited in the Notes are included for the most part in the Bibliography, which is intended to be selective, not exhaustive.

It is a pleasure to acknowledge the gracious assistance of friends who have given generously of their knowledge and time that this might be a better book than I alone could have made it. I am indebted particularly to Arvel B. Erickson, Professor of History in Western Reserve University, who first directed my attention to the topic for this study, and made invaluable suggestions and corrections on the entire manuscript through several drafts. He has taught me more than formal education can ever impart. I wish to thank also the staff of the Public Record Office, especially E. K. Timings, whose familiarity with the manuscripts of that depository is astounding, and the late Stanley J. Rich, formerly superintendent at the P.R.O., whose recent death makes me even more aware of the friendship, peace of mind, and will to work that I found in his home. Dr. David M. Rogers, of the Bodleian Library, gave me the benefit of years of careful study in recusant history in a lengthy conversation one fine spring afternoon. Dr. D. M. Barrett, whose work on the religious history of Oxfordshire during the seventeenth century is well known, helped me with the Bankes Manuscripts, which she is presently calendaring. To the Reverend Bernard Fisher, archivist, and the Reverend David Norris, librarian of the Westminster Archives, I owe many thanks, not only for permission to use the manuscripts in Archbishop's House, but also for providing such pleasant rooms in which to read them over several months. Research at the British Museum and the Berkshire Record Office in England and at the Western Reserve University and Cleveland Public Libraries here was greatly facilitated by the careful attention of devoted personnel. Several of my colleagues at Kent State, especially R. H. Jones and J. M. Powell, made helpful comments on portions of the manuscript. I owe much to my wife and parents, whose constant encouragement provided intangible strength in weaker moments.

This book could not have been completed without the generous financial aid provided by the Social Science Research Council, which made possible an extended residence in England. I wish to single out particularly Dr. Elbridge Sibley, executive associate of the Council, whose kindness and encouragement have meant a great deal to me. The preparation of the final draft of this book was financed by a timely gift from the Kent State University Alumni Fund. Portions of this study have appeared, in somewhat different form, in *The Catholic Historical Review, The American Ecclesiastical Review,* and *Recusant History.*   M. J. H.

RAVENNA, OHIO
October 1961

CONTENTS

The Catholics in Caroline England

Chapter One

THE LETTER OF THE LAW

THE CHEERING THRONG of Londoners who, on November 23, 1558, tramped several miles out of the city to greet their new Queen, Elizabeth, did so out of more than mere curiosity or love of pageantry. Their exuberant welcome manifested the popular reaction to the excesses of Mary Tudor's reign. Since Elizabeth was neither a daughter of Rome nor a pawn of Philip II of Spain, her ascent to the throne heralded the end of English subordination to Spanish politics and freedom for Protestants from religious persecution. Although many Englishmen welcomed the change in monarch, few must have been as comforted as those peers and gentry who had built their family titles and landed wealth upon the ruination of the monasteries that followed Henry VIII's break with Rome.[1] Of course, since Elizabeth had not shown a strong preference for any religious group, few could be sure at first what she would do about religion, and, indeed, for a time the religious convictions and practices of Catholics as well as Protestants went unchallenged by the Crown. But within nine months of Elizabeth's coronation on January 15, 1559, she and Parliament set their policy. Through the Acts of Supremacy and Uniformity, Parliament established an English Protestant national church under a Protestant Queen and made disloyal dissenters of obdurate

[1] Numbered notes will be found at the back of the book, pp. 161–86.

Catholics. Elizabeth replaced seven of Mary's councillors with Protestants and excluded from office all Catholic bishops who had refused the oath of supremacy.

Most of the Catholic lower clergy accepted the reinstitution of Protestantism, as did the majority of their parishioners. But a small minority of staunch Catholics resisted the Elizabethan religious settlement. To this resistance the Government responded by enacting a series of penal laws[2] that affected the family life, the economic welfare, the personal liberty, and the peace of mind of practicing Catholics (and religious dissenters in general). The purpose of this chapter is to describe, as briefly as possible, the nature of these Elizabethan and Jacobean penal laws.

From 1559 to her excommunication by Pius V (*Regnans in excelsis,* 1570), Elizabeth endeavored to induce Catholic conformity through light fines and occasional imprisonments, hoping thereby to avert full-scale persecution. The Northern Rebellion of 1569, in which Catholics were involved, and the return to England of Catholic missionaries after 1574 awakened privy councillors and Parliament to the threat of Catholic rebellion. Elizabeth remained calm, telling her subjects that so long as they conformed outwardly to the law by attending Anglican services regularly, no one need fear that his religious convictions would be challenged. Even so, stricter penal laws were enacted in 1571 and 1581 which effectively thwarted the mild Catholic reaction to the Elizabethan settlement. Events during the 1580's, including the assassination of William the Silent, the Babington Plot, and the culmination of the grand "Enterprise" in the Armada of 1588, did not lessen the apprehension of Elizabethan statesmen about the seditious designs of scheming Jesuits and treasonous recusants.[3] Each new crisis demanded fresh penal legislation, as in 1585 and 1587. Beyond doubt, the anti-Catholic laws would have been harsher but for the restraining hand of Elizabeth.

Parliament reinstituted Protestantism through two statutes passed in 1559, one acknowledging the supremacy of Elizabeth in the English Church, the other establishing uniformity of worship.[4] The Act of Supremacy named the Queen as Supreme Governor of the Church of England and provided her with the means to exercise ecclesiastical jurisdiction; it also imposed an oath of supremacy[5] upon ecclesiastical and secular officers (extended in 1563 to include those taking Holy Orders, university graduates, schoolmasters, and lawyers), who were to acknowledge "that the Queen's Highness is the only supreme governor of this realm," and to "utterly renounce and forsake all foreign jurisdictions, powers, superiorities and authorities."[6] Catholics, who necessarily recognized the Pope's spiritual sovereignty, could not in good conscience take such an oath.

The Act of Uniformity, which may be regarded as the first penal law, revived the second Act of Uniformity of Edward VI. The Prayer Book of 1552, with slight additions and alterations, became the recognized standard text for "celebrating of the Lord's Supper openly or privily, or matins, evensong, administration of the sacraments, or other open prayers." Any clergyman who refused to use the Prayer Book forfeited a year's income and was imprisoned for six months, and upon second offense was imprisoned for one year and deprived of his benefices. Furthermore, any written or spoken criticism of the Book brought a fine of 100 marks for a first offense and 400 marks for a second. Failure to attend Anglican service on Sundays and Holy Days carried a shilling fine for each absence.[7]

An Act of 1563[8] strengthened and expanded the Act of Supremacy by imposing the penalties of *Praemunire*,[9] and required that minor officials and university graduates take the oath of supremacy. Although Parliament enacted no penal legislation thereafter for eight years, religious uniformity was rigorously enforced in the interval, especially from 1567 to 1569.[10]

Elizabeth faced the first true crisis of her reign in 1569. Mary

Stuart, the Catholic Queen of Scots, unable to resolve her quarrel with the rebellious Protestant lords of Scotland following her marriage to Lord Darnley, escaped imprisonment at their hands in May 1568 by fleeing to England. Elizabeth granted Mary asylum, even though in Catholic eyes Elizabeth was illegitimate and Mary was the rightful Queen of England. Certain northern earls quickly took up Mary's cause, and some Catholics joined them in the quickly suppressed Northern Rebellion of 1569. Though the Catholics as a whole had been loyal, Catholic complicity in rebellion, and the unfortunate excommunication of Elizabeth by Pius V soon afterwards, prompted Parliament to enact new penal legislation.

The excommunication of Elizabeth simplified matters for the majority of English Catholics, who had scrupulously wavered over the treasonous and moral implications of revolt so long as Elizabeth was not formally declared a heretic. They were now faced with the choice of becoming traitors for refusing to recognize Elizabeth's claim to the throne, or of being excommunicated by their church. The necessity of this choice was given emphasis by Elizabeth's increasing deference to Government men like Sir William Cecil, the Principal Secretary, who sought to prove that good Catholics were automatically bad Englishmen.[11]

The result of the Northern Rebellion and the excommunication of Elizabeth was the enactment of three penal laws in 1571. The first of these Acts pronounced it to be high treason for anyone to question Elizabeth's rightful place as Queen, or to regard her as a heretic, schismatic, or usurper. The second Act was directed at papal authority to issue bulls in England. After July 1, anyone who received, propagated, or employed written or printed orders emanating from Rome or its agents was guilty of treason. Anyone who aided such a person became liable to the disabilities of *Praemunire,* as were persons who imported "crosses, pictures, beads or suchlike vain and superstitious things from the bishop or see of Rome."[12] The third law of 1571, the so-called Fugitive Act, forbade dissenters, including Catholics, to leave the country for the purpose of evading the penalties under the penal laws, or to be trained as missionaries. Accordingly everyone going abroad was to procure a license, and emigrants already on the Continent were to return to England and conform to the Establishment within six months of a proclamation to that effect. Failure to do so was punishable by permanent forfeiture of the emigrant's land and goods.[13]

The Government had good reason to be concerned about clandestine emigration to the Continent, for there had been several waves of moderate to heavy Catholic emigration during the Elizabethan period. During the first ten years of the reign the refugees consisted primarily of the surviving members of the various regular orders that were dispersed at the dissolution of the monasteries. Some secular priests, some dons and students of Oxford and Cambridge Universities, and a few laymen, mostly sons of noble families, also left England at that time. A smaller but important body of Catholics who had been involved in the Northern Rebellion emigrated to towns in the Low Countries and France, mainly Brussels, Louvain, Antwerp, Bruges, and Douay. More Catholics left to escape the disabilities imposed by the penal laws of 1571; others after the execution of Mary Stuart in 1587. Thereafter Catholic emigration gradually diminished. [14]

Not unexpectedly, the activity of these English Catholic refugees centered mainly around education. Colleges for English youths sprang up at Douay, Saint-Omer, and elsewhere to train hundreds of priests for the English mission.[15] The small band of about one hundred seculars in England in 1585 swelled to over five hundred by 1597.[16] Of course, not all the exiles became priests or nuns. Whether religious or laymen, most of the emigrants left their fortunes behind and drew upon Spanish and papal pensions, or upon money sent by solicitous relatives.[17]

The return of large numbers of Catholic missionaries naturally worried the Government. Since they could not survive in England without the support of patrons, an Act was passed to root out the missionaries by punishing their benefactors.[18] Accordingly, the penal law of 1581 strengthened the Acts of 1571 (bulls and foreign emigration) by imposing the death penalty for high treason on priests who proselytized among the Protestant community, and forbade Catholics to sustain missionaries or to keep secret their work on pain of indefinite terms of imprisonment.

In addition, the law of 1581 put pressure on contumacious recusants who refused to conform to the Establishment. If they were caught attending mass, they faced imprisonment for a year and a fine of from 100 to 200 marks. Still more severe was the provision that imposed a ruinous fine of £20 a month on Catholics who missed Anglican service on Sundays and Holy Days for more than one month. At the same time, the fine of a shilling a Sunday remained in force. It is apparent that the Government hoped to induce conformity by making it virtually impossible for most recusants to pay the fines. Furthermore, with this Act the Government clearly instituted, by practice if not by intent, a long-term policy of treating recusancy as a fruitful source of revenue. The money gathered from fines was to be divided in three equal parts among the Crown, the parish in which the penal laws had been violated, and the informer who caused a recusant to be convicted.[19] Unhappily, as we shall see, the financial rewards offered for informing were, for the most part, sufficiently large to enable a gang of scoundrels to make a living at it.

A new penal law in 1585[20] differed from the earlier laws of 1559, 1563, and 1581 primarily in its emphasis on priests, whose very presence in England was now regarded as an act of high treason. The preamble to the new Act set forth Parliament's conviction that the missionaries were planning to "stire up and move sedition, rebellion and open hostility," at the expense of the Queen and the Established Church. Although scholars to-day may doubt whether the English Catholic clergy posed a threat to national security, Elizabeth, her councillors, and her Parliaments had no such doubts.[21]

The new Act required all English-born Catholic clergy who had been ordained abroad since the Feast of St. John the Baptist, 1559, to leave the kingdom within forty days of the prorogation of Parliament then in session. Priests who remained beyond that time, or subsequently returned, were guilty of high treason, a crime punishable by hanging, drawing, and quartering. Persons who knowingly relieved, comforted, aided, or boarded a cleric would be charged with felony. English students enrolled in continental seminaries were to return within six months, and to submit to the Establishment within two days of debarkation by taking the oath of supremacy before the bishop of the diocese or two justices of the peace of the county in which they landed. Englishmen could not assist seminarians on the Continent either financially or in any other way under pain of the penalties of *Praemunire*. Through such heavy punishments against priests, seminarians, and their benefactors, the Government hoped to starve out the emigrants and force their return, thus killing the missionary movement.[22]

In addition, everyone was bound to report the whereabouts of a Catholic priest to the constabulary within twelve days of acquiring such information, on pain of fine and imprisonment. Justices of the peace who kept secret the residence of a priest for over twenty-eight days incurred a 200-mark fine. Even conformed recusants could not come within ten miles of the Queen without permission, on possible pain of death. The Government did indeed restrict the foreign travel of every Englishman, but Catholics were watched more closely than others. In effect, no one except mariners and merchants could leave England without a license signed by either the Queen or four privy councillors.[23]

Violators of the penal laws of 1581 and 1585—"prisoners for

religion," as they were called—filled the London jails. Inadequate records preclude an accurate count of Catholics imprisoned in that city for recusancy, but the number was undoubtedly larger than the prison lists for 1583, 1584, 1586, and 1588 would suggest. Philip Hughes concludes that the contemporary estimates of the Spanish ambassador and Father Robert Persons are unrealistic, and that the certificates of the keepers of prisons are inaccurate: the prison list for 1583, for instance, gives the names of 103 Catholics, including only twenty-nine priests and four women, and the list for 1588 includes seventy-three Catholic prisoners, only thirteen of them priests.[24] Other Catholics undoubtedly would have joined them following the discovery of the Babington Plot in August 1586, but for the work of the executioner. The brainchild of a Derbyshire gentleman recently turned Catholic, the plot involved the rescue of the imprisoned Queen of Scots; her execution in the following February, after conviction under the penal law of 1585, temporarily removed one cause of Catholic conspiracy.

Oddly enough, the penal laws of 1587 apparently had little relation to the Babington Plot and the beheading of Mary. In the new Act, Parliament sought to correct abuses that had crept into the enforcement and collection of the £20 monthly fines against recusants authorized under the Act of 1581. Hoping to save their estates from confiscation by the Government to satisfy arrears in these fines, some recusants made conveyances of their property while, at the same time, continuing to derive benefit from it. The Act voided all such conveyances of property made by recusants since the accession of Elizabeth. Moreover, recusants were to pay their £20 monthly fines regularly at Easter and Michaelmas Terms directly to the Exchequer. The penalty for not doing so was severe: "if default be made in any part of any payment," the Queen could "take, seize, and enjoy all the goods and two parts as well of all the lands, tenements and hereditaments, leases and farms of such offenders . . . leaving the third part only . . . for the maintenance and relief" of the recusant and his family, until such time as he conformed. This provision of the Act not only trapped wealthy recusants who sought to avoid paying fines but also penalized less affluent recusants who could not meet the ruinous fines. In addition, the Act was designed to root out "all frauds and delays heretofore practiced . . . [by justices of the peace and local courts] to the hindrance of the due and speedy execution of [the Act of 1581]." Accordingly, the justices were ordered to certify to the Exchequer before the following Easter Term all convictions for recusancy that had not so far been reported.[25]

In the six years between the death of Mary Stuart in 1587 and the meeting of Parliament early in 1593, the zeal of Catholic missionaries in England and the resolve of obdurate recusants remained undiminished. The Parliament of 1593 accordingly enacted two new measures to strengthen the laws against missionaries and to immobilize recusants.

By the first Act,[26] persons over the age of sixteen who refused to attend Anglican service at least once a month, or who, beginning forty days after the then current session of Parliament ended, sought to dissuade any Englishman from obeying the ecclesiastical laws, would be jailed "without bail or mainprise until they shall conform." Protestant dissenters were required to conform by formal submission before a bishop, minister, or justice of the peace within three months of conviction under the Act or abjure the realm. But "no popish recusant or semi-convert shall be compelled or bound to abjure by virtue of this act." The Act also stipulated that since "every person having house and family is in duty bound to have special regard to the good government and ordering of the same," heads of families, after having been warned by the ecclesiastical or judicial authorities, could not harbor a recusant on pain of £10 fine. However, this provision was not applicable to the wives, children, and other close relatives of recusants who were heads of families. Violators of this Act would forfeit all their property and goods for life, but their heirs could inherit their estates and their wives could retain their dowries.

By the so-called Five-Mile Act,[27] the second of two penal laws passed in 1593, Parliament endeavored to control the travel of recusants. Catholics were prone to "secretly wander and shift from place to place . . . to corrupt and seduce her Majesty's subjects," the preamble states, while "hiding their most detestable and devilish purposes under a false pretext of religion." In a move to combat these "traitorous and most dangerous conspiracies," recusants over the age of sixteen were commanded to return to their permanent homes and never thereafter venture beyond five miles of them except by license. Infraction of the law carried a penalty of loss of goods, chattels, and property for life. Recusants without permanent abode were to reside at their birthplace, where they should register, within twenty days of arrival, with a constable, headborough, or tithingman of the town, and with the minister or curate of the parish. Justices of the peace learned of these new registrants in their districts at the Quarter Sessions through the local officers of Government. Recusants who failed to return to their homes, or who returned but would not submit and conform to the Establishment, and who were without property yielding at least a twenty-mark profit annually, were to leave the kingdom. To disobey an order to leave, or to return without permission, was a felony.

The Act also required a person suspected of being a Catholic priest "to answer directly and truly [to duly constituted examiners] whether he be a jesuit, or a seminary or massing priest." If such a person refused to confess his priesthood, he would be imprisoned indefinitely without benefit of bail until he did so.

The foregoing penalties against recusants could be discharged if they went to divine services and submitted to the ecclesiastical laws before being convicted under the Act. In submitting, a recusant had to take a prescribed oath acknowledging that he had offended God by denying the lawful Government of the realm, and by breaking the laws requiring church attendance. Moreover, the conforming recusant was to renounce the authority of the Pope in England, and promise to recognize and observe all the laws and statutes governing uniformity of worship. The officiating clergyman had to record the submission and pass on the information to his bishop within ten days.

The laws of 1593 were the last enacted against Catholic recusants during Elizabeth's reign. Her Government had enforced religious uniformity by imposing financial and corporal penalties, and though its work had been accomplished without much cruelty toward recusants, the threat to their well-being could never be far from their minds. Government pressure and the pressure of conscience brought other pressures in their train. Some Englishmen regarded Catholics as traitors and contemptible cowards whose allegiance to Rome outweighed their loyalty to the Queen. And not least of all, Catholics undoubtedly suffered the visceral tensions, the frustrations, and the mental depression of those whose principles are under attack.

It was no wonder that Catholics heaved a deep sigh of relief when Elizabeth died, and looked forward to the accession of James I. Although the new King had been brought up as a Calvinist and nourished an abiding aversion for the Catholic Church, the Pope, and the priesthood (he especially abhorred the Jesuits), he had been moderate toward the Catholic Scots, even after some had plotted rebellion against him, and there was good reason to expect that he would be equally moderate toward the English Catholics. James's wife, Anne, had become a Catholic convert in Scotland, and James himself hoped that a religious compromise could be reached with the Catholic Church.

James had no intention at first of treating the English Catholics badly. The recusancy fines were collected as usual in May 1603, but they were suspended thereafter for about a year and a half. Of the lay Catholics the King asked loyalty and outward conformity to the Church of England. But the Catholic priests James could not trust.[28] He did not trouble the Catholic laity for almost two years, but he sought to prevent the education of young English Catholics in Continental seminaries. Accordingly, Parliament passed a statute in 1603[29] which obliged students to return to England within a year on pain of £100 fine and loss of property. No one under twenty-one could thereafter go abroad without the written consent of the King or six privy councillors. Port officials who permitted Catholics to slip by were to be dismissed and fined. Owners of ships that ferried Catholics to the Continent were to lose their vessels, and sea captains their jobs and property. Parliament also provided more carefully for the punishment of teachers who were not certified by a bishop. Recusant schoolmasters and their employers were liable to fines of forty shillings for each day they taught. Half of all the money raised through this Act was to go to the King,[30] and the other half could be acquired by those who would sue for it in the courts of record in Westminister "by action of debt, bill, plaint or information."

James was under constant pressure from the Anglican bishops, the judges, and the Puritans to abandon his policy of leniency. When it became clear that this policy would not be successful in bringing about conformity, James yielded. He reactivated the Elizabethan anti-Catholic laws in February 1605 and ordered rigorous enforcement of them. Within the year the Gunpower Plot shocked the nation,[31] and the reality of Catholic conspiracy could no longer be questioned. Although James rightly recognized that the Catholic community as a whole was loyal, he could not forget that the plotters meant to kill him. As for Parliament, the fact that only a handful of conspirators were involved signified little to the intended victims, and parliamentary leaders at once decided on a general policy of reprisal.

The result was the two penal laws of 1606, the most disabling religious legislation promulgated since 1581. The preamble to the first Act[32] made clear Parliament's growing apprehension over papist treachery:

> For as much as it is found by daily experience, that his Majesty's subjects that adhere in their hearts to the popish religion, by the infection drawn from thence, and by the wicked and devilish counsel of jesuits, seminarians, and other like persons dangerous to the church and state, are so far perverted in the point of their loyalty . . . unto the King's majesty, and the crown of England, as they are ready to entertain and execute any treasonous conspiracies and practice, as evidently appears by that more than barbarous and horrible attempt to have blown up with gunpower the King, Queen, Prince, lords and commons in the house of parliament assembled, tending to the utter submersion of the whole state, lately undertaken by the instigation of jesuits and seminarians, and instructed by them to that purpose, which attempt by the goodness of almighty God . . . [was averted] (2) and where divers persons popishly affected, do nevertheless, the better to cover and hide their false hearts and with the more safety to attend the opportunity to execute their mischievous designs, repair sometimes to church, to escape the penalty of the laws in that behalf provided.

The "church papist," to which Part 2 of this preamble makes reference, was a problem to Anglicans and Catholics alike. As one contemporary put it, such a person "parts his religion betwixt his conscience and his purse, and comes to Church not to serve God but the King." Such pseudo-Catholics frequently took the oath of allegiance, instituted in 1606, and attended Anglican services as often as the law required, but they carefully avoided the Anglican Communion in the hope of retaining their ties with the Roman Church. Some "church papists" belonged to old Catholic families that had conformed up to a point to the state religion; others considered themselves Catholics even though they compromised their religious principles by submitting to escape fines. There is no way of knowing how many there were, but their number probably grew in late Elizabethan and early Jacobean times. The fact that the first of the two penal statutes passed in 1606 required Anglican converts to take Communion once a year is evidence that the Government was concerned with more than a few "church papists."

This first Act of 1606 also contained an oath of allegiance by which the Government sought to distinguish between loyal and disloyal Catholics. A loyal Catholic, James believed, would willingly acknowledge him as rightful sovereign, deny the authority of the Pope to depose excommunicated princes, and renounce the abhorrent doctrine that heretical kings could be lawfully murdered.[33] That James suffered an occasional twinge of fear at that thought is not surprising. Plots against Elizabeth had arisen, and the Cardinal of Como, writing to a nuncio, Filippo Sega, at Madrid in 1580, reported the Pope's opinion relative to the possibility of assassinating Elizabeth. At that time, Gregory XIII (d. 1585) reputedly believed that "that guilty woman [Elizabeth] of England rules over two such noble kingdoms of Christendom and is the cause of so much injury to the catholic faith, . . . there is no doubt that whosoever sends her out of the world with the pious intention of doing God service, not only does not sin but gains merit."[34] Although few Catholics could have condoned regicide, the attempt on James's life in the plot of 1605 undoubtedly convinced many Englishmen that the Romanists would kill the King should the Pope command them to do so.

Catholics of easy conscience readily took the oath, but scrupulous Catholics, although loyal to the Crown, were greatly troubled. The oath required Catholics to accept by implication the proposition that the Pope was not in every way spiritually sovereign, for among Catholics his authority to excommunicate was explicit. If a Catholic took the oath, he contravened two briefs by Paul V which forbade taking such an oath; if a Catholic refused the oath, he incurred the disabilities of *Praemunire,* at the least. James intended that the oath should distinguish between papists who were obedient to civil authority and "the perverse disciples of the Powder Treason." The oath was imposed upon Catholics of all classes, but, in general, the lower-class Catholics in the southern sections of the country felt the pressure of the law more acutely than their more affluent coreligionists, especially in the North.[35] Little wonder that the oath stirred up a hornet's nest within the Catholic community and precipitated a pamphlet war between James and the Papacy. The Jesuits resolved the quandary of whether to take the oath by mental reservation, also called the doctrine of equivocation, by which the oath might be recited without intention of being bound by it. Others, such as Father Thomas Preston, George Blackwell the archpriest, and Leander Jones, tried to convince Catholics that the King meant them only to swear civil obedience to him, not to renounce papal jurisdiction. The issue not only divided the clergy, but also made impossible a compromise over religion between England and Rome throughout the early Stuart period.

The second penal law of 1606[36] further restricted the right of a recusant to travel or to practice a profession. Section xii of the Five-Mile Act of 1593 was changed to require the signatures of four justices of the peace to validate travel beyond the five-mile limit. Recusants, except those in business or trade, could neither reside in London nor venture to within closer than ten miles of the city under penalty of £100. Law, pharmacy, and medicine were closed to recusants; they could not take a degree from Oxford or Cambridge; and they could not be officers in either the trainbands or the navy. A Protestant who took a Catholic wife was denied public office of any kind, although it would appear that in practice this provision was relaxed in a number of cases.

The same Act penalized the partners in mixed marriages. The widowed Catholic wife of a Protestant forfeited two-thirds of her dowry as well as the right to be the executrix of his will. Men who married outside the Church of England lost any claim to their wives' property. Children born to recusants were to be baptized only by Anglican clergymen, within a month of their birth, on pain of £100 fine. Persons who buried a recusant anywhere except in an Anglican cemetery forfeited £20. The usual provision forbidding Catholic education abroad remained unchanged, as did the restrictions governing the importation of popish primers, psalters, rosaries, catechisms, missals, and breviaries. Constables and churchwardens were instructed to watch closely for "relics of popery" and to burn any that were found. Parliament also ordered that crucifixes taken from recusants be defaced at the Quarter Sessions and be returned to them so mutilated. Search parties were commanded to confiscate, upon a warrant signed by four justices of the peace, the armor, gunpowder, and munitions of a recusant, leaving him only such weapons as might be required for his personal protection. Confiscated armor and weapons were to be stored at the recusant's expense.

According to the first Act of 1606, only those who had been convicted for recusancy, who had failed to receive the Anglican Communion twice a year, or who admitted that they were recusants were obliged to take the oath of allegiance. A law of 1610, entitled "An act for administering the Oath of Allegiance, and reformation of Married Women Recusants," widened the field. Now "all and every person and persons, as well ecclesiastical as temporal," over eighteen years of age, regardless of sex, social or financial status, or station in life, had to take the oath. The penalties of *Praemunire* were to be imposed against anyone who would refuse the oath, except female married recusants—formerly exempt from most of the penalties under the penal laws—who could now be imprisoned for refusing the oath. Their incarceration could be avoided, however, if their husbands paid £10 a month or gave up one-third of their lands for their wives' recusancy.[37]

Such were the penal laws affecting Catholics during the reigns of Elizabeth and James. Under James, proclamations for the enforcement of the laws appeared regularly, as in 1606, 1621, and 1624, but to little effect. A total of seventeen priests and six laymen, excluding the Gunpower Plot conspirators, suffered death because of religion during the Jacobean period. On the whole, however, most Catholics escaped the stigma of recusancy and the penalties it brought. Despite parliamentary pressure James showed more leniency toward the Catholic laity than they might have expected, and Catholic persecution was diminished during the last years of his reign, largely as a result of his sporadic negotiations with Catholic Spain and France over a marriage treaty. But Protestant memories and prejudices ran deeper than reasons of state. As James rushed into the proposed alliance with Spain in 1623, his Protestant subjects looked on with grave apprehension and distrust of the Catholics.

Chapter Two

UNREALIZED HOPES

B Y 1623, TWENTY YEARS after his ascendancy to the coveted English throne, James I had degenerated into a sullen, sick, and prematurely aged man. Gout and arthritis tormented his body and plagued his spirit. Dread of assassination by Spanish-bred Catholics needlessly worried him, and the family affairs of George Villiers, the handsome royal favorite, seemed to interest him quite as much as matters of state. Above all, he had lost touch with the pulse of public opinion, which had turned against him as a result of monopolies and purveyances, long periods of arbitrary personal rule, insensitivity to demands for the suppression of Catholicism, and the proposed Spanish alliance.

The Thirty Years' War, from which James wished to stand aloof, touched England when Frederick, Elector of the Palatinate, who had married James's daughter Elizabeth in 1613, was deprived of his throne. Parliament called for war against Spain to restore Frederick and Elizabeth and to aid the Protestant alliance against the Hapsburgs, but James opposed a war that he felt would bring England only expense and defeat. Instead, he sought to bind England and Spain in an alliance that would effect the withdrawal of Spanish troops from the Palatinate and the restoration of its prince. Accordingly, in 1622 James renewed in earnest the long-standing negotiations with Spain for a marriage between Prince Charles and the Infanta

Maria. Spain had no intention of sacrificing its political ambitions in Europe to placate the anxiety of the English Protestant King over his wayward children. Yet King Philip IV and his chief minister, Count Olivares, showed interest in the marriage in the hope of forestalling active English assistance in the cause of European Protestantism. Count Gondomar, the Spanish ambassador to England, worked hard for the marriage to ensure English neutrality in the war. Gondomar seems also to have believed that the marriage might eventually bring about the reconversion of the English people to Catholicism.[1]

A marriage between Charles and Maria involved serious religious differences. Spain insisted that the penal code be repealed and that full liberty of worship be permitted the English Catholics. The Infanta was to have a public church staffed by a bishop and priests of her own choosing, and complete control of the Catholic education of any children born of the union with Charles. Such conditions should have turned James against a Spanish alliance, but thoughts of a substantial dowry and of the peaceful restoration of Elizabeth and Frederick so filled his mind that he half promised to accept the terms, without realizing their impact upon English public opinion and subsequent religious policy.[2]

The marriage negotiations proceeded slowly, and Charles was an impatient suitor. In an unguarded moment James agreed that Buckingham and Charles should go to Spain to woo the Infanta in person. On second thought, James pleaded with his "sweet boys" to stay. But Buckingham and Charles got their way as usual and left London incognito as Tom and Jack Smith on February 17, 1623, with Francis Cottington and Endymion Porter, amid James's hysterical cries that he would never see them again.

The four vagabonds traveled by way of Paris, where Princess Henrietta Maria, the gay younger sister of Louis XIII, caught her first glimpse of Charles. Their unexpected arrival in Madrid

startled the Spanish Court as much as it annoyed Sir John
Digby, the English ambassador, whose careful negotiations toward a treaty giving advantage to England now had less chance
of success. The Spanish received Charles coldly but politely,
and bargaining over the treaty terms went on inconclusively
through the spring and early summer. Meanwhile, the love-
starved Prince and his ever present Steenie sat through formal
receptions and dinners without once being left alone with the
Infanta. Charles, thinking himself passionately in love with her,
became annoyed at the prudish Spaniards' obvious attempt to
keep the courtship frigid.[3]

Charles ultimately made his influence felt in various ways.
At one point he shocked the Spanish by leaping over a wall into
an orchard where the Infanta sat alone. This boyish act was no
less irresponsible than his promises to the Spanish that the penal
laws would be suspended immediately and repealed by Parliament within three years if they would consent to the marriage.

These promises led to a draft treaty, and after further negotiations the marriage treaty was signed at Madrid on July 25,
1623. Beyond doubt, Spain got the better of the bargain. No
definite agreement was reached about the dowry, the Palatinate,
or the time of marriage. James, Charles, and the privy councillors were to take oaths never to reimpose the penal laws, and
the Infanta would remain in Spain for at least a year after the
marriage. The oaths were taken on July 20, and instructions
went out to suspend the prosecution of the penal laws until the
Privy Council could formulate a general pardon for all English
Catholics. The pardon, published on September 8, stated that
in view of the impending marriage of Charles, and the desire to
treat those of the Princess Maria's faith with "all clemency and
mildness," James had resolved to lessen the severity of the anti-
Catholic laws. He further promised to pardon all recusants
within five years, and to be lenient toward them in the meantime.[4]

James encountered strong opposition to the obvious surrender to Spain. Some councillors feared that a sudden and full relaxation of the penal code would arouse "a gen'all impression if not a Mutynie" among the Protestants. Other councillors insisted that only Parliament had the right to rescind the laws. Several justices of the peace argued that pardoning the Catholics was utterly unprecedented.[5] The generality of Englishmen manifested their feelings in the wild jubilation that broke out upon Charles's safe return to London on October 6. Bonfires illuminated the city, church bells rang for hours, and rich men gave banquets in the streets for the poor.[6]

But after the trouble England had taken to arrange the marriage, it never took place. The unhappy time that Charles and Buckingham spent in Spain made them less enthusiastic about a marriage treaty that would bring no advantage to England. Charles's ardor for the Infanta turned to resentment, and Buckingham could not forget the insults he had endured. Before long, though James would have continued the Spanish alliance, anti-Spanish feeling rendered the marriage impossible. Parliament met in February 1624, debated the Spanish question, and recommended that the treaties be dissolved. Charles and Buckingham undertook preparations for war against Spain, and Parliament promised them assistance. Plans were made for a grand alliance against Spain, and to that end negotiations were begun with France toward a marriage between Charles and the Catholic Princess Henrietta Maria.[7]

A treaty with France presented difficulties, not the least of which was James's promise to Parliament on April 23, 1624, that the English Catholics would be given no concessions through any future marriage treaty. The Comte de Tillières, French minister to England, told James bluntly that King Louis would allow the marriage only upon a written guarantee of religious freedom for the English Catholics.[8] The promise to Parliament notwithstanding, James surrendered to Buckingham's insistence that the negotiations with France be speedily undertaken.

Sir Edward Herbert, the English ambassador at Paris, assured James that the religious difficulties over the marriage could be easily overcome. Viscount Kensington and the Earl of Carlisle hurried to France to learn Louis's views on the marriage and on support for England against Spain.[9]

Talks with Cardinal Richelieu commenced on June 10, 1624, and continued for several weeks. The French proposed a draft treaty requiring James to honor Henrietta's religion, to provide her with public and private chapels staffed by French clergymen, and to suspend the oath of allegiance for Catholics. Kensington, a Puritan, balked as such proposals. He objected most strenuously to an article that would have had James respect intercessions by Henrietta on behalf of English Catholics troubled by the penal laws. Moreover, the thought of an English king bowing to the whims of a fifteen-year-old French princess seemed to Kensington ludicrous, but to his amazement James accepted this condition with no more than halfhearted concern.[10]

The final draft of the treaty, consisting of thirty clauses, was ratified in December 1624.[11] It differed little in essence from the abortive Spanish treaty, with the notable exception that it went even further in theoretically protecting Catholics against persecution. Henrietta was to be allowed public chapels in each of her royal palaces, to be staffed by twenty-eight priests and a bishop. She also would have charge of the education and religious training of any children born of the marriage. Her right to choose French Catholic domestics and courtiers would be limited only by the formal approval of the English King. A concession to England, important in the light of later developments, recognized James's prerogative to replace Henrietta's lay suite with Englishmen.[12]

Although James had publicly promised his recently dissolved Parliament that no concessions would be made to Catholics in consequence of a French alliance, Richelieu insisted that James accept the following secret clause as a *sine qua non* of ratification:

> The King of Great Britain shall give to the King [Louis XIII] a special written statement signed by him, his most serene prince, his son, and a secretary of state, by which he promises, upon the faith and word of a King, that in the knowledge of his dear son, and lady, the sister of the most Christian king, he promises to all his Roman catholic subjects the greatest freedom and privilege, in whatever concerns their religion, that they would have had by virtue of the articles agreed to by the marriage treaty with Spain: provided always, in this regard, that his Catholic subjects be unmolested in their persons as well as in their goods, in the practice of the said religion, and in their Catholic way of life, provided always that they conduct themselves modestly and as good and true subjects render obedience to their king, who, through his goodness, will never restrain them contrary to their religion.[13]

The Crown thereby unequivocally guaranteed that Catholics could practice their religion privately so long as they obeyed the law.

Once committed to this policy, James honored his commitment by ordering the immediate release of imprisoned recusants, the return of all fines taken from them since Trinity Term of 1624, and the full suspension of the penal code. Writs went out to judges, sheriffs, and constables advertising these immunities and ordering them to restore the land and goods taken from recusants during the year.[14] Although James himself issued the orders, in many places they were not carried out. As a matter of fact, in London and in several of the northern counties the harassing of Catholics seems actually to have increased. In some ways, therefore, the French match created more problems for the Catholics than it solved.

James, who had long suffered from a combination of painful

diseases, including arthritis, gout, and gallstone attacks, died on March 27, 1625. Against the advice of physicians, he had continually overindulged a craving for melons and cool ale, and had persistently gorged himself at table. Weakened by pain and premature old age, he suffered in succession the tertian ague, frequent convulsions, high fever, and dysentery that finally killed him. Few Englishmen seem to have lamented his passing, and fewer still put much stock in the report of surgeons that "proved" his high qualities of character by autopsy. They found his heart great and soft (generosity and kindliness), his bile black (melancholy), and his head stuffed with brains, "a great marke of his infynite judgement."[15]

Soon after James died a rumor spread that Catholics had poisoned him. The accusation probably stemmed from the fact that Lady Buckingham, the Duke's Catholic mother, had applied medicinal plasters to the King's abdomen and wrists, and that the Duke himself had given James a white powder two weeks before his death.[16] Although the remedies did him no good, they undoubtedly did him no harm. But a Catholic attendant at the King's side was enough to worry a fanciful Protestant. Another rumor had it that James became a Catholic during his last hours, but this likewise had no foundation in fact. James took Communion from the Bishop of Lincoln, who said later that James had professed his devotion to Protestantism.[17]

In fact, the Catholics grieved and worried at James's passing as they had rejoiced at Elizabeth's. The Tuscan ambassador, Amerigo Salvetti, reported that the Catholics offered prayers for James, and for Charles also, perhaps out of anxiety that Charles might not choose to continue the religious truce.[18] Many of the Catholic nobility wished to attend the funeral, but the Privy Council reportedly made this difficult by refusing them the customary black mourning cloth.[19] A number of Catholic emissaries, including the Marquis d'Effiat and the Duc de Chevreuse, attended the interment. Signor Pesaro, the Venetian

ambassador, stayed away. He said that according to his understanding the diplomatic corps were not invited, and that he suspected the Council of intentionally excluding him. The Councillors rectified their "oversight" by suspending the steward, Sir
Lewis Lewknor, from office.[20]

Now that Charles was king, the marriage arrangements took
on greater importance. The union of the Catholic princess and
the Protestant prince could not be made without papal dispensation, and Urban VIII hesitated for some time before granting
it; he wanted first to be certain that James, and then Charles,
would lay aside the oath of allegiance and provide Henrietta
with a church open to the public. In the end, Richelieu, through
the agency of Père de Bérulle, confessor to Henrietta, obtained
the dispensation on December 1, 1624.[21] Urban believed that in
sanctioning the union he was taking the first strong step toward
the goal of his life's work—the restoration of Catholicism in
England. Henrietta did not intend to disappoint him. Her letters to the Pontiff and to her brother plainly prove that she considered her marriage an apostolate for the liberation of her
coreligionists from persecution. To Urban she promised un-
yielding devotion to the Church, unfailing energy in its cause,
and a sound Catholic education for her children. She gave
Louis her word that she would promote "what may be useful
and advantageous to the religion and to the Catholics of Great
Britain." It may be presumed that she did not open the several
Books of Common Prayer that were sent her by pious Englishmen who hoped for her conversion.[22]

Richelieu married the royal couple by proxy at the great west
door of Notre Dame on May 11, 1625. Soon thereafter Lord
Holland reported to Charles on the qualities that he would find
in his fifteen-year-old bride: surpassing beauty, the deepest respect and love for her intended, and wisdom beyond her tender
years.[23] The ambassador naturally told Charles what he wanted
to hear, and did not mind stretching the facts a little to do so.

Actually, Henrietta was not a beautiful woman, though she had a pleasant appearance. Van Dyck's portraits of her, like his portraits of Charles, are flattering. She was a frail girl with large, soft eyes, a rather long nose, and full, sensuous lips. She wore her hair in ringlets silhouetting her oval face. In an age when smallpox marred the beauty of many a woman, Henrietta could boast of a smooth, ivory complexion that became the envy of her suite. She was gay, frequently frivolous, sometimes childish, and generally stubborn. Her charm commanded attention, and she knew how to use it to advantage. At first she spoke English hardly at all, but she improved in it as the years went by. Sewing, singing, acting, and dancing amused her most of all.

Preparations for her arrival had been going on for months. Rooms were made ready in Whitehall for her French attendants, and artisans rushed to complete a new chapel in Somerset House. Meanwhile, a room was coverted into an oratory.[24] At last Buckingham journeyed to Paris to fetch the bride. He arrived on May 14, stayed a week, and accompanied the royal entourage to Boulogne; on June 11 English ships ferried them across the Channel to Dover. Bride and groom met there for the first time, dined, and left in the morning for London, which they reached in four days.[25]

Some festivities followed, but nothing like those that had heralded the return of Charles from Spain. On the first Sunday of her residence in London Henrietta became ill. The formal proclamation of the marriage, and the state dinner to celebrate it, had to be postponed until the following Tuesday, on which occasion the articles of the treaty were read in French to the assembled guests.[26] Buckingham and the Duc de Chevreuse also honored the royal couple at banquets, but beyond these occasions there was little conviviality, for the plague had again broken out in London. Parliament and the King moved to Oxford in July, and Henrietta busied herself with the arrangements of more comfortable quarters for her confessor, Bérulle, and his Oratorian brothers, who were already grumbling about English inhospitality.[27]

If the marriage of Charles and Henrietta gave Catholics hope that their situation might improve, they were disappointed. Just before Parliament assembled in June 1625, Charles showed his good faith by issuing five mandates that renewed James's order suspending the penal laws,[28] but the Privy Council, when apprised of recusant activity, authorized investigations and arrests.[29] In August, Tillières reported to Louis that neither the change in monarch nor the marriage had altered the customary attitudes of Parliament and the Privy Council toward Catholics.[30] A proclamation soon went out from the Council ordering judges to enforce the penal code and recalling English seminarians from Continental schools.[31] Charles eventually fell into line by denying English Catholics the right to attend mass in royal and ambassadorial chapels.[32]

Despite the secret clause of the marriage treaty by which James promised to permit Catholics religious freedom, and the proclamations by James and Charles ordering the suspension of the penal laws, Catholics continued to be punished for their religion. From June 1624, when Richelieu began negotiations with the ambassadors of King James, to January 1625, when James ordered the recusancy laws suspended, the English Catholic clergy watched events with ever deepening skepticism. "Fear and tremor have enveloped us," William Farrar wrote from London, "especially since this treatie with ffrance that many are affraied to write [to friends] what otherwise should seeme expedient."[33] An anonymous priest in the North complained that "sicknesse raynethe much and so doth persequution not withe standinge the treaty with france."[34] Father Henry Clifford's letter to a colleague typifies the anxiety among the Catholics:

> In England we are not so sure [of the effects of the French marriage] because in the remoter parts from London p'secution is [carried on] with rigoure both upon the lands goodds

and psons of catholiks, and some are come up to sollicite the
side of the french Ambassadour, who is much p'plexed finding not the playne and reall effects in their [the English]
promises that he expected: yet the Cardinal Richlieu from
france has [written] . . . a very courteous and friendly lre
assuering our catholicks . . . all assistance for their peace
and benefite.[35]

The letters of Thomas Rant, a secular priest of London, point
up the futility of the French ambassador's intercessions with the
Government. Men still paid the weekly twelvepence fine for
missing Anglican services, Rant relates, and presentments and
indignities continued without interruption. In London in 1624,
Catholic prisoners were still held in Newgate, and the Lord
Mayor's constables were daily breaking into the homes of recusants, looting shops, and imprisoning their Catholic proprie-
tors.[36] By November, the persecution had fallen off somewhat
in London, where the pursuivants were temporarily suppressed.[37]

Elsewhere in the country there seems to have been little
change.[38] In Berkshire, Staffordshire, and Leicestershire, Catholics still paid heavy fines.[39] While Londoners burned bonfires,
heard the roar of cannon at the Tower, and even danced in the
streets in celebration of the French match,[40] the recusants of
Lincolnshire were suffering at the hands of Justice Sir Nicholas
Sanderson. In Botsworth Parish, for instance, churchwardens
forced their way into the home of a tradesman named Christopher Cromell, beat him, and imprisoned him in Lincoln Castle
even though he was a consumptive who could not earn the
money to pay his fines. A woman of eighty-five, Mrs. Huggett,
and another identified simply as "old mother Odlyn" were both
thrown in jail for failing to pay their twelvepence fines. The
churchwardens also arrested without warrant a weaver, William Smith, as well as the wife of another recusant, and trailed

them at horse tail for half a mile.[41] There is no reason to suspect that such incidents were peculiar to Botsworth Parish.

Rumors of Catholic plots against the Government, accentuated by Parliament's condemnation of papists and the beginning of opposition to the French suite, gripped the nation during the spring and summer of 1625. Reports of supposed conspiracy poured into the Privy Council from every corner of England. Justices of the peace in Buckinghamshire warned of great gatherings of scheming recusants. From the Bishop of Chester came a letter about "great and unaccustomed resorte to the houses of recusantes."[42] In Cornwall, Dorset, and Somerset, constables discovered letters which indicated that Catholic insurrection there was imminent. Sir Francis Coke, speaking of Catholic activity in Derbyshire, believed "that certainly the papists have some designs in hand."[43] At Newark, a suburb of Leicester, Catholics reportedly took over the parish church and scoffed at attempts by churchwardens to arrest them.[44] Recusants supposedly thronged to Milford Haven, Pembrokeshire, where they fought off constables who tried to imprison them, and in King's College, Cambridge, a Bedfordshire scholar named Richard Carpenter allegedly organized a fraternity of Catholic students.[45]

Such reports so worried the Privy Council that they ordered the disarming of every known recusant. Circular letters dated October 4, 1625, went out to the Lords Lieutenant of the several shires authorizing the confiscation of all weapons held by recusants except those needed to protect their persons and property. The Council laid the burden of responsibility for this action squarely on Catholic shoulders: they had offended King Charles beyond forgiveness by accusing him of cowardly submission to Parliament's demands. The Council further charged that papists planned "stires and tumultes"throughout the realm so as to bring about in England a Christian commonwealth ruled by the

Pope. The Crown had "too large and too cleare proofe" of Catholic treason, the Council added, to delay suppression longer. Therefore, they explained,

> althoughe wee do not misjudge or condemne all . . . Romish Catholiques, but believe that many of them will not imploye theire armes and lives in his [the Pope's] service, yett because wee are not able to distinguishe betweene the well and worse affected wee have seconded with our advise . . . to take out of possession of all Romish recusantes convicted or justly suspected . . . all such martiall municions, armes and weapons as shalbe found in theire houses.[46]

The confiscated weapons were to be stored at the expense of the recusants, who could claim them only in the event of a national emergency. Little did the Council then suspect that in one such crisis, Alexander Leslie's Scottish invasion of England, unarmed recusants would prove to be among the most loyal subjects of the King.

The formidable task of searching the homes of Catholics for hidden weapons that they were allegedly collecting for a general rebellion took about two months. The quantity of arms found was infinitesimal. A search in the hundreds of Bergeveny, St. Kenffreth, Raglan, Usk, and Trelech in the South Wales marches, for example, turned up nine corcellets, nine pikes, two "fowlinge pieces," one pistol, one "glaive," one musket, and one "curesse" from the homes of thirteen recusants, six of whom were women.[47] In five hundreds of Derbyshire, Sir Francis Coke uncovered no arms other than those belonging to the trainbands, but he seems to have stumbled upon a Catholic center in Appletree hundred where there was a house containing two chapels, crucifixes, and forty to fifty beds, lately used. Few arms were found in Dorset, Somerset, or Cornwall.[48] If the results of the arms hunt were any guide, most Catholics must have had little quarrel with the message of a widely distributed anonymous pamphlet, *The Advice of a Catholic to his Fellow-Catholics in England,* which exhorted recusants to submit humbly to the afflictions of the times without murmur or fail in their duty and loyalty to the Crown.[49]

But if many Catholics necessarily accepted with resignation the enforcement of the penal laws despite James's and Charles's proclamations suspending these laws, most were shocked by such duplicity. English Catholics naturally assumed (as Louis XIII assumed) that Charles would shape religious policy as much as Elizabeth and James had done. But none of them understood well enough the temper of the times or Charles's character. There is little reason to associate the King with those who hated Catholics. Indeed, he understood and sometimes sympathized with the Catholic point of view (if only out of pique with the other side), but he was too easily swayed by love for a favorite or a show of authority. He was anything but a strong king. He was reluctant to quarrel and cowardly at times in the face of opposition, and he often was bullied into taking actions he deplored. His speech impediment, his shyness, and his uncontentious manner left him a prey to more aggressive disputants.

His mother, herself a convert to Rome,[50] had first interested Charles in the cultural brilliance of Italy and its Catholic life. According to the papal agent George Conn, writing in 1638, Charles believed in the decrees of the first four ecumenical councils, the three ancient creeds, and the theology of the Church Fathers. Charles would not accept papal sovereignty, of course, but neither did he like his title of "Supreme Governor" of the Established Church. He recognized the efficacy of auricular confession, and set an example by sometimes going to confession himself. He occasionally fasted, often gave alms to the poor, venerated relics and the crucifix, and saw little essential difference between the Thirty-nine Articles and the Roman Catholic Creed.[51] With Catholics he had little quarrel over dogma, and he was disinclined to persecute them because of religion. On this point Parliament disagreed.

The Parliament that opened on June 18, 1625, was eager to suppress Catholicism, especially since Charles had ordered the penal laws suspended on May 1. Salvetti, the Tuscan ambassador, noted that as writs went out for the election of the Commons, the "Puritanical faction . . . [was] exciting tumults that they make sure of a majority." He added prophetically that the Commons would undoubtedly raise a debate on religion and condition a grant of money to the Crown upon the satisfaction of their grievances.[52] On June 22, Sir Francis Seymour suggested that the lower House petition the King to enforce the penal laws and to restrain Catholics from attending mass at the chapels of Catholic ambassadors. Other Members supported the motion made by Sir Edward Giles and seconded by Sir Robert Phelips that the penal laws be enforced. One Member, mindful of the severity of the plague in London at that time, warned the Commons that they had more to fear from the "plague of souls" than from the dangers to the body. Sir John Eliot spoke about religion on June 23, and John Pym and Sir Edwin Sandys drafted a petition on religion that was sent up to the Lords on the 30th. Meanwhile, the Commons learned that Charles had forbidden English Catholics to serve the Queen and to attend mass at any Catholic chapel.[53]

"The Petition of both Houses for Execution of the Laws against Popery, and for advancing true Religion" was presented to Charles on July 7. It included a list of reasons why there had been a "mischievous increase of Papists." Recusancy could hardly be controlled, Parliament asserted, if royal officers ignored their duty to enforce the penal laws. Because of this laxity the papists moved about at will and flaunted their religion in the face of the law by regularly attending mass at the foreign embassies. Continental seminaries were allowed to train missionaries whose return to England meant an increase in the strength of the Catholic party that endangered the Established Church. Seditious Catholic literature induced poorly educated Anglican clergymen to abandon their faith. Worst of all, the Crown permitted Catholics to hold high positions in the Government. Such evils required drastic remedies. Schoolmasters must be taught dogma in universities in which the ancient disciplines were restored. The number of educators should be increased, and the pluralities of the clergy reduced. Catholic priests must be banished from the realm, imprisoned recusants kept away from other prisoners, English Catholics banned from Court, and repossessed recusant estates reconfiscated.[54] Charles answered the petition against recusants briefly but favorably on July 11, promising to enforce the penal laws.[55]

Parliament adjourned for three weeks and reconvened at Oxford on August 1. On that day religion was the second point of business. Sir Edward Giles told the Commons of a pardon that Charles had granted on July 12 for a Jesuit and several other priests imprisoned at Exeter. That was the day after the King's answer to the petition against recusants. Out of surprise at Charles's apparent breach of faith, the Commons were quiet. Only Eliot spoke at length on the pardons, and he confined himself to scolding the ministers of the Crown, as though they, not Charles, were to blame.[56] The House of Lords, generally less vituperative than the Commons in criticizing the Crown, this time chided Charles for having gone back on his promise to protect the Established Church against recusants. Sir Edward Conway, speaking for Charles, answered that the French marriage treaty obligated the Crown to free imprisoned priests. Lord Keeper Thomas Coventry supported Conway before the Lords, but they were not disposed to accept any explanation based on the unpopular French match. (Only a month earlier, on July 4, they had voiced their displeasure over the liberties allowed recusants and the French Catholic life permitted at Court.) One peer went so far as to call the Queen the "Princess of papists," and spoke against allowing Englishmen to hear mass in her chapel.[57]

On August 2, the Commons resumed debate on Richard Montague, an Essex rector who had been the subject of much criticism during the previous session at Westminster. Montague was the writer of two pamphlets, *A New Gag for an Old Goose* and *An Appeal to Caesar,* which represented the high Anglican point of view and which were thought by the Commons to condone Catholic ritual and dogma. *An Appeal to Caesar* made a good case for the similarity of Catholic and Anglican theology, and openly criticized the plainness of Puritanism. In *A New Gag for an Old Goose,* an answer to an anonymous Catholic pamphlet, *A Gag for the New Gospel,* Montague held that the Roman Church was as valid an institution as the Church of England, and that confession and absolution, and the use of statuary and pictures in church, were acceptable practices. He also defended the sacramental nature of ordination and denied the Calvinist doctrine of predestination.

The Commons were as eager to suppress "Catholic" practices and beliefs in the Established Church as they were to thwart Catholicism itself. During the Westminster session, on July 7, a committee headed by John Pym had reported on their investigation of the Montague pamphlets. Pym called the writings "factious and seditious" and "a great encouragement of Popery," and condemned them as contrary to the Articles of Religion defined by Parliament. The Commons ultimately laid three charges against Montague, the most important of which was his contempt for the lower House, and committed him to the custody of the sergeant-at-arms.[58]

Montague was released on bond during the recess. At Oxford, when the Commons summoned him to answer questions of the committee on religion, he pleaded illness. Charles sought to protect Montague by making him King's chaplain, and several bishops strongly supported him. Such formidable support notwithstanding, the Commons stood firm: it would not admit that any of the King's servants were above censure in Parliament. King Charles addressed Parliament briefly on August 4, and for the next two days the Commons discussed money for the fleet, Buckingham, and English foreign policy. On the 8th the royal favorite spoke to the Lords and Commons as though they were schoolboys at the feet of an arrogant headmaster. Buckingham spoke mainly of foreign policy, but he also made remarks about the Catholics. After Charles's full answer to the petition against recusants had been read, Buckingham assured his audience that the penal laws would be enforced. But he also implied that the Members were not to meddle in matters of religion, which only the King and his bishops could consider.[59] Grievances over religion, with reference to Charles's pardon of the priests at Exeter, again occupied the Commons on the afternoon of August 11, and an innocuous protestation was prepared to assure the King of the Commons' loyalty, devotion, and readiness to reform abuses in the realm. Charles expected a vote of supply; the Commons would not grant it, and Parliament was dissolved on August 12.[60]

Two days later, without regard to England's obligations in the marriage treaty, Charles formally renewed Catholic persecution. He issued a proclamation recalling English seminarians and revitalized the recusancy laws against Catholic missionaries. This decision to abandon the Catholics probably grew from the strained relations between the Commons and the Crown over the French treaty. Rather than vote a supply, the Commons had reiterated their grievances in religion, not the least of which was the favor shown Catholics. Perhaps the Tuscan ambassador assumed rightly that Charles ordered the penal laws enforced out of anxiety that the Commons might not otherwise grant him money.[61] Whatever motivated Charles, Henrietta was furious and reproached him bitterly. Charles replied that he was the King, and that he would not tolerate her meddling in politics.[62]

Since Buckingham had advised Charles to break the treaty, Henrietta's protest may have been prompted in part by jealousy of the Duke's inordinate influence over her husband. But Charles expected simply that Henrietta should love and obey him in whatever he did.[63]

Henrietta herself was not without fault. She made little effort to fit into the English way of life in an age when her subjects were riding the crest of nationalism, and lived instead as though she were home in France, surrounded by doting cavaliers and indulgent, matronly ladies-in-waiting. She rarely appeared in public, preferring to be with her French friends, who were as contemptuous of the English as she was. Worst of all, within a year of her arrival, Henrietta had alienated many of the most influential Protestants. It is not surprising that they should have grown suspicious of her and the French staff in Somerset House. There was talk of how Henrietta had formed a little colony in London that was controlled by the French cabinet. Others fancied French domestics plotting to subvert the Established Church, and still others accused the French ambassadors of forwarding state secrets to Richelieu. It did not help soothe English tempers either to see Catholic priests parading about the streets of London in clerical gowns.[64]

Charles liked the French even less. He blamed them for his trouble with Parliament, and suspected with reason that they were turning Henrietta against him. In the hope that Henrietta might acquire English friends who would counteract the inordinate influence of French companions, Charles assigned the Duchess of Buckingham, the Countess of Denbigh, and the Marchioness of Hamilton to her bedchamber. Street women could have pleased Henrietta more! The ladies were Buckingham's wife, sister, and niece—all Protestants. Henrietta reminded Charles that he had violated the marriage contract a second time by appointing English Protestants to her household, but he simply ignored her.[65] To make matters worse, parliamentary pressure induced Charles to dismiss some of the French, including the three ambassadors extraordinary (the Duc de Chevreuse, the Marquis d'Effiat, and M. de Ville Sereine) and thirty-five servants.[66]

If Englishmen were undecided about the adverse influence exerted by the French at Court, the Titchfield incident resolved the question. Charles had made over a guardroom of his country house at Titchfield into an Anglican chapel. Although Henrietta much preferred London to the country, she sometimes stayed at Woodstock or Titchfield, and she was upset by the sight of Anglican clergymen conducting services under her nose. On the last Sunday in September 1625, while at Titchfield, she decided to do something about it. Charles having gone to Beaulieu, she assembled her ladies and had them stomp up and down the aisle of the chapel, talking and laughing at the top of their voices while the minister was delivering a sermon. They later made him the butt of a practical joke by firing a pistol from behind a hedge near which he was sitting.[67] The incident suggests the tensions that the French suite created. Had Henrietta maintained a measure of dignity in battling what she believed to be inroads upon her prerogatives in religion, she might have been able to accomplish something worthwhile to lessen the burdens of her coreligionists. But she allowed pride and stubbornness so to take hold of her that she turned many quiet Protestants into active anti-Catholics. The renewal of persecution was as much her doing as it was the Government's.

Although little could be done to salvage the marriage treaty in English eyes, Louis XIII nevertheless sent a special ambassador, M. de Blainville, to do what he could to settle the quarrel. Before he set foot in England, Charles had his agents Holland and Carlisle complain to Louis about the French suite.[68] Thus, when Blainville disembarked at Dover, the Privy Council merely arranged that his passage to London should be comfortable and that he should be provided with suitable rooms. Thereafter he was virtually ignored.[69]

Charles would not grant Blainville an audience until October 11, and then their conversation came to nothing. Blainville asked that England honor its obligation to free the Catholics from the burdens of the penal laws. Charles replied that the treaty was nullified because the recusants had been disloyal. After all, Charles added, he had promised to favor the Catholics only if they conducted themselves prudently, and he judged that they had acted otherwise. Finally, Charles insisted that since neither the French nor the English took seriously the secret clause guaranteeing freedom of worship to Catholics, he was not obligated to honor it.[70]

Blainville naturally left the meeting dissatisfied. During the next three months he sulked about London, making several halfhearted attempts to change Charles's mind and writing complaints to Richelieu. Blainville's dispatches reek with self-effacing pity. They tell how he was being "persecuted" and describe his unceasing efforts to better the plight of the Catholics. He repeatedly exaggerated minor incidents, and he went so far as to suggest that unless he could personally resolve the current crisis, the cause of the Catholic Church in England was doomed. Such a man could hardly contribute to Anglo-French understanding, and it was a stroke of good luck for the Catholics that he left England in April, *persona non grata*.[71]

Chapter Three

THE FRENCH QUEEN'S CATHOLIC COURT

IGNOMINIOUS FAILURE haunted Charles, Buckingham, and England in the last months of 1625. Buckingham and Charles planned a grand Protestant league under English leadership to crush Spain and her Catholic allies, even though the country was near bankruptcy and Parliament was unwilling to finance the scheme. On September 8, England and the Dutch States-General joined in a close offensive and defensive alliance whereby the Dutch would supply twenty ships and would blockade the Flemish harbors. Denmark and the north German princes stayed in the war on a promise from Charles of £30,000 a month, which he had little hope of raising. The overtures Buckingham made to France for help against Spain in the Palatinate foundered on several grounds. French merchant ships, thought to be carrying Spanish goods, were captured by English men-of-war. Six English merchantmen leased to France for eighteen months were employed by Richelieu against the Huguenots at La Rochelle. And not least of all, Charles was having trouble with Henrietta and her French Catholic courtiers. Meanwhile, a combined fleet of English and Dutch ships crammed with irresponsible pressed troops under Sir Edward Cecil, a good soldier who had no experience at sea, made for Spain. The drunkenness of the English soldiers and the lack of food and supplies at Cádiz robbed Buckingham of victory and the Spanish gold he needed to implement his foreign policy. On October 5, the Privy Council ordered that the recusants be disarmed, and on November 3 the enforcement of the penal laws was resumed.[1]

If Charles and Buckingham were worried by difficulties in war, diplomacy, and finance, the generality of Englishmen were equally troubled by disease and depression. The dreaded plague, reputed by some to be a curse sent by God for the sin of tolerating the Catholics, erupted once more in April, gained hold in late spring and summer, and in a few places survived the winter of 1626. In London, where the pestilence seems to have been the worst, the narrow, water-soaked lanes and alleys were littered with garbage which fed the black rats that carried the disease to every corner of the city, and fires burned in front of every sixth house to purge the air. During August, cartmen were burying in common graves as many as four thousand carbuncle-ridden bodies a week.[2] Parliament, as we have seen, moved to Oxford to escape the plague, and the King left London for Woodstock. In southeastern England entire sections of towns were depopulated, and rows of merchants boarded up their shops. Commerce all but stopped, artisans were left jobless, and gangs of thieves roamed the countryside, robbing the living and the dead. Money became scarce, and with business at a standstill a serious economic depression set in. One Londoner, writing late in 1625, remarked that "the want of money [is] so great as the like [has] . . . not been known," and that not even the servants of the King had been paid for months.[3]

During these troubled months Henrietta Maria spent money as foolishly as ever, buying jewels valued at £3,000 and paying £1,667 in household expenses during July 1625, even while she owed another £6,663 to artisans who had been decorating her chapel in Somerset House. During 1626 she spent £14,260 on "personal items,"[4] and from June 1625 to October 1627 the cost of maintaining her Court ran to £89,378 in addition to the £18,166 she received from her land and houses.[5] In view of the state of the English treasury, Henrietta might well have set an example by being more frugal. Yet Charles showed as little common sense in putting up £10,000 for paintings that caught his fancy.[6]

Fear of the plague and the general disorder that it created, as well as the preparations for the Spanish war, delayed the coronation of Charles for nearly ten months. It did not take place until February 2, 1626, and even then it went off with less pomp than was customary. Charles quite naturally expected that Henrietta would be at his side, but while arrangements were being completed for the coronation she announced tersely that she would not be crowned by a Protestant bishop or attend the ceremony in Westminster Abbey.[7] She believed that it would be sacrilegious to be anointed Queen by the Archbishop of Canterbury and to participate in the ritual of the Established Church. She told Charles that she would only agree to be invested in a separate Roman Catholic ceremony conducted by her own Almoner, the Bishop of Mende.[8] Henrietta was following the advice of the Faculty of Theology in the Sorbonne, who declared that her coronation in a Protestant church by Protestant prelates would be heretical.[9] Charles, however, adamantly insisted that if she would not be crowned by his Archbishop she would not be crowned at all. Finding that she could not be swayed, Charles tried to induce her at least to attend the ceremony in a latticed box so situated that she could not be seen, but she balked even at this.[10] She did not participate in the procession to Westminster Abbey, but watched it from the bay window of the old gatehouse which then extended over the roadway leading from Whitehall to the Abbey.[11] It was not without serious consequence later that Charles accused Blainville of having talked Henrietta into avoiding the coronation.[12]

Most of the Catholic peers and gentry in London attended

the ceremonies, "not without scandal to other Catholics," the Tuscan ambassador noted.[13] Doubtless they understood better than Henrietta or the French Court at Paris that there was nothing to be gained by insulting Charles; and they could reflect that Canon Law only forbade participation in, but not attendance at, Protestant religious services. (However, to be on the safe side, they probably left the Abbey before the sermon was delivered.)[14] Certainly Blainville's refusal to attend the festivities convinced many that the Catholics actually were implacable foes.[15]

Not only did Henrietta refuse to witness the coronation, but she also humiliated and disappointed Charles on the occasion of the formal opening of Parliament. Charles, eager to have Henrietta enjoy the ceremony, told her on February 5 that he wished her to watch the solemnities from the Countess of Buckingham's rooms rather than from their gallery windows. Henrietta readily agreed, but the next day when it was time to walk across the courtyard to the Countess's quarters, she would not go: it was raining, she said, and she did not wish to be drenched. Neither Charles nor Buckingham could convince her that it was not raining, and Charles angrily left the room. It seems likely that Henrietta imagined the rain so as to please Blainville, who had cautioned her not to associate with the Countess of Buckingham.[16] What upset Charles most was that he had suggested her rooms to counteract Blainville's advice. Once the procession had passed, Charles sent Buckingham to scold Henrietta and see that she was confined to quarters. The Duke, haughty as ever, suggested that Henrietta apologize for her bad manners. Her reply was to order him from her sight,[17] and for three days the royal couple spoke not a word to each other. Charles rightly blamed Blainville for what had happened and ordered him out of London.[18] Eventually Henrietta mollified Charles by staging a masque in his honor at Durham House; Blainville attended as inconspicuously as possible.[19]

The people of London have always made royalty a part of everyday conversation, and it was natural that gossip about the petty quarrels of the royal couple should make the rounds. The average Englishman could not have missed the point of the inordinate influence that the French had been exerting over Henrietta. The sight of French Catholics living sumptuously at Court gave rise to caustic criticism of the Queen, and her most ordinary actions became topics for censure. Her bursts of frivolity and her periods of piety were alike construed to be evil manifestations of an evil Queen who practiced an evil religion.

Henrietta liked to meditate and to pray, and she frequently went off alone to do so. During Holy Week in early April 1626, for instance, she and her ladies lived like cloistered nuns in Somerset House, where a long gallery had been divided into cells for them. There they passed the week in spiritual exercises, meeting but once a day to chant the Psalms according to the Benedictine rule. On Holy Thursday Henrietta walked through the rain to her chapel in St. James's, perhaps to allay troubled thoughts of failure in her apostolate. When, on Good Friday, Charles forbade Catholics to attend mass in her chapel, her fears and melancholy returned.[20]

Henrietta's harmless and quite accidental visit to Tyburn on June 26 was viewed in some quarters as another of her scandalous deeds. After a long day of prayer in her chapel, Henrietta, in the company of the Bishop of Mende, the Comtesse de Tillières, Père de Sancy (her confessor), and Mme de Saint-Georges, who had raised her from childhood, rode in a coach to the end of the brick wall beside Hyde Park. There she left the coach to walk across to Tyburn tree, a famous place of execution to which victims had been dragged through the city from the Tower. Since 1571 a permanent triangular gallows had stood there as a sentinel to the murderers and martyrs alike who had swung to their deaths. Nothing was more natural than that the Queen should kneel in prayer before the gallows for five minutes or so, paying her respects to the Catholics who had given their lives for their religion. Several passers-by noticed her while she prayed.[21]

Charles probably learned of the visit to Tyburn from one or another of these witnesses. The story he heard was that Henrietta had led barefoot a pilgrimage to honor dead Catholic traitors. The account by John Pory, a learned London gossip,[22] might very well have been the one Charles believed. The French priests—"hypocritical dogges," Pory calls them—made the "pore Queen to walke a foot (some add barefoot)" to Tyburn to honor martyrs who had shed their blood in defense of the Catholic cause.[23] So reported, the incident seemed to Charles a further insult by the intolerably brash Frenchmen who had purposely humbled the Queen.

By this time, Charles and his subjects had had their fill of the French. English plans to use the marriage treaty as a stepping-stone to an Anglo-French military alliance against Spain had foundered upon the flat refusal of Louis XIII to wage war for the recovery of the Palatinate, or to help Mansfeld's bedraggled corps in Germany. After France made a separate peace with Spain in April 1626, Charles could drop the pretense of cordiality that he had shown France while there was still hope of a military alliance. In view of Anglo-French relations since the signing of the marriage treaty, it is little wonder that the English exaggerated the petty annoyances created by the French at Court. The obstinacy and haughtiness of Henrietta and Blainville and the singing of Catholic masses in the Queen's chapel were in themselves hardly serious matters, but seen in the perspective of European politics and the traditional Protestant fear of Catholicism they took on inordinate importance in turning the English against the French.

The increasing influence of the French courtiers over Henrietta nurtured Charles's growing hatred of them. He blamed them for his domestic troubles and used their conduct as an excuse for his own violation of the religious articles of the marriage treaty. As early as November 20, 1625, Charles wrote to Buckingham at The Hague that there soon would be sufficient cause "to put away the Monsers" either on the ground that they had alienated Henrietta's affections or on the ground that they had plotted with English Catholics against the Established Church. All that was necessary to expel the French, Charles remarked, was positive proof of conspiracy.[24] A month later Charles notified the Bishop of Mende that English attendants would be substituted for the French.[25] Charles wrote to Buckingham a second time, saying that Henrietta had begun to mend her manners, probably at the advice of her French friends, who feared they would be sent home.[26] For some months thereafter Charles seems to have calmed down about the French, but perhaps his silence merely indicates that he was increasingly preoccupied with the serious parliamentary troubles that had arisen.

The plans Charles made to expel the French finally materialized early in August 1626. In the knowledge that Louis would take strong exception to the deportation of the French suite, Charles sent Dudley Carleton to Paris to be on the spot when the news broke. The French were apparently aware that something ill was brewing in London, for the Bishop of Mende advised Richelieu to be cautious in believing whatever Carleton might say.[27] After dinner on the evening of July 31, Charles took Henrietta aside and told her point-blank that the French would have to go. Secretary Conway was sent to tell them that their days in England were numbered, and that in the meantime they should move immediately from their quarters in Whitehall to Somerset House.[28] Their protests notwithstanding, the Guard hurried them into St. James's Park where Charles himself is said to have scolded them.[29]

John Verney, a Gallophile contemporary biographer of Henrietta, has left one version of what Charles supposedly told the startled Frenchmen.[30] The King claimed that they had tried his patience to the breaking point by their constant interference in his marital relations. At that, the Bishop of Mende begged Charles to specify what they had done, and Mme de Saint-Georges could only say that Henrietta would vouch for her conduct. But Charles refused to be specific and merely told the French that they must leave England. They probably felt better when Charles assured them that their dismissal would not mean the loss of their gratuities. That evening Charles ordered Buckingham to be sure that the French left town the next day: "I command you to send all the French away to-morrow . . . by faire meanes (but strike not longe in disputing) other-ways force them away, dryving them away lyke so manie wyld beastes."[31]

The yeomen of the guard brought coaches, carts, and barges to Somerset House in the morning to carry away all but a few specifically mentioned Frenchmen; realizing that complaint was futile, those who were to be deported quietly left the palace.[32] In the three days' journey to the Channel the party stopped overnight at Rochester, Canterbury, and Dover, where Captain George Allen picked them up for the trip to Calais.[33] They left England loaded with gifts of jewels and money totaling £22,500. In spite of this, Henrietta's Master of the Horse claimed he should have been given all of the Queen's stable, including the saddles, and the Bishop of Mende demanded £2,000 to defray what he said had been personal expenses in operating the chapel.[34] Only a handful of the original French suite of nearly three hundred persons stayed behind with Henrietta, and Charles immediately appointed the core of a new English suite by assigning to Somerset House several noblemen as well as two priests named Potter and Godfrey.[35] Besides these, the Duchess of Buckingham, the Marchioness of Hamilton, and Lady Carlisle accepted posts as ladies of the bedchamber.[36]

Henrietta was at first upset, but she soon learned that life without her French friends could be quite pleasant. She had a fit of temper the night Charles told her that they were to go, and she wrote the Bishop of Mende that she had never been so lonely and depressed.[37] In turn, the Bishop spread word to the French Court in Paris that Charles was keeping Henrietta a virtual prisoner in her palace, and that her confessor could scarcely say mass without danger to his person.[38] The Bishop's account was echoed by the Comte de Tillières, who had sped to Paris on Carleton's heels to describe firsthand the English insults to French honor.[39] Louis pieced together enough truth from what he heard to know that his sister had been basely treated. To learn the details he sent to England a special ambassador, Marshal François de Bassompierre.

Louis could have chosen no better man for the delicate task of assuaging English anger while at the same time upholding French rights. Bassompierre had already made his mark as a soldier under Henry IV and Louis XIII. He had led victorious armies in wars with Savoy (1602) and with the Turks in Hungary (1603), and he had been rewarded with a Marshal's baton in 1622. Men knew him best for his strong character, his acute sense of humor, and his intimate knowledge of foreign affairs—all good qualities in a diplomat.[40] He could listen well, too. To the English he must have seemed an unusual Frenchman, especially by contrast with his countrymen the Bishop of Mende, Blainville, and Mme de Saint-Georges, whose virtues did not include humility and patience. Yet the new ambassador could not be bullied. Charles, Buckingham, and even Henrietta learned to their surprise that at the appropriate moment Bassompierre could be firm.

For a week after his arrival in London on September 27 he was occupied with the normal round of state visits from the principal governmental officers whom Charles sent to sound him out. The studied chill with which Bassompierre was first received by Buckingham, who wished to repay France for the cold reception Richelieu had given Carleton, soon warmed into a surprisingly close friendship.[41] Aware that the Duke and Henrietta had been at each other's throats since the departure of the French household, Bassompierre set immediately about the task of settling their differences, which he managed with considerable (if temporary) success.[42] The Marshal knew also that Henrietta had repeatedly irritated her husband by her childish contentiousness, and several times reproved her for picking quarrels with Charles.[43]

Bassompierre finally met with Charles for two hours at Hampton Court. The King, as husbands sometimes do to those who are willing to listen, complained to the ambassador of Henrietta's bad conduct. So well did Bassompierre listen that he managed to win Charles's confidence, and before the conversation concluded for the day, he had broached the sensitive subject of French prerogatives in the marriage treaty. He reviewed the marriage difficulties and won Charles's consent to have the provisions of the treaty studied by a commission of his own choosing.[44] He ultimately arranged conferences for the writing of a new treaty, in spite of English opinion that was strongly opposed to any concession to France.

Ten English commissioners, including most of the important privy councillors,[45] sat with Bassompierre for better than two weeks in early November 1626. The English immediately brought up all the old grievances against the French household in general, and against the Bishop of Mende in particular: that the French priests spied for Richelieu and fomented plots with English Catholics to subvert the Established Church; that Henrietta was humiliated and bullied by the Bishop, who forced her to follow the monastic rule, as evidenced by her meditations and fasts and the barefooted pilgrimage to Tyburn; and that he poisoned her mind against Charles and the English way of life. Bassompierre listened patiently to the charges and had the good sense not to deny them. His reply was disarmingly simple:

though the allegations might be true, he said, it seemed to him that the English were nonetheless bound to honor their treaty obligations. By avoiding arguments and conceding on minor points here and there, he not only won the respect of the commissioners but also won substantial concessions from them, including their promise to mitigate the severity of the penal laws.[46]

The talks concluded on a note of conviviality at a sumptuous banquet which Buckingham arranged to honor Bassompierre and the new Anglo-French accord.[47] Bassompierre seems to have gained more advantages than anyone could reasonably have expected. The two nations agreed that Henrietta would be permitted a suite whose nucleus, and particularly those who would attend her person, would be French, though not the same persons who had been banished. She would have ten priests as well as a bishop and a confessor and his coadjutor to serve her chapel. Two ladies of the bedchamber should be added to her corps in addition to three chambermaids, two physicians, a surgeon, an apothecary, a chamberlain, a secretary, a valet of the private chamber, a baker, a cook, and a few kitchen servants, all of her own nation.[48] The English also promised to complete the Catholic chapel and cemetery at St. James's and to build a new chapel for the Queen adjacent to Somerset House, her principal residence.[49] According to the Venetian envoy, Bassompierre was willing to give the assurance that France would pay the £100,000 still due on Henrietta's dowry if Parliament would provide £10,000 a year toward her maintenance, but no agreement was reached on this point.[50]

Before leaving England, Bassompierre held several more conferences with Buckingham in the hope of eliciting a concrete promise of toleration for English Catholics. The Duke was unusually sympathetic, but he obviously could not change the Government's religious policy over parliamentary opposition.[51] On December 2 Bassompierre left London with gifts of diamonds and pearls, the respect of Charles and his ministers, and sixteen priests who had been released from prison into his custody.[52]

Louis XIII, Rome, and the English Catholics soon found fault with the way Bassompierre had settled Anglo-French differences, and the ambassador himself was skeptical of the effect of his mission. The Most Christian King would accept nothing less than the terms of the original treaty, and disavowed Bassompierre for not getting them. The Pope joined Louis in denouncing the compromise. The English in turn were angered, and Buckingham wrote Richelieu that Charles felt freed from any obligation regarding Henrietta's suite. The English Catholics' displeasure with Bassompierre grew out of the belief that he had not adequately served their interests, for persecution went on as always, even during the negotiations. It did not improve their opinion of him, either, that he had used his position to make a handsome profit from the exportation of several thousand English hides.[53]

With Bassompierre gone, life settled down to rather dull routine for Henrietta, and she was probably glad of it after so much domestic turmoil. Her personal conduct seems to have been greatly influenced by her talks with Bassompierre. For the next two years, only an occasional minor misunderstanding adversely affected the relations between her Court and the nation. For instance, one of her musicians, a lute player named Galtier, spoke too freely about his dislike of Buckingham and was accused of intending to murder the Duke; he was imprisoned in the Tower until the accusation against him was proved to be mere gossip.[54] Similarly, in June 1628, Henrietta's surgeon was accused of forwarding state secrets to Richelieu and of criticizing Buckingham.[55] Neither the lute player nor the surgeon was convicted of maligning the favorite, and in truth, if this were a crime, many of England's stoutest hearts might have been as justly convicted of it.

During this time, too, Henrietta seems to have captured a corner of Charles's heart. In the summer of 1627, Buckingham was busy preparing and leading the disastrous expedition to the Island of Ré, so that Charles had more time for Henrietta. "I cannot ommit to tell you," Charles wrote to the Duke, "that my Wyfe & I wer never better togeather, . . . shoing her selfe so loving to me . . . upon all ocasions that it makes us all wonder and estime her."[56] That October the Queen was pregnant. A self-styled oracle named Lady Eleanor Davis, the wife of Sir John, formerly Attorney-General, predicted that Henrietta would bear a son who would die the day of his birth. On May 13, 1628, Charles James was born at Greenwich, about two months prematurely, and expired that same evening after being baptized in the rite of the English Church over the protests of Henrietta and her confessor.[57]

It was also during Buckingham's absence that Charles became alarmed over the efforts of priests in London to convert members of the royal household to Catholicism. Catholic catechisms and devotional books given to some Protestant courtiers impressed them with the elaborate doctrines and imposing ceremony of the Roman Church; by comparison, the Established Church appeared dull and emotionally unsatisfying. The books so greatly influenced thinking among the ladies at Court that Charles immediately took steps to discourage proselytization and the use of the Catholic prayer books.

Charles chose John Cosin,[58] then a young rector beneficed in Durham and the protégé of Bishop Richard Neile in the circle of Laud and Montague, to edit a prayer book in which pomp, color, and music should be played up to show that the Established Church could also provide her children with emotional satisfaction in religion. Cosin's *Manual of Private Prayer* was published in 1627. In form and flavor the prescribed prayers bore a striking similarity to Catholic practice. Cosin marked certain days to be set aside for abstinence, meditation, and rejoicing, and thoroughly analyzed the Apostles' Creed and the Lord's Prayer. He set forth the times of the day, much like a monastic rule, at which Psalms were to be sung and corporal works of mercy to be undertaken. He explained the Ten Commandments with admirable clarity and even recommended the Sacrament of Penance for those troubled by uneasy consciences.⁵⁹

Critics of the *Manual of Private Prayer* became alarmed at its popularity. William Prynne for one, just then emerging as the rock of Puritanism, could not let the challenge pass unanswered. To his earlier tract, *The Unloveliness of Lovelocks,* which condemned the current fashion among courtiers of wearing their hair long to the shoulders, he added in 1628 an equally violent diatribe, *A Briefe Survay and Censure of Mr. Cozens His Couzening Devotions.*⁶⁰ There is little that Prynne did not find loathsome in Cosin's prayer book. It "smells, nay, stinkes of Poperie," Prynne wrote, and "it is fraught with contradictions . . . scandalous, and prejudiciall to our owne [church], and advantagious onely to the Church of Rome." Like many other Protestant critics of the Established Church, Prynne erroneously thought of colorful religious ceremony as peculiar to Catholicism. What irked him most, though, was that Cosin had substituted new devotions "stolen out of Popish Primers, Prayer Bookes, and Catechismes" for the prayers found in the 1560 and 1573 editions of Elizabeth's prayer book. Not even the frontispiece escaped criticism: Cosin's crest could be identified as "an undoubted Badge, and Character of a Popish, and Jesuiticall Booke."⁶¹ Prynne dedicated his tract to Parliament, which in the previous two years had shown itself critical of High Church ritual in its censure of Montague, Neile, and Roger Manwaring.

For all its importance, this controversy meant little to Henrietta, who in the winter and spring of 1629 felt really happy for the first time since coming to England. She had lost her first baby, but little time passed before she was again pregnant. Buck-ingham was dead, Charles was attentive, and she seems to have forgotten the first four unhappy years of her marriage. She also had matured sufficiently to accept the reality of practical politics —that all her tears and flashes of anger would not alter the fact of Charles's continuous violation of their marriage treaty—and to wait patiently while her husband and brother sent their war-ships to the Channel during the Anglo-French naval war of 1627–29. Charles also realized the sweetness of conjugal bliss and governmental tranquility. His troublesome Parliament had been dissolved, and he turned to Henrietta to forget the real pain of Buckingham's death. English Catholics were delighted by the course of events, since both parliamentary sessions and the quarrels of the royal couple over religion inevitably hurt them. The penal code might never be rescinded, but with Par-liament gone and the King content, it might not be enforced so severely.[62]

At Susa, on April 15, 1629, England and France put an end to their intermittent war. Like most wars, it had settled few of the grievances over which it had been fought. The questions of religious toleration for English Catholics and the reinstate-ment of the French suite did not come up for discussion at the peace table. Louis XIII promised to allow the Huguenots free-dom of worship, but before long he brought them to submission in spite of English protests. Although Charles had just made peace with Spain, Louis thought the time propitious to drag England once more into an alliance against Philip IV. To that end there came to London on June 28 a new French ambassa-dor, Claude de Châteauneuf.

Almost immediately he sensed that Charles, lacking money and all hope of getting any from a hostile Parliament, could not be cajoled into war. Moreover, Lord Treasurer Richard Weston, whom Charles assigned to discuss with Châteauneuf plans for resumption of trade, the revocation of the letters of marque, and the mutual return of prisoners of war,[63] was as tight-fisted a manager of money as could be found to guard the dwindling resources of the Crown. He would not listen to talk of war that would probably bankrupt England for the sake of France. Thus thwarted by both Charles and Weston, Châteauneuf turned to Henrietta, in the hope that her influence over Charles might be exploited to political advantage for France.

Louis also instructed Châteauneuf to arrange for the erection of a small chapel in London to be staffed by Jean Barrault, Bishop of Bazas, whom Henrietta had personally chosen to replace the Bishop of Mende, and eight secular priests. As for the kind and number of other servants who might be allowed Henrietta, Châteauneuf was to learn her pleasure.[64] To his surprise, she told him that she was too much in love with Charles to bring up controversial subjects that might turn him once more against her. Indeed, Charles had become an ardent lover, showering gifts of jewelry on Henrietta almost daily, kissing her frequently in public, and resenting like a jealous schoolboy any suggestion that Frenchmen be permitted to intrude on his marital happiness. Even the presence of Mme de Ventelet, one of the ladies-in-waiting who had stayed behind in 1626, and who was the soul of discretion, irked Charles.[65]

But Châteauneuf was not easily discouraged by the royal couple's lack of interest in his proposals. He conferred privately with Henrietta on several occasions during July and August, impressing her with the fact that Marie de' Medici, her mother, would not be happy until some of Henrietta's worthy countrymen could be sent to attend to her spiritual and temporal needs. She should at least have a bishop as Grand Almoner, a learned physician, and an older companion, such as Mme de Saint-Georges, with whom she might share her little secrets. Henrietta eventually admitted to Châteauneuf that she would enjoy the company of a few French ladies-in-waiting with whom she could converse and attend chapel. The Countess of Buckingham and Lady Savage were kind ladies, she added, but they were away more often than not.[66]

Châteauneuf had a more difficult time with Charles. He told the ambassador bluntly that nothing definite regarding the return of the French household had been promised Bassompierre in 1626. Henrietta might be allowed a few more priests if she felt she needed them, Charles added, provided they were neither Jesuits nor Oratorians. Seculars, Benedictines, or even Capuchins would be acceptable, but under no circumstances would a French bishop be allowed at Court.[67] The reasons for excluding Jesuits and Oratorians were obvious: the clergy in the original household had been Oratorians, and two generations of Englishmen, notably including James I, had associated Jesuits with political intrigue. (Moreover, the discovery of ten Jesuits at Clerkenwell in March 1628 had caused such a furor in Parliament that Charles could not risk another scandal.) Benedictines appealed to Charles because they were known to oppose the episcopal jurisdiction in England of the Catholic Bishop of Chalcedon. As for a bishop, the Protestant bishops would not tolerate the rival claims of a French Catholic bishop in their midst.[68] Charles finally agreed to allow Henrietta eight Capuchin monks and two Capuchin lay brothers, but no bishop.

Charles and Châteauneuf also discussed the cost of a chapel to be built adjacent to Somerset House in accordance with the agreement of 1626. Châteauneuf insisted that even a small building, tastefully decorated, would cost 40,000 livres (£2,000), but Charles answered that 20,000 livres would be enough, even with the addition of rooms to house the Capuchins. But for the time being no decision was reached.[69]

His mission finished, Châteauneuf remained in London to await the arrival of the new French ambassador, M. de Fontenay-Mareuil, and the Capuchins,[70] who disembarked at the Downs in February 1630. Charles showed them every courtesy and lodged them temporarily in a fine house close by Somerset

House. The Capuchins, in contrast to their haughty Oratorian predecessors, undertook their priestly labors in a quiet manner, ministering to hundreds of Catholics who flocked to mass and to the sacraments in the Queen's chapel.[71]

The arrival of the Capuchins and the apparent freedom of worship permitted the Catholics in London provoked a storm of protest in Protestant circles. On March 10 the Privy Council issued another of its periodic proclamations forbidding Catholics to attend mass in the ambassadorial and royal chapels.[72] Denunciatory pamphlets appeared, crowds milled outside the Capuchins' house, and Henrietta was scathingly criticized. Puritan meetinghouses shook with the tremor of polemical sermons against her. Bernard, a London lecturer, publicly beseeched God to "open the queen's majesty's eyes, that she may see Jesus Christ, whom she has pierced with her infidelity, superstition, and idolatry," and Dr. Alexander Leighton, a Scottish preacher living in England, called Henrietta "an idolatress" and a "daughter of Heth."[73]

Henrietta had too much on her mind to worry about the slanderous remarks of enemies, for the birth of her second child was imminent. Charles objected to the attendance of a French physician at the birth, but Marie de' Medici nonetheless sent M. de Poix, who arrived early in May, well in time for the event. On Saturday, May 29, 1630, Henrietta bore a healthy son, who would later become Charles II. Poix was not in attendance.[74] The King had silently ignored his requests for an audience during the last weeks of Henrietta's pregnancy, and as late as two months after the birth he had not yet been formally received at Court.[75] This was Charles's way of showing Paris that he alone would direct the affairs of his marriage.

The question arose whether the baby prince would be baptized a Catholic or an Anglican. Both Charles and Henrietta spoke their minds in the matter, and in the end Charles had his way. The marriage treaty, which had specified that children born of the French match would be reared Catholics until their thirteenth birthday, was clearly a dead letter, and Bishop Laud's advice that the heir to the throne be baptized in the Church of England understandably weighed more heavily with Charles than Henrietta's wishes. The proud father named Frederick and Elizabeth of the Palatinate the honorary godparents, and as a political gesture he extended similar honors to Louis XIII and Marie de' Medici. The French King's silence indicated his displeasure.[76]

The christening took place amidst splendent pageantry on June 27 at St. James's, but not in the Queen's chapel. There was cause enough for grand ceremony, for Prince Charles was the first male heir born to a reigning English monarch since Jane Seymour bore Henry VIII a son in 1537. The chapel decorations were gorgeous: Turkish carpets covered the floor, rich damask draped the stairways, altar, and baptismal font, and curtains of crimson taffeta hid the drab gray walls. Mary, Marchioness of Hamilton, carried the ermine-swaddled baby from the nursery to the chapel, preceded by the Aldermen of London in scarlet gowns, the peers of the realm, the heralds, the pursuivants-at-arms, and the Gentlemen Ushers. Next came the two deputy godfathers, the Duke of Lennox and the Marquis of Hamilton, and the Earl of Bedford carrying a basin of holy water. The royal almoner, the Bishop of Norwich, met the procession at the chapel doors and led it to the altar, where Laud read evening prayer while a choir, accompanied by two organs, sang the Lord's Prayer. Watching from their seats in two galleries on the second floor along each wall were numerous dignitaries. Laud then baptized the baby according to the prescribed form in the Book of Common Prayer. Thereafter a herald recited Prince Charles's titles, and Laud delivered an appropriate sermon, read the Collect for the day, and prayed for the King, Queen, and prince. No contemporary document records the presence of Henrietta at the christening, and it is not certain whether she was in the chapel.[77]

On the day the child was born, Charles named as governess

the Countess of Roxburgh, a Scottish Catholic. But after two weeks of listening to complaints about a "romish" Scotswoman being entrusted with the heir, Charles changed his mind. He then gave the honor to the Countess of Dorset, the wife of Edward Sackville, Lord Chamberlain to the Queen.[78] But the lady who was given the actual task of rearing the boy was a Mrs. Wyndham, who had extraordinary influence over him throughout his youth.[79]

During the next two years the Catholics at Court and in London enjoyed a time of relative quiet. While Charles worked at tasks that kept him away from his family for long periods at a time, Henrietta sewed, supervised her household, and took a great interest in the operation of her chapel under the capable administration of the pious Capuchins. She was occasionally troubled by quarrels with Bishop Laud, whom she disliked intensely, and she was greatly distressed to hear of the expulsion from France of her mother, Marie de' Medici, who in the summer of 1631 failed in a plot to oust Richelieu and fled to the Netherlands. Almost immediately she appealed to Henrietta to intercede with Charles for political asylum, but he would not hear of it. He already had his hands full in the Palatinate and could not risk offending France. Soon thereafter, on November 4, 1631, Henrietta gave birth to her first daughter, Mary, who was baptized by Laud.

In the same two years the circle of royal advisers changed, to the advantage of the Catholic party. Dudley Carleton, Viscount Dorchester, never a friend of the Catholics, was succeeded as Principal Secretary by Francis Windebank, who later proved to be sympathetic to Rome. The new Lord Treasurer, Richard Weston, and the Chancellor of the Exchequer, Francis Cottington, both had close family ties with the Catholic Church: Weston's wife and daughter-in-law were Catholics, and Cottington had himself been a Catholic as a youth in Spain. Others, like Endymion Porter, who had a Spanish Catholic mother, and

Tobie Mathew, soon to become a Catholic convert, were influential courtiers. Of the others in high office, only Laud, who became Archbishop of Canterbury in 1633, and Thomas Wentworth, the newly appointed Lord Deputy of Ireland, were vehemently opposed to the lenient policy toward recusants that Charles was then pursuing. In view of the attitudes of influential privy councillors, the absence of a troublesome and intolerant Parliament, and Charles's growing leniency toward the Catholics, it is not surprising that by 1634 a fresh Catholic revival was beginning to take shape at Court.

Another factor in the revival was the erection of a small Catholic chapel on the tennis grounds adjoining Somerset House.[80] Plans to build such a chapel had been discussed in the marriage treaty negotiations in 1624 and during Bassompierre's mission in 1626, and again during Châteauneuf's conversations with Charles in 1629–30, but work was not begun for two years more. There is no doubt that a larger chapel was needed, for the chapels in St. James's Palace and in Somerset House were too small to serve even the Catholic courtiers.[81]

Workmen began to lay the foundation for the new chapel in 1632, and on Friday, September 14, the Feast of the Veneration of the Holy Cross, Henrietta, in the presence of Charles and an audience of about two thousand persons, laid the first two cornerstones. Abbé Jacques du Perron, Henrietta's Grand Almoner, blessed the building, and a choir, as good as the one at Notre Dame de Paris, according to one contemporary, chanted Psalms and prayers. Some in the gathering may have been alarmed that Charles had permitted the chapel to be built at all; others may have been more astonished that a silver plate bearing the profiles of the King and Queen, as well as the names of the resident Capuchins, was fixed to the cornerstone in commemoration of their sponsorship. That night cannons at the Tower boomed in celebration of the event, and bonfires burned at the homes of the Catholic ambassadors.[82]

The following spring, Henrietta, though in delicate health because of a succession of pregnancies, was again pregnant.[83] Laud and Charles left late in May for Edinburgh, where his long-delayed Scottish coronation took place on June 18 at Holyrood Castle. They stayed a month, during which time Laud became aware of the decayed state of the Established Church there and Charles met with the Scottish Parliament. They would have remained in the northern capital longer had not Charles's anxiety over Henrietta's health necessitated his speedy return to London.[84] On October 14, the peal of church bells and bright bonfires heralded the birth of their second son. Henrietta again begged Charles to allow the baby to be baptized a Catholic, but Laud advised against it and christened the child James, after his grandfather, according to the Anglican rite.[85]

Two months later the baby suddenly grew feverish, and there was serious doubt that he would survive. Sickness in children was to be expected, especially in the early seventeenth century, but inevitably something more than ordinary circumstance was suggested as the cause of the illness. One of the baby's two nurses was a Catholic, and she was accused of having given him a sinister popish potion. The illness passed, but the attention focused upon the nurse brought out the fact that at the time of her appointment she had refused the customary oath of allegiance required of all state employees. She had been dismissed, but was reinstated through the intercession of Henrietta, who claimed that her Protestant nurse had gone mad. Once returned to duty, the Catholic nurse again refused the oath, and was questioned, threatened, and badgered until she finally accepted an ordinary oath of fealty that would assure her loyalty to the Crown.[86] Such an incident, although it had little bearing on the development of Catholicism in England, goes a long way to illustrate the continuing fear of Catholics that was at the root of their persecution.

Chapter Four

THE ARENA OF POLITICS

BEYOND DOUBT, the Parliaments from 1625 to 1629 were sincere in their worries over the Roman Catholic issue. Petitions on religion mentioned the growth in numbers and strength of the Catholic community and Charles's seeming leniency toward Catholics, and emphasized the increasing danger to the Crown and the Church. But for all the surface rhetoric, the growing tension between the King and Parliament on this issue was essentially part of the larger conflict over Divine Right. Elizabethan Parliaments had also, of course, opposed the principle of Divine Right, but the Crown then usually managed to thwart adverse criticism by the adroitness of its privy councillors, who not only led the debates in the lower House but also headed important committees.[1] Moreover, the war with Catholic Spain and the fear of Catholic plots served to unite Crown and Parliament against a common enemy. Between Charles and his Parliaments, however, there was no such mutual bond. Parliament suspected Charles of deliberately appeasing the Catholics, not only at Court in deference to the Queen, but throughout the realm by his failure to enforce the penal laws. The threat of "popery" was debated openly on the floors of both Houses, and the speeches on this issue of such men as John Pym, Sir John Eliot, Sir Walter Earle, and Sir Robert Phelips commanded national attention.

Catholics themselves hoped that they would benefit from

the growing rift between the Commons and the King. Some
hoped merely that Charles would dissolve Parliament, always
a welcome move since proclamations for stricter enforcement
of the penal code usually coincided with parliamentary sessions.
Others looked to a widening of the breach between the Puritans
and the Established Church; in the event of a crisis, Charles
might perhaps defend the Catholic as well as the Anglican
point of view, the two religions being similar in so many respects.[2] Still others saw grounds for hope in Buckingham's
increasing unpopularity. According to the Venetian ambassador, Buckingham's support of full enforcement of the penal
code might result in Parliament's lightening the harshness of
the laws simply to discredit him.[3]

Such speculation was of course unrealistic. There was no
reason whatever to expect Parliament to change its policy toward Catholics. If anything, it was more determined than ever
to suppress Catholicism in England, and within three weeks of
its convening on February 6, 1626, it had turned to the Catholic
question. On March 4 the Commons framed a bill to restrain
the emigration of Catholic children to the Continent. On the
20th, they considered and approved for presentment to Charles
a list of Catholics and suspected Catholics in public office.[4]
The Commons were also disturbed by the fact that Catholic
peers could still sit in the upper House, although they rarely
did so, and it even considered a proposal to investigate the
Lords for recusancy.[5]

Behind many of these proposals stood John Pym and his
committee on religion, one of the most important policy-making
groups in the Commons.[6] This committee framed bills, presentments, and remonstrances, created subcommittees to examine special problems regarding religion, inquired into
charges of recusancy, censored "popish" books, and employed
pursuivants to ferret out Catholics.[7] Pym directed the work of
the committee with the genius and energy that were to make

him the undisputed manager of the Commons in the early years of the Long Parliament. Scarcely a week passed in which he did not report on measures proposed by his committee to curb recusancy and "romish" practices in the Church of England.

Shortly before Easter 1626 the Commons were stirred by a report about living conditions among prisoners in the Clink, a jail in Southwark, wherein several priests who had taken the oath of allegiance were allegedly kept in protective custody. On the Commons' advice, Attorney-General Robert Heath sent John Tendring (marshal of Middlesex), Sir George Paul (a justice of the peace in Surrey), and several pursuivants to search the prison. Arriving on Good Friday morning, April 7, they found four priests, including Thomas Preston, the Benedictine, in unusually comfortable quarters. The Clink adjoined the palace of Richard Neile, Bishop of Winchester, and he had, it seemed, allowed Preston to break in a wall giving access to a four-room apartment. Tendring, testifying later before the committee on religion, said that Preston had three servants, (presumably the three priests living with him), a library valued at £2,000, and the necessary articles for celebrating mass; he also had five bags of money, £100 in loose change, and several packets of letters. He apparently enjoyed the right to leave the prison at will and to have visitors.

While Tendring was searching the Clink, he received an order from Archbishop George Abbot countermanding his warrant and directing him to confiscate nothing.[8] The committee on religion, learning of Abbot's order, conducted a hearing to determine the facts in the case. Abbot testified before the committee that Tendring had unjustly disturbed Preston, who was being maintained at the expense of the Crown to protect him from angry coreligionists. Preston, Abbot said, had taken the oath of allegiance and had turned state's evidence against one or two colleagues, who were later imprisoned. In return

for Preston's cooperation, King James had instructed Abbot and
Neile to provide for him comfortably and to allow him full
liberty of person and conscience.[9]

Preston's case specifically, and the whole tenor of Charles's
policy toward Catholics, aroused Parliament to prepare a "Petition against Recusants in Authority,"[10] which it sent to the
King in June 1626. It listed the Catholics who held important
posts in the Government—for the most part, peers in the strongly
Catholic northern counties who served as commissioners of
sewers, justices of the peace, and deputy lieutenants. Among
the names were Henry, Lord Dunbar (deputy lieutenant in the
East Riding of Yorkshire); Henry, Lord Abergavenny; John,
Lord Tenham; Edward, Lord Wotton; Henry, Lord Morley;
John, Lord Mordaunt (all commissioners of sewers); and John,
Lord St. John (captain of Lidley Castle in Southampton). Particular charges were made against Francis, Earl of Rutland (lord
lieutenant of Lincoln), and Emmanuel, Earl of Sunderland
(lord lieutenant of Yorkshire and lord president of the North).
The committee charged Rutland with obstructing the prosecution of recusants in the North Riding of Yorkshire and with
countenancing Roger Conyers, a Catholic teacher who had been
refused a license. The charges against Sunderland were more
serious: he refused to attend church on holy days and violated
them by hunting; he neither fasted nor received Communion;
he would not disarm recusants; and he employed as assistants
only recusants.[11]

The Commons heard the petition read during a violent
thunderstorm that swept over Westminster in the afternoon of
June 12. The subsequent torrent of rain undermined a high
supporting wall of St. Andrew's Cemetery, which caved in and
laid open the graves of a dozen men. The rotting coffins split
and a number of decomposed bodies were washed some distance
down the street. A few bystanders said they saw "a spirit at the
same time . . . upon the waters, which did sore affright"

them.[12] If the Catholics interpreted this as a sign of God's displeasure, the Commons interpreted it differently, and approved the petition.

After several perfunctory expressions of Parliament's faith in the Crown, the petition exhorted Charles to execute the penal laws in spite of the marriage treaty with France. One article condemned the harboring of "fruitless Ambassadors" who spied for Cardinal Richelieu while growing fat on English stipends too large for their station and needs.[13] Since Charles had but recently expelled most of the members of Henrietta's French suite, he was glad enough to have the approval of the lower House. And indeed, he accepted without dispute all the articles in the petition. But when the Commons, after drawing up articles of impeachment against Buckingham, asked Charles to remove him from office,[14] he lost patience, and on June 15, 1626, he dissolved Parliament.

Nineteen months passed before the pressing need of money forced Charles to call his third Parliament. In the interval, war had broken out with France, and Charles had aroused English anger with a forced loan, arbitrary arrests, and the billeting of troops. Despite the King's efforts to ensure a sympathetic House by attempting to dictate elections to it, the new Commons included many of his old opponents,[15] and it was clear that enforcement of the penal laws would once again be an issue. The Tuscan ambassador thought that Charles might be lenient to the Catholics out of gratitude for their generous contributions to the forced loan,[16] but there is no real evidence that Catholics had been any more willing to part with their money than the many Protestants who refused to pay rather than compromise their opposition to unparliamentary taxation.[17]

Parliament convened on March 17, 1628, and the Members resumed debate on many of the topics that had engaged their attention in the previous session. The ensuing year was one of the most significant in the constitutional history of England, with important resolutions against unparliamentary taxation and arbitrary imprisonment and lengthy debates on Buckingham, on the wars with Spain and France, and on the Petition of Right. We shall necessarily confine ourselves to the actions taken by Parliament on the Catholic issue.[18]

No Catholic could sit in the House of Commons, where all Members had to take the oath of supremacy. In the spring of 1628 the lower House, under the leadership of its committee on religion, took steps to ensure that no Catholic had slipped in. On Monday and Saturday afternoons the committee usually met to consider questions involving religion and to recommend proposals to be debated in the committee of the whole. At a Monday meeting just before Easter the committee on religion recommended, as they had on earlier occasions, that the Commons observe a day of fast and Communion on April 6 in St. Margaret's Church, Westminster. Accordingly, on that day a subcommittee composed of William Bulstrode, Miles Fleetwood, Robert Harley, Edward Giles, James Perrott, and Robert Pye issued certificates to the Members of the lower House who took Communion. Those who refused were to be suspended from Parliament until they complied.[19] There is no record of anyone's refusing Communion, and it is unlikely that the religious persuasion of any Member could have been concealed.

In April, the House of Lords petitioned Charles to enforce the penal laws rigidly and to restrain the activities of the Oratorian priests, who were accused of subverting the faith of Protestants by openly preaching and proselytizing in the streets of London.[20] The petition probably resulted from the Clerkenwell incident, which had been brought to the attention of Parliament in mid-March, a few days before it opened.

George Long, a justice of the peace in Middlesex, learned that the former home of John Talbot, Earl of Shrewsbury, in Clerkenwell just north of London, was being used by a small community of Jesuits. They were arrested and their goods and papers seized. The letters revealed Jesuit missionary activity as well as facts concerning their dispute with Richard Smith, the Catholic Bishop of Chalcedon, then resident in England;[21] and one letter (thought by Gardiner to have been a forgery)[22] suggested that the Jesuits were collaborating with the Commons to discredit Buckingham. The Venetian ambassador believed that the letter was intended to stop the harsh criticism of the Duke by the Commons and to humiliate them into granting subsidies.[23]

The accusation aroused the suspicions of the Commons, and the committee on religion asked Secretary Sir John Coke and Attorney-General Heath to testify in the matter. Coke alleged that the French ambassador was behind a popish plot and that the Jesuits planned to meet him at Clerkenwell on the Feast of St. Joseph (March 17)[24] to make final arrangements for their conspiracy.[25] Heath submitted a written report, "The Discovery of the Jesuits' College at Clerkenwell," in which he explained that the Privy Council had been aware of Jesuit activity in Clerkenwell since Christmas of 1627, when it assigned several pursuivants to watch the Talbot house. Soon thereafter, Heath added, Justice Long and a pursuivant, Humphrey Cross, searched the premises and captured several men hiding in the basement behind a newly bricked-over wall. The prisoners refused to admit that they were priests, but their "massing stuff" and letters incriminated them.[26]

In attempting to prove that a Jesuit plot was imminent, Heath drew attention to the forged letter,[27] which he said had been written by a Jesuit to his superior in Brussels, but he denied that the Commons were conspiring with Jesuits against Buckingham. Although the alleged plan to discredit the Commons failed, some, including the suspicious Puritan pamphleteer William Prynne, believed the story. It may have been that Heath and Coke purposely twisted the truth in an effort to force the Commons into granting a subsidy. For whatever purpose the letter was intended, the Commons apparently were unaware that the St. Joseph's Day meeting had been called simply to conduct the ordinary promotion of novices in the Jesuit order.[28]

All this talk of a Jesuit plot led Parliament to draw up another petition calling for the enforcement of the penal laws. The Clerkenwell letters had revealed the presence of a bishop and a corps of ecclesiastical officers within the Catholic community in England, and the fact that the Jesuits and the Benedictines had strong organizations.[29] The lower House was annoyed that such a large number of regular clergy could thrive in spite of the penal laws, and some Members even suggested that Charles had made a pact with the Catholics to restrain recusancy proceedings if they would help fill his treasury. Even further, the Commons, aware that Catholic children who went to the Continent for an education frequently returned as missionaries, proposed that the state adopt as wards the children of recusants to ensure their being reared in the Anglican Church.[30]

The "Petition of both Houses Concerning Enforcing the Laws against Recusants" was approved on March 29, 1628, and submitted to Charles two days later. It recounted the old grievances against Catholics and asked especially that the Jesuits be restrained. Charles was warned of the increasing boldness of the Catholics in accepting a bishop to direct their religious life, of the significance of the re-establishment of religious houses for the regular orders, and of the growing strength of the Catholic community, which dared to support an assembly of Jesuits who challenged the authority of Parliament. Parliament asked Charles to confine Catholic priests to the prison castle at Wisbech, as his father had done, and to forbid Catholics to come within ten miles of London. Parliament would allow Catholic ambassadors their chapels, the petition said, but attendance at them by English Catholics would not be tolerated. The petition also pointed out that although the composition of recusants' estates had brought in great revenue, because of fraud and "patched up . . . colourable leases, contracts, and preconveyances" little of the money had actually been deposited with the Exchequer. Charles accepted the petition and swore to "keep Religion amongst us free from Innovation and Corruption."[31]

Some weeks later, apparently disgruntled by the weak and unacceptable answer that Charles had at first given it on the Petition of Right, the Commons became involved in a series of impassioned debates, touched off by the speech of Sir John Eliot on June 3. This now famous denunciation of England's foreign and domestic policies laid the blame for all the country's misfortunes squarely at the feet of Buckingham, though his name was never mentioned. At intervals for a week thereafter the Commons labored over a statement of grievances—a remonstrance—which was approved by the committee of the whole on June 11, 1628. The remonstrance, composed of eight articles drawn up under the direction of Eliot, Pym, Sir Thomas Wentworth, and John Selden, dealt with religion, government, and charges against Buckingham. Of interest here is the first article, "Fear of innovation in Religion," in which the Commons accused the Countess of Buckingham of assisting papists, criticized Bishops Neile and Laud for preaching "popery" in St. Paul's Cathedral, decried the alarming increase of recusancy, particularly in London, and denounced the liberty of conscience permitted Catholics through the composition of their estates. The petition demanded that the penal laws be enforced to prevent Catholics from influencing persons of quality who protected them. Finally, it reminded Charles for the third time that he had promised three years before at Oxford to ensure the "purity" of the English Church.[32]

A few days after this remonstrance was approved, the Lords' committee on recusants and the Commons' committee on religion jointly submitted for the consideration of both Houses a

bill "To restrain the Passing or Sending of Any to be Popishly-
Bred Beyond the Seas." It was considered and approved by the
lower House on June 20, 1628,[33] and after a conference between
the two Houses, the Act was passed.[34] It differed little from an
earlier Act of 1603 (1 Jac. I, c. 4) which authorized seizure of
the property and income of anyone who permitted his child to
attend a Continental Catholic school or seminary; and it re-
enacted the customary "escape clause," whereby those who
returned to England within six months, submitted to the
Establishment, and took the oath of allegiance were excused the
punishment due their crimes.[35]

Meanwhile, on June 17, the remonstrance had been read by
the Speaker before the Commons and the King. Charles, who
was at the moment displeased by the murder of a Dr. Lambe,
supposed to be the astrologer for the Duke of Buckingham,
answered curtly: he had not expected a remonstrance, he said,
in view of his gracious acceptance of the Petition of Right, and
he would give the articles as much consideration as they de-
served. He had listened to harangues against the French suite,
against Catholics, and against Buckingham, and although he
cared little for the welfare of his Catholic subjects, and nothing
for the French, he was deeply grieved and annoyed with Parliament's constant criticism of his favorite. The time was ripe
to dismiss Buckingham, but Charles was not yet ready, as he
would be in 1641, when the Strafford affair occurred, to abandon
a friend in order to save himself. Instead, he prorogued Parliament on June 26 and published a proclamation commanding the
strict enforcement of the penal laws against Catholics.[36]

It was not long, however, before this point of contention, at
least, between Charles and Parliament was resolved: on August
23 Buckingham was murdered by John Felton.[37] With Buckingham dead, Charles had every reason to anticipate less diffi-
culty during the second session of his third Parliament, which
opened on January 20, 1629. But the Commons at once ap-

pointed a new committee on religion, composed of Sir Walter Earle, William Coryton, Sir Richard Grosvenor, Sir Robert Phelips, Selden, and Pym (chairman),[38] and seemed ready to make religion again its chief concern. When Sir John Coke offered, on the 26th, to present a bill for tonnage and poundage, discussion on it was tabled in favor of debate over grievances in religion. Several Members, including Francis Rouse and Edward Kirton, warned the Commons of the encroachments of popery and Arminianism, which were paving the way for the subordination of Protestantism to Rome. The following day, Pym spoke on the important issue of the Commons' right to consider questions of religion. Indignation among the Members had been aroused by a declaration of December 1628, in which Charles had defended the Thirty-nine Articles, reasserted the exclusive rights of Convocation in matters of religion, and forbidden discussion of various interpretations of the Articles, particularly those that raised the doctrine of predestination.[39] According to Charles, Parliament had no right to consider religious reform.

Against this contention Pym advocated the combined supremacy of King and Parliament. What men craved, Pym asserted, was a return to the purity of practice typical of Edward VI's reign and exemplified in the writings of Peter Martyr and Martin Bucer. Only Parliament, he said, could successfully meet the danger of Catholicism and Arminianism. His plea, supported by Eliot on January 29, struck an old note, but it had never before been sounded so strongly. Both Pym and Eliot made it clear that they considered Parliament the watchdog of the English Church, and they rejected, by implication, the exclusive sovereignty of the King in Convocation to govern it.[40] On January 30 a committee of the lower House, in the name of Parliament, asked Charles for permission to hold a day of fast and prayer, ostensibly for the spiritual intention of improving "the deplorable estate of the reformed Churches abroad."

Charles gave permission, but he added sarcastically that fasting was becoming an unnecessary adjunct of every parliamentary session.[41]

The Commons next attacked Arminianism, in the person of four high-ranking Anglican clergymen who were favorites of Charles. Two of them, Montague and Cosin, had long been enemies of the Commons. The other two, Robert Sibthorpe and Roger Manwaring, had delivered sermons in 1627 upholding the King's right to exact forced loans without parliamentary approbation, maintaining that the King's will was supreme and unquestionable. Since Arminianism rejected predestination and recognized the continuity of the Established Church with the pre-Reformation Church in doctrine, ceremony, and episcopal government, the increasingly powerful Puritan Members of Parliament loathed it quite as much as they loathed Catholicism. Parliament brought charges against the four clergymen on various grounds. The Crown pardoned them. The Commons were infuriated and ordered an investigation of the pardons.[42]

A subcommittee on pardons, led by Phelips and Christopher Sherland, was appointed to look into Commons' suspicion that Charles himself had pardoned the clergymen. Attorney-General Heath told Phelips that Charles had ordered the pardon for Montague, and that the pardons for Sibthorpe, Cosin, and Manwaring had come through Bishop Neile. Phelips angrily insisted that the King had been abused in his mercy by giving pardons to the "greatest enemies to the church and state, that were standing under judgment of the parliament." Heath objected that Commons' indictment against Cosin was based on the erroneous assumption that he had repudiated the sovereignty of the King over the English Church. Eliot, rejecting this explanation, severely criticized Cosin and implicated Bishop Laud in the pardons. Oliver Cromwell, a young, virtually unknown Puritan of the Fens, rose to warn the Commons that Neile and Manwaring were preaching "flat Popery" at St. Paul's.

Cromwell's speech touched off a new series of denunciations of the menace of Arminianism and Catholicism.[43] There the matter dropped, but the vital issue of the Commons' right to consider questions of religion had once more been raised.

From February 13 to 19 the Commons again discussed the Clerkenwell Jesuits. Selden told the Commons that ten Jesuits had been arrested but that no legal action had been taken against them until December 1628. Of the three who were tried at the Middlesex Quarter Sessions, two were acquitted (although "plain treason" was proved); a third was sentenced to death, but Chief Justice Sir Nicholas Hyde reprieved him. None of the priests was held, despite their refusal to take the oath of allegiance. Such a miscarriage of justice shocked the Commons. Pym spoke of how diligently the lower House had worked to stem the growth of popery, only to have its efforts reversed by the courts. The Commons alone, Pym said, had framed a petition and an Act against recusants; evasions of recusancy fines had been investigated; and papists had been removed from political office. Parliament had done everything possible to preserve true religion, yet recusants went unprosecuted and proclamations against them were simply ignored. Eliot, echoing Pym, charged Hyde and the Earl of Dorset, who had carried the order of the King authorizing the release of the Jesuits, with criminal negligence. While the Jesuits are undermining the state and the English Church, Eliot said, "the over-officiousness of ministers of state . . . interpose themselves to preserve these men to all our ruins." A statement by Secretary Coke confirmed the suspicion of the Commons that Charles had authorized the Jesuits' release. The Commons, furious though they were, could only submit to the decision of the King.[44]

As the session drew to a close, religion continued to occupy the Commons. They were adjourned between February 23 and 25, but on the 24th the committee on religion completed a set of resolutions on religious grievances for consideration by the committee of the whole the following day. The resolutions were a summary of the debates of the entire session against Catholicism and Arminianism. The Members reaffirmed their confidence in the strong purpose of the King to maintain the faith and ascribed the misdirection of religion to the influence of his ecclesiastical advisers, notably Laud and Neile. Such men, the resolutions asserted, purposely favored and countenanced Arminians, to the disadvantage of orthodox clergymen who supported the Prayer Book, the Homilies, and the Catechism. Catholicism went unchecked. In England, the resolutions said, there had been "an extraordinary growth of Popery," so that in some counties there had been an increase of two thousand recusants since Elizabeth's reign. Moreover, Catholics went publicly to mass "in multitudes without control," thereby scandalizing the Court. And what were the reasons for this growth of recusancy? The answer read like another Millenary Petition: officers of the Crown were negligent in executing the penal laws; popish books, like those by Montague and Cosin, were licensed for popular consumption; the purity of the English Church was poisoned by popish practices such as bowing, making the sign of the cross, and using pictures, lights, and altars. In future, it concluded, anyone speaking or writing contrary to orthodoxy should be punished; bishoprics should be conferred only upon pious, orthodox men; heretical books must be burned; and recusants must be disciplined.[45]

But the Commons were not given a chance to debate the resolutions for the King adjourned Parliament until March 2. On that day the Commons were asked to adjourn again, until the 10th, but refused; they would adjourn, they declared, in their own good time. Then the doors were locked, and as the Usher of the Black Rod pounded on them outside with a message from the King, Eliot denounced Arminianism as the harbinger of popery. The King's guards were said to be on their way to force entry into the Commons. Hurriedly, Denzil Holles read three resolutions drawn up by Eliot. Two concerned tonnage and poundage. The third stated that anyone who brought in innovations in religion, or sought to introduce or extend popery or Arminianism, would be a capital enemy to the kingdom and the commonwealth. The Members at once voted to adopt the resolutions and then adjourned. Eight days later Charles dissolved Parliament. It was not to meet again until 1640.[46]

Chapter Five

THE MISSIONARIES

MANY PROTESTANTS in Caroline England thought of Catholic missionaries as seditious rebels plotting intrigue in dingy rooms in Long Acre Street, or in the great halls of Catholics' country houses. The intentions of these rebels were genuinely feared by men who had heard of or perhaps even witnessed the trials of the Jesuits Edmund Campion and Robert Persons, and who had been shocked by the Gunpowder Plot. Nothing could be more probable to Protestant patriots than that the missionaries hoped to overthrow the monarchy and the Established Church in order to reunite England with Rome.

In truth, as one might expect, the missionaries were neither strong enough nor sufficiently united to justify their formidable image in their enemies' mind. Lacking proper supervision, they were badly split over the question of church government. The rift between the seculars and regulars that had first become apparent in Elizabethan times grew wider during the residence of the Bishop of Chalcedon, whom most of the regulars refused to recognize, and widened again after his departure in 1631. Most of the clergy took no part in the dispute, but the few clerics who did speak out weakened the morale and faith of Catholics, who needed unity above all in order to withstand the rigors of the penal laws. Among these few, the staunchest opponents of the Bishop of Chalcedon were the Jesuits.

Priest-hunting had by now become a government habit, but

those sought most zealously were always the disciples of Ignatius Loyola. Warrants for the apprehension of Jesuits were issued virtually every month by the Privy Council, usually through the office of the principal secretary. In January 1627, for instance, Secretary Conway instructed local constables throughout the realm to watch for the "notorious Jesuit" George Muskett (a secular!),[1] and in February a similar warrant authorized the arrest of a Jesuit with a "flaxen beard inclining to whitish" who frequented the home of the French ambassador in Fleet Street.[2]

Secular priests, particularly those making their way into England disguised as travelers, also caused the Government anxiety; a number of them were arrested in 1625 and 1626 while trying to slip past port authorities. Constables apprehended two such priests at Canterbury, and the mayor of Dartmouth seized a "priest from Douay" who had sailed from Newhaven.[3] William Hale, the mayor of Plymouth, discovering Father Gilbert Brodyn of Brussels on a ship that had lately dropped anchor, had him committed to jail in Devon.[4] Fathers John Taylor and James Redoch were arrested at Newcastle soon after disembarking.[5] Occasionally, priests were stopped even before they could leave Dutch or French ports. William Trumbull, English resident at Brussels, prevented several clerics from sailing in August 1625, after learning of their attempts to procure forged passports.[6]

Raids on recusants' homes in search of priests were not unusual. In Drury Lane, London, where many Catholic families resided, constables arrested two seculars posing as servants of Sir Thomas Gerard,[7] and in Rochester, Father Hoard (alias Gervase Hambleton) was imprisoned along with his brother Peter, a physician.[8] A memorandum of June 1630 gives some details about the history and appearance of several priests: George Gage of the English College in Rome had a slit nose; William Price (alias Jones), the president-elect of Douay College, had much land and money bequeathed to him by deceased English gentry; Father Rawlins had conducted Elizabeth Lyon across the Channel to Brussels, where she had entered a nunnery; and Father Parkinson kept a house and servants "as though he were a country farmer."[9]

Such prosperity as that of Price and Parkinson was indeed rare among the secular clergy, who for the most part worked amid poverty and deprivation. Many of the regulars, it is true—particularly the Jesuits—found comfortable homes with well-to-do families like the Arundels of Wardour, the Vauxs of Harrowden, and the Savages,[10] but seculars usually had no permanent home or regular income. Their plight grew so serious, in fact, that in October 1630 the clergy of London drafted a proposal to establish a common fund for the support of their indigent brethren working in areas where penitents were too poor to support them. In addition, archdeacons were asked to exhort Catholics in their districts to contribute 40*d*. a year toward the support of the Bishop of Chalcedon, the colleges of Douay and Lisbon, and the Vicar General and his staff in London.[11]

The letters of the Catholic clergy often mention their need of money. Father Thomas Greene, an elderly archdeacon and rural dean of Essex, notified the Vicar General in 1635 of the general ignorance of Catholics in his county in matters of the faith, a result, he believed, of their being too poor to support priests. Wealthy Catholic families had resident clergymen in their homes the year round, but they sometimes would not permit them to attend the poor for fear the attention of the Government might be aroused and fines imposed. Greene suggested that these rich families should raise money to support priests who would have charge of the poor. "A poor man's priest," he cautioned, "must be apostolical in spirit, zealous for souls and fond of hard work, and no lover of his back or belly and diligent to instruct."[12] In 1633, Father George Leyburn asked Peter Fitton, the seculars' agent in Rome, to beseech the Pontiff for money to alleviate "the great miserie and hurt wch doth happen unto the clergie" of England.[13] Three years later, Leyburn wrote to the Bishop of Chalcedon: "I never knew us [the seculars] in a worse estate for moneys . . . [because] little summes come in, and thos [at] Lisbon doth devoure now [our money, and] our cheef friends never thinke of providing any charityes for the discharge of common expences."[14] In 1636, Father John Southcot admitted to a friend named Edward Hope that the seculars were in dire need of money.[15] Even the Benedictines, who were rarely in need during this period, seemed to have been pressed for funds. William Price, a Benedictine in London, took the trouble to ask a friend in the North to contribute what he could to the dwindling treasury of the order.[16]

In desperation, the seculars were sometimes forced to borrow money at high interest rates. Southcot promised in the name of the clergy to repay out of their common fund any money that wealthy Catholics could lend them, at the rate of 8 per cent a year per hundred pounds. Alban Jernegan lent the clergy £100 on February 11, 1635, but it would appear that few others did.[17] In January 1638, Richard Worthington borrowed £300 at 8 per cent interest a month toward the support of Douay College.[18]

Happily, the clergy did on occasion come into some funds. A London gentleman, Sir Thomas Roper, gave Southcot and John Farmer a piece of land in Buckinghamshire valued at £440 a year.[19] Father Thomas Keightley of Grays Thurrock Manor in Essex willed his younger brother Edward the income from his manor, and Father Francis Lockwood of Yorkshire likewise bequeathed a large estate to Thomas Killigrew and Robert Reade. When the Jesuit Richard Ireland moved from England to France, he reportedly left about £2,000 in the care of his brother William.[20]

Although it is now impossible to determine accurately the number of seculars and regulars resident in England during

Charles's reign, it is certain that there were a good many more in 1630 than there had been in 1603. Despite the controversy between the two clerical groups over the jurisdiction of Bishop Smith between 1625 and 1631, and the consequent acrimony that left them in want of effective leadership, most Catholics generally had access to priests at no great distance from their homes. With the exception of the Southwest, particularly Cornwall, Devon, and Wiltshire, there seems to have been at least a skeleton corps of clerics who ministered to the faithful, if only at irregular intervals.

One responsible authority has fixed the number of priests in England in 1669 at about 230 seculars, 120 Jesuits, and 80 Benedictines—430 in all—and almost double that number in 1631, or about 850 priests.[21] Another, Dom Leander Jones, estimated in 1634 that there were over 900 priests—500 seculars, 250 Jesuits, 100 Benedictines, 30 Franciscans, 20 Dominicans, and eight Capuchins. He added, significantly, that the number was greater than the need.[22] Whatever their strength, during the 1630's the ranks of the regulars apparently multiplied faster than those of the seculars. Southcot, writing to Peter Fitton in Rome in 1633, lamented the growing strength of the regulars, who, he said, were taking permanent posts in districts where seculars could not be provided in sufficient numbers.[23] One must remember, however, that his evaluation of the number and distribution of the regulars may have been influenced by his animosity, as a secular, toward the more comfortably situated Jesuits and Benedictines.

As one might expect, there were far more priests in the North, where Catholics made up a sizable proportion of the population, than there were in the Midlands or the Southeast, which were becoming Puritan strongholds. Since the time of Elizabeth the drain of population from the Southwest, mainly from Cornwall, had left few Catholics there, and in consequence fewer priests to attend them. In Wales there appear to have been an unusually large number, and London and its environs had more than a fair share, though the Catholic population there was dwindling.[24]

The correspondence of seculars helps to give some notion of the geographical distribution of the clergy. For example, just prior to the resignation of Richard Smith in 1631, the seculars drew up testimonials disavowing their parishioners' concurrence with the prominent Catholic gentry who questioned Smith's episcopal jurisdiction. The testimonials were generally signed by the archdeacon or dean of each district, together with a handful of his priests. Most of the clergy, it is true, had no opportunity to add their names, but the number of those who did ought certainly to give some indication of the total number of priests in each district. The districts that reported and the number who signed were as follows: Wales, 27; Staffordshire, 13; Essex, seven; Lincolnshire, three; Hampshire, three; Yorkshire, 11; Sussex, ten; Berkshire, four; Bishopric of Durham, eight; Suffolk, six; Northamptonshire, four; Norfolk, eight; Derbyshire, two; Worcestershire, nine; Kent, one; London and Middlesex, 19.[25] A letter by Southcot, dated February 8, 1633, lists by name 14 seculars and four regulars in Sussex, and two seculars, one Benedictine, and five Jesuits then working in Lincolnshire.[26] A similar list of October 1634 names four priests in Worcestershire, four in Sussex, three in Lincoln, two in Kent, and nine in Yorkshire.[27] A petition addressed to the Pope in 1632 by Father John Colleton and the priests of Essex, Suffolk, Kent, Norfolk, Bedfordshire, Buckinghamshire, Sussex, Middlesex, Herefordshire, the district of London, and the Bishoprics of Canterbury and Ely, is signed by 29 seculars.[28]

An indication of the number of priests in London is given by a record compiled in 1632 by John Southcot. "Seculars Imprisoned" names 17 seculars, seven Benedictines, four Jesuits, and one Dominican in five London jails; "Seculars Out of Prison" names 24 seculars, nine Jesuits, two Benedictines, one

Dominican, and one Carmelite. The only duplication in names is that of Southcot himself. The total of these two lists, with the addition of the eight Capuchins who served Henrietta Maria, accounts for 73 priests in London in 1632. Southcot also lists ten names for Berkshire, ten for Somerset, seven for Norfolk, and 22 for Warwickshire.[29] According to a recent authority, there were 31 Jesuits in the London area early in 1634.[30] One may conclude from the foregoing statistics that the Catholics of most counties and bishoprics of England did not want for priests, but one cannot go much further in estimating the actual number of priests in any county, or in the country as a whole.

The procedure by which a secular secured a station was uncertain and circuitous. The case of Father John Trumble, interrogated by Sir John Coke and Sir Robert Heath in 1626, was not unusual. Trumble stated that he served in Flanders for twenty-five years before journeying to England. He was first a chaplain to the Bishop of Cambrai, then a pastor near Ghent, and finally a preacher in Saint-Omer at the Church of SS. Martin and Margaret. Disguised as a traveler, he crossed the Channel from Calais to Deal in a small English vessel and went on to Canterbury, where constables apprehended him. It had been his intention to proceed to the residence of Bishop Smith, if he could find it, and there seek approbation to serve Catholics in England. Thereafter, Trumble was to present himself to Father George Muskett, "said to be living in London," and then to Father Cuthbert Trollop in the North. He hoped there to be placed "in some home of a Recusant as other priests do."[31] What is most curious about Trumble's journey is that he expected to find Smith, Muskett, and Trollop, all of whom he had never met and could not recognize by sight. However, it can be surmised that a chain of command over the secular clergy existed in 1626, and that there were fixed routes, circuitous to be sure, which missionaries could follow until they were finally assigned to stations.

How many Catholics did the missionaries of England serve?

The question cannot be answered with authority. Unfortunately, contemporary commentators usually neglected to explain exactly what they meant when they wrote of "church papists," recusants, Catholics who accepted the oath of allegiance, and Catholics who questioned papal supremacy. Should all of these be counted? Until we can determine in some way what "Catholic" meant, we can do little more than consider all the various estimates and try to arrive at a reasonable guess.

I have relied here largely on Brian Magee's findings. William Paget, Lord Privy Seal under Mary Tudor, wrote Protector Somerset in 1548 that only one-twelfth of the nation favored the new religion. The Spanish ambassador put the Catholic population in 1559 at two-thirds, and in 1605 the Venetian ambassador believed that at least half the population was still Catholic. The Spanish ambassador, Gondomar, whose figures, though obviously far off the mark, are most often quoted, breaks down the population about 1617 as follows: recusants, 300,000; Catholics attending Protestant worship, 600,000; atheists, 900,000; Puritans, 600,000; other Protestants, 1,200,000; total, 3,600,000. Two papal agents, Gregorio Panzani and George Conn, put the number of Catholics at 150,000 (1637) and 200,000 (1638) respectively. Here it is obvious that they meant only recusants, not all Catholics. An anonymous correspondent in 1667 estimated that there were then no more than 24,000 recusants. Summing up, Magee believes that the Catholic population in the reign of Charles I was something more than 7½ per cent of the total.[32] If from 1603 to 1660 the population is put at between 4,000,000 and 4,500,000,[33] the number of Catholics would be about 320,000 to 360,000. How many of these had been recusants there is no way of knowing. Magee concludes that there were only about 27,000 in the whole country in 1647.[34]

Of all the problems that plagued the Catholic clergy of Caroline England, none was more perplexing than that of church government. This problem had two main historical phases:

the archpriest controversy (1594–1623) and the quarrel over the jurisdiction of Bishop Smith (1625–31). Since the former has its historians,[35] and the latter soon will have its,[36] we may here confine ourselves to a broad review of the troubles.

In 1594, after the death of Cardinal William Allen,[37] the recognized leader of the English Catholics since 1581 when he became Prefect of the Mission,[38] several prominent seculars petitioned Rome to appoint a resident English bishop. Accordingly, in 1598, Clement VIII consecrated George Blackwell archpriest of England, investing him with episcopal jurisdiction over all the clergy. But a group of regulars, mainly Jesuits and Benedictines, immediately challenged his authority on the grounds that it compromised their clerical freedom. Several times thereafter the Jesuits appealed to the Pontiff, without success, for the archpriest's dismissal. Meanwhile, Queen Elizabeth, in a move to intensify the dispute and break down Catholic opposition to the Crown, appeared to favor the seculars against the regulars. After the enactment of the Jacobean oath of allegiance in 1606, the quarrel among the clergy became more serious; some of the seculars saw no harm in the oath, and a few took it to escape persecution. The archpriest Blackwell himself took the oath and advised others to do the same, even though Pope Paul V had forbidden it. Not surprisingly, the Pope punished Blackwell for disloyalty by stripping him of authority in 1608. Neither of Blackwell's successors as archpriest, George Birkhead (1608–15) and William Harrison (1615–21), could overcome the ecclesiastical hegemony of the masterful Jesuits or settle their quarrel with the seculars.[39]

For two years following Harrison's death in 1621 no prelate whatever was in charge of the English mission. Then the cheerful prospect of toleration for Catholics at the time of the Spanish marriage negotiations gave a group of seculars, headed by John Bennett, the opportunity to appeal once more for the appointment of an English bishop.[40] Accordingly, in June 1623, an aged priest named Dr. William Bishop[41] became Vicar Apostolic for England with the title of Bishop of Chalcedon. He died less than a year after taking office, but not before he had inadvertantly alienated the regulars by subjecting their sacerdotal faculties, (i.e., the right by which they administered the sacraments) to his approbation, and by appointing archdeacons and rural deans to supervise local administration.[42]

Dr. Richard Smith, a proud man with a flair for organization, succeeded to the bishopric of Chalcedon in April 1625. Within two months of his appointment he had established a badly needed system of church government that included a chapter (the central group of administrative asistants to a bishop within a diocese), vicars, archdeacons, notaries, and registrars. He also claimed to have ordinary jurisdiction over the regulars as well as the seculars. He set up his headquarters in the home of Lady Mordaunt at Turney, about three miles from Bedford, and frequently stayed also with Lady Dormer in Buckinghamshire, or at Chandeis near Allobury. From these points he sometimes traveled west, or as far south as Sussex, in a four-horse carriage accompanied by his assistants. He seldom went to London, but employed several subordinates, including John Colleton, dean of the English seculars, and George Muskett in Kent and Middlesex, to carry out his orders there.[43]

Pope Gregory XV, in his brief time in office, had been careful to invest Smith with episcopal authority, thereby empowering him to settle the serious differences between the two groups of clergy. But the English Jesuits once more blocked the way, maintaining, as before, that a bishop could not effectively rule the Catholics in a kingdom in which he had to hide. They also maintained that they were responsible only to Richard Blount, their provincial, and were not bound to acknowledge Smith's authority. To make matters worse, Smith pointedly refused to permit some of the Jesuits to administer the sacraments, and he planned to appoint an ecclesiastical court empowered to excommunicate, probate wills, and govern all aspects of Catholic life.[44]

The correspondence between Smith and Blount set the tone for the whole disagreement. In a letter of May 1628, Smith quoted Blount as having scoffed at his jurisdiction as "a thing in the aire," and asked him if he had made such a statement; if he had, Smith said, it must be immediately rescinded as "false and seditious." And he ended the letter coldly: "Wherefore . . . [I hope] this briefe admonition will suffice for you and all yours." Blount answered in kind: "Your Lp. gave me occasion to reflect how true that saying is: *Veritas odium parit.* I could not but much wonder at the tenor thereof." Blount flatly denied that he had "divulged any false and malicious rumors notwithstanding whatsoever I may have written," and charged that Smith had not obeyed the Pope's order.[45]

The order in question was in a letter from the new Pope, Urban VIII, instructing Smith to desist from further quarrel with the regulars and to extend approbation to them without delay.[46] So directed, Smith complied in a letter to the superiors of the regular clergy in February 1628, which did in fact acknowledge his obligations. "Since we may be sure that their [the Catholics'] confessions made to Regular priests may be valid without doubt," Smith admitted, "we do here approve the Regulars now in England to hear . . . confessions. This holds true even for those Regulars who have not sought our approbation."[47]

The fact that the Pope restricted Smith's authority indicates the extent to which the bishop had imposed his will over the regulars to the detriment of the faithful. Since many of them had taken the sacraments from regulars, Smith's refusal to validate their faculties had put in doubt the spiritual welfare of hundreds of penitents, causing them serious anxiety. One Catholic gentleman named William Cape was so worried about the efficacy of his confessions to a Jesuit that he visited the bishop himself for advice. During their conversation, Cape relates, he told the bishop that regardless of his rights under Canon Law to approbate faculties, he did wrong to invalidate so many confessions simply to prove his point. To this Smith gave no satisfactory reply, and it was not until the papal order resolved the issue that Cape, and undoubtedly many other Catholics, could rest easy.[48]

With the help of the Pope, the regulars had won the first round of their fight with Smith. They then pressed their advantage by bombarding him with letters, petitions, and pamphlets in the hope of inducing his resignation.[49] The most significant of these writings was the *Protestatio Declaratoria* (1631), a protestation against Smith's jurisdiction as bishop in ordinary which was signed by dozens of prominent Catholic laymen in an effort to prove that Smith's supporters were wrong in maintaining that a majority of the laity recognized his claim. We "heir make our protestation . . . & declare under our hands," the document begins, "that wee doe hold the said Rd. Bp. of Chalcedon not to bee in any sorte Ordinary in England, neither can wee submitte ourselves to any such authority in this kingdome, as our case stands." Eighty-six signatures, including those of such leading Catholic gentlemen as Vaux, Abergavenny, Rivers, Baltimore, and Brundenell, and such prominent families as the Howards, Widdringtons, and Herberts, attested to the formidable opposition to Smith among the laity[50]—though no doubt most of them acted under the influence of their regular confessors.

Whether the signers of the *Protestatio Declaratoria* spoke for a majority of English Catholics cannot now be determined, but Smith was certainly not without substantial support among another group of laymen. Many Catholics of the gentry and lower classes respected and supported him, despite their fears about their spiritual welfare. An anonymous correspondent of June 1628 boldly remarked that in his county alone (which is unnamed) he could get five hundred signatures in favor of the bishop, among which there would be only a half-dozen of gentlemen, the rest being of the lower classes.[51] George Leyburn, writing in the same year, estimated that the number of lay Catholics opposing the bishop was "very small."[52] Lord Arundel of Wardour, a staunch defendant of episcopal jurisdiction, said in 1627 that the gentry who claimed to speak for all lay Catholics against the bishop ignored the opinions of thirty-nine out of every forty.[53] John Paulet, fifth Marquis of Winchester, came out in support of the bishop, as did fifty-three peers and gentry.[54]

So hot a controversy could not fail to attract the attention of the Government. In 1628 Secretary Coke compiled a dossier on Smith which included information on his residences in Bedfordshire and Buckinghamshire, and the names of some of the seculars on his administrative staff. The Privy Council learned of the quarrel between Smith and the regulars from the papers found at Clerkenwell, and an order for Smith's arrest was issued on December 11, 1628. Another order a few months later, on March 24, 1629, offered £100 for his capture. Pursuivants were brought in to lead the search, but despite a plan by the Council to have Smith trapped by an apostate Catholic named Edward Morgan, Smith escaped.[55] Eventually, the councillors realized that he had lost control of the English Catholics and that his capture would be of little consequence, and thereafter they ignored him.

By 1631, Smith's position had become untenable. His efforts to placate the regulars, to win over influential peers and gentry, and to make peace with the Benedictines, all had failed.[56] Sometime between July 12 and September 21 (probably on August 24),[57] he left England for Paris, where he spent the remainder of his life under the patronage of Richelieu and Mazarin. Surprisingly enough, he considered neither his departure nor his resignation as bishop *de jure* to be permanent—he said as much in a letter to Urban VIII in December, and he appointed John

Colleton his coadjutor "during his absence."[58] He also retained Peter Fitton as his agent in Rome to work toward his restoration.[59] Until his death in 1655, Smith never ceased to hope that he would one day return to England as its Catholic bishop, and he kept in close touch with English affairs in a voluminous correspondence with Leyburn, Fitton, Colleton, and Southcot, as well as with Douay and Lisbon Colleges.

The controversy between the two clerical groups went on throughout the 1630's. Every passing year seemed to make each group feel increasingly bitter toward the other:[60] both wrote hundreds of letters and pamphlets about the need for a bishop and mustered support either for or against from every quarter. They appealed to Rome, to the Catholic peers and gentry, and even to Charles and Henrietta to speak their minds in the matter. Leander Jones, Gregorio Panzani, and George Conn went to England at various times to do what they could to settle the quarrel, but their attempts failed, and by 1640 the Catholic community as a whole was even weaker than it had been in 1603 or 1625.

The essential source of this weakness was not so much the Catholics' numerical inferiority as their inability to organize legally. The suppression of Catholicism under Elizabeth and James I had impaired the traditional system of church government by outlawing the forces of hierarchy and centralization, in effect by driving the leaders underground. As a result, clergy and laity formed small, isolated groups without an effective spiritual leadership beyond the group itself. The ties with Rome were weakened, and lesser loyalties took their place: the regular turned to his order, the secular to his parish or his station, the layman too often to a narrow self-concern. The need for a bishop was widely conceded, but the charms of decentralization had been tasted and were not lightly to be surrendered.

Perhaps no bishop could have restored order in the circumstances, but the choice of Richard Smith was especially unfortunate. It is clear that Smith badly bungled his episcopacy. His challenge to the long-standing prerogatives of the regulars was technically within his authority, and was welcome enough, as we have seen, to those who had nothing to lose by it, but no move could have been less in accord with the necessities of the situation and the temper of the times. Rome understandably chose not to endorse his policy, but the damage was done.[61]

Chapter Six

THE TOILS OF THE LAW

I T IS A MORE OR LESS commonly accepted view that the marriage of Charles I to a Catholic princess greatly eased the lot of English Catholics—that, under Charles I, the penal code was rarely enforced, especially after 1629, the clergy were allowed to minister to their parishioners without much governmental interference, and the Catholic community as a whole enjoyed a time of relative quiet. When one looks beyond proclamations and petitions, however, and into obscure documents that concern the lives of the people, especially those in the counties, one sees a different picture.

Some Catholics, it is true, were able to escape the recusancy laws altogether, but these were chiefly of the upper class—members of families who had sufficient influence to enlist the sympathy of, or to intimidate, local constables and churchwardens who were assigned to carry out the recusancy laws. Many other Catholics were not so fortunate. For them, recusancy might mean, at the very least, a frightening day or two at the Quarter Sessions, or lengthy interrogation by the local constabulary. Beyond that, there were fines, imprisonment, the loss of goods and land, not to mention restrictions on baptism, marriage, and burial.

Charles I had a number of regular sources of revenue, but they were often inadequate, especially after 1629. As the heir to the constitutional, financial, and religious quarrels between James and Parliament, Charles had to beg and borrow his way through a troublesome reign in which a frugal and hostile Commons frequently failed to vote sufficient funds to meet the rising cost of Government.[1] With no Parliament at all between 1629 and 1640, the problem of finance became acute. Forced loans, ship money, distraint of knighthood fees, deforestation penalties, and recusancy fines were imposed, but all of these measures, except the last, were unpopular and generally unsuccessful. Only in fining Catholics, in pounds and shillings, could the King avoid the unparliamentary taxation.

Before 1625 penalties for recusancy had provided some income for the Crown, but in decreasing amounts. Few Catholics could long afford the monstrous £20 monthly fines or stand to lose as much as two-thirds of their land and all their goods, and many of them either fell into arrears or did not pay at all. It was largely for this reason that Charles restored the practice of composition. This was a contract between the Government and a recusant whereby the recusant agreed to compound, that is, to pay an annual rent based upon the assessed value of two-thirds of his landed property, often in lieu of arrears in recusancy fines. Once a Catholic compounded, he was technically no longer liable for subsequent violations of the penal code. It will be seen, however, that in practice composition was not a guarantee against further fines.

King James had occasionally permitted recusants to compound, but the widespread adoption of this system began in July 1626. In answer to complaints by recusants about the ominous nature of their financial penalties, Charles said that he would permit them to earn a living "so that in the course of time they would [not] become mendicants and . . . be supported by the Parishes." And he added, "we do not seek their ruin but rather their conversion . . . without slackening Our hand in the prosecution of the laws against them." Thereafter,

Charles ordered, recusants would be allowed to lease two-thirds of their confiscated land at prevailing rents within three months (May 16) of the promulgation of a royal proclamation to that effect.[2] If recusants had not compounded for the seized portions of their land by that time it would be leased to anyone except other recusants. It is unlikely that Charles sanctioned composition through any compelling sympathy for the financial welfare of his Catholic subjects, or because of sympathy with their dogma. Rather, it would appear he did so to assure a larger return of income from them at a time when recusant revenue had fallen off sharply and the Government needed money badly.[3] The final words of Charles's proclamation authorizing composition—that he hoped it would yield £150,000 a year— belie his stated purpose of converting the recusants.

A recusant often had little choice but to compound. Upon being presented at the Quarter Sessions he was usually fined. If the fine happened to be light, he could pay it without undue hardship, especially if he were presented seldom thereafter; but repeated convictions often led to heavier fines, loss of part of his property, or even imprisonment. A recusant, deprived of a part of his source of income, fell into debt with the Government, which sometimes gave him the alternative of imprisonment or composition. Naturally, he chose the latter; and then, as a rule, he was interrogated by the sheriff or a deputy of his county, and referred to either of two royal commissions for compounding. The commissioners assessed the annual income of his property to determine what rent should be charged on two-thirds of it (one-third after 1635). The compounder, having agreed to pay the rent fixed by the commissioners, signed the book of compositions and received a warrant certifying the transaction. The commissioners then forwarded the record to the attorney-general's office, which drew up a contract of composition and sent it with the other particulars of the case to the Office of the Pipe in the Exchequer, where the lease was recorded and returned to the compounder. After that the case was periodically reviewed to see that the rental payments had been made regularly, or to renew or alter leases.

How much rent recusants might have to pay depended largely upon the whim or disposition of the commissioners who assessed their property. Most of the commissioners came from good gentry families, but high-ranking ecclesiastics (such as the Archbishop of York and the bishops of the Northern Province) and peers frequently sat on boards of composition—men, for the most part, of considerable governmental experience. The Northern commission for compounding, which sat at York under the leadership of Emmanuel Scrope, Earl of Sunderland, had jurisdiction over recusants' estates north of the Trent. Its membership of from forty-one to forty-eight persons changed frequently, but Sir Edward Osborne (vice-president of the Council at York), and Sir Henry Slingsby (brother to Sir William, commissioner on fees) served throughout the 1630's; others, such as Sir John Savile, Sir John Hotham, Sir Arthur Ingram, and Sir William Dalton, sat for shorter periods at different times.[4] The second commission for compounding, with its headquarters at Westminster, technically had jurisdiction over all England, although it normally dealt with recusants' estates south of the Trent. Its membership, made up largely of Exchequer officers under the Lord Treasurer, included prominent men such as Archbishop George Abbot, Lord Keeper Thomas Coventry, Sir Dudley Digges, Sir Thomas Walsingham, Sir William Twynsden, and Sir Edwin Sandys, who served at irregular intervals.[5]

These men generally treated the Catholics fairly, and as often as not seem to have been lenient in assessing recusants' estates. (Laud and others thought they were too lenient, and one memorandum of the Privy Council to the commissioners in the North draws their attention to the sharp decrease in recusant revenue from Yorkshire, Durham, Northumberland,

Cumberland, Westmoreland, Lancashire, Nottingham, Derby, Stafford, and Chester.) One Philip Anne, for example, whose annual income before composition had been £500, afterward paid only £20 rent on the two-thirds of his estate that the Government confiscated, although his father had been assessed £80 on the same land the previous year (1628). Another recusant named Chomley, with an annual income of £800, paid £25 rent in 1629 despite his having inherited a brother's estate which brought in another £120.[6]

Lenient compositions in the North ceased with the administration of Thomas, Viscount Wentworth, as president of the Council (1630–33). Bent on augmenting recusant revenue, he ordered composition rents to be increased, an action for which some commended him and others, even Protestants, criticized him. Charles Wandesford, an officer of the Exchequer, praised him as a "light and Comfort to the whole country . . . for the Papists already hang down their Heads like Bulrushes, and think themselves like Water spilt upon the Ground." Wentworth served justice so well, Wandesford added, that "the Rust of the Laws made against . . . [the Catholics] . . . which hath almost eaten out the very Iron" was filed off.[7] George Calvert, Lord Baltimore,[8] a Catholic, demanded of Wentworth "true justice," not severity, towards recusants. Even Lord Treasurer Richard Weston questioned Wentworth's harsh policy, saying, "you proceed with extreme Rigour, valuing the Goods and Lands of the poorest at the highest Rates, or rather above the value, without which you are not content to make any Composition."[9]

Hundreds of recusants compounded for their sequestered estates. Henry Foster, a Catholic who owned property near Copdocke in Suffolk, was convicted of recusancy three times between June 1626 and February 1634 "for not repayring to Church to heare divine service by the space of three monethes." Following his second conviction on March 20, 1632, having fallen in arrears on his £20 monthly fines, Foster appeared before High Sheriff Sir Robert Crane, who, on a writ from the Court of Exchequer, sequestered Foster's "demesne" valued at £16 13s. 4d. a year. A third conviction for recusancy led to an enquiry on April 10, 1634, before Sheriff Sir Edmond Bacon, who ordered the seizure of the remainder of Foster's estate for the duration of his life. On November 13, 1634, Foster compounded for two-thirds of all of his estate, consisting of "diverse messuages, Landes, tenements and one water mill," at an annual rental of £8 4s. 5d., payable semi-annually. His arrears in fines were canceled and he could be penalized no further for recusancy.[10] Foster's composition is noteworthy in that it not only brought the Government financial profit but also made it possible for him to earn a living.

The case of Francis Mathews, a recusant of Sherborne, Dorset, was typical of the Government's policy of making composition over an extended term of up to forty-one years. Convicted on April 20, 1625, for failing to attend Anglican services, Mathews was deprived of his land and goods (presumably he had been found guilty of the same offense several times before). On July 5, 1638, he made composition on two-thirds of his land for sixteen years at an annual rent of £12. That the Exchequer periodically verified the regularity of Mathews's payments is proved in a certificate signed by Sir Henry Croke, clerk of the pipe, on February 25, 1639.[11]

A third record of composition involves a Lancashire Catholic named Edward Scaresbreck, who was convicted on August 20, 1635, for repeated violations of the penal code. All of his property was seized by the Crown for the duration of his life. Deprived of his means of livelihood and facing poverty, he had little choice but to compound for £16 6s. 8d. in rent on two-thirds of his land. In addition, he had to pay arrears in fines owing from a previous conviction in the Michaelmas Term of 1633. The Government reviewed his recusancy in June 1640 with an eye to harnessing him with further penalties, but what happened after that is not known.[12]

The case of Henry Wilford, a well-to-do yeoman of Quendon, Essex, is proof that composition was not a guarantee against further financial penalties. He was cited for recusancy four times between 1625 and 1640, in each instance having to pay fines—the fact that he owned several estates totaling hundreds of acres explains his ability to pay them. Finally, after selling most of his property, he compounded for the remainder in January 1634. But early in 1639 the Barons of the Exchequer suddenly held Wilford accountable for arrears in fines amounting to £3,580. Because he could not raise such an enormous sum of money, the Crown confiscated all his land, two-thirds of which was leased to Sir Edward Wardour for rent.[13]

But few recusants suffered so heavily. For most, the commutation of rentals on land, fixed by law until 1635 at two-thirds of the annual rental, was often reduced to a third, fourth, or even a fifth part.[14] Encouraged to compound by this lenient policy, many recusants did so on the understanding that they would thereafter be excused from further fines. Yet leniency in composition was not the rule in Yorkshire in the 1630's, when recusant land was assessed at high rates and infractions of the penal code such as Catholic christenings and marriages were severely punished even after the offenders had compounded.[15] In Durham, too, Bishop Thomas Morton repeatedly abused Catholics in this way. His sentences grew so harsh, in fact, that the Franciscan Christopher Davenport, a friend of the Court, interceded with the Privy Council, which ordered Morton to moderate the penalties.[16]

Some of the money collected from recusants never reached the King at all but stayed in the pockets of dishonest officials along the way. In 1626 the Government prosecuted James Conyers, a churchwarden of Guisborough Parish, Yorkshire, for stealing "divers sommes of [recusant] monie."[17] On another occasion the Privy Council questioned the honesty of several sheriffs of Midland counties, who allegedly charged Catholics more rent than their composition contracts called for.[18] Commissioners for subsidy in Leicestershire could not explain to the satisfaction of the Privy Council what had happened to a portion of the money collected from recusants during 1628.[19] Sir Henry Spiller, sometime Exchequer officer and justice of the peace for Middlesex, was cited in three successive Parliaments for irregularities concerning recusant revenue.[20] Archbishop Abbot asked Bishop John Bridgeman of Chester to investigate the meager financial returns from Catholics within his diocese. The embezzlement of recusant revenue at last became such a problem that the Government cautioned the commissioners for compounding to surrender cash only to authorized agents of the Crown.[21] Even the Clerk of the Pipe, Sir Henry Croke, admitted exacting excessive fees and made a financial settlement with the Crown in 1638.[22] Andrea Rosso, the Venetian ambassador, knew of corruption among officials handling recusant revenue; his comment that only £2,000 of the £40,000 collected in 1625 ever reached the Exchequer, is surely exaggerated, but it does indicate what must have been fairly widespread knowledge of the dishonesty.[23]

The Government, naturally dissatisfied with the small returns, tried hard to increase the yield. Henry Stanley and Philip Farrell were hired at twenty marks a year each to audit accounts of recusant revenue.[24] King Charles also considered granting Stanley, then an auditor in the Mint, a monopoly to collect arrears in rent when he promised to raise £6,000 the first year and £20,000 a year thereafter. Had Charles actually done so, Catholics might have been subjected to the evils of tax farming. Instead, he made Stanley clerk of recusants' fines and gave him several assistants to record property transfers to the Crown.[25] Lord Keeper Thomas Coventry (himself a commissioner), per-plexed by the "smallness of . . . Revenue yearly answered by the forfeitures of popish Recusants," accused several commissioners of misreporting the true values of recusant property, and ordered circuit judges to conduct enquiries toward reassessing lands.[26] Such measures helped little. Although there were receivers-general in the North (Sir John Savile, 1628–29; Viscount Wentworth, 1629–40) and in the South (George Fielding, 1628–39) to direct the collection and safekeeping of recusant revenue, the appointment of far too many deputy-receivers and collectors increased the opportunity for dishonesty.[27]

The lack of complete records as well as poor bookkeeping by Government auditors makes it impossible to determine the total revenue from recusants. According to Professor Frederick Dietz, who has studied the Exchequer during the early Stuart period,[28] the annual recusant receipts between 1625 and 1630 did not exceed £5,300 out of a national revenue of some £640,-000 in 1625 and £500,000 in 1630. But in the next five years they rose quickly, from £6,396 in 1631 to £26,866 in 1634. From 1635 through 1640 the average yield was £15,428. The annual revenue from all sources between 1630 and 1640 averaged about £450,000.[29] These figures on recusancy fines do not include money taken in composition rents, or at least not most of it. And when it is remembered that some money was stolen, or in other ways lost to the Crown, it becomes clear that the actual income from recusants must have been greater than the figures would now indicate.

The smallness of most parishes (averaging about three hundred inhabitants in the rural areas) necessarily drew people into close association, and the bonds so engendered were often quite as strong as religious beliefs. It is not surprising, therefore, that the local constables and churchwardens often neglected their duties rather than point accusing fingers at Catholic neighbors. Pressure from superiors sometimes compelled them to enforce the law,[30] but ordinarily, so long as Catholics made no issue of their religion or became nuisances, they left them alone.

The justices of the peace, however, were not so casual in fulfilling their duties concerning recusancy. Above all, the justices had to be of suitable moral character, which meant in Stuart times that they must adhere to the official form of worship. No one in the counties carried such a heavy burden of responsibility. Since Elizabethan times all manner of administrative work had been thrust upon them: they regulated labor and wages, made and implemented highway legislation and the poor laws, meted out justice to misdemeanants and felons, and carried out a multitude of orders from the Government. Their work with recusants alone would have been sufficient to keep them busy. Priests had to be reported to the Council within twenty-eight days after arrest (27 Eliz. I, c. 2), and could be imprisoned without recourse to bail for giving evasive answers to questions (35 Eliz. I, c. 2). Justices could also deport recusants who refused to conform within three months of conviction (21 Jac. I, c. 28) and fine those who traveled beyond five miles of their homes without license (3 Jac. I, c. 5). Two justices together could tender a recusant the oath of allegiance, license his travel abroad, or search his house for books and religious articles (3 Jac. I, c. 5). At least two justices, one of the quorum,[31] were required to sentence a woman to prison for refusing to conform within three months of her identification as a covert recusant (protected by her husband), unless he bought her freedom with a £10 monthly fine or two-thirds of his land (7 Jac. I, c. 6). Any two justices might also summon a suspected recusant to appear at the next sessions to take the oath of allegiance, and retain his £20 bond if he failed to do so.[32]

The justices did their real work at the Quarter Sessions, where the legal officials of the shire met four times a year for two or three days to pass judgment on minor crimes. Once every three months two or more justices in every division of the county sent warrants to the constables and churchwardens of the parishes within their limits to present under oath, at least fourteen days before the sessions, the full names, residences, and offenses of known or suspected recusants. The constables then brought these persons to court for questioning and indictment.[33] After the clerk of the peace had read the names and charges of all prisoners as well as the new statutes passed since the previous session, the high constables of the hundreds made their presentments of prisoners, including recusants. Then, while the jury considered its verdicts in cases of petty larceny and traverses (objections to indictments at previous sessions for minor offenses like trespasses and assaults and battery), the clerk compiled a list of recusants presented by the high and petty constables and the juries of the several hundreds, and submitted it to the grand jury. Recusants against whom indictments had been returned were bound over to appear at the next sessions; those who had been indicted at the previous session were imprisoned, ordered to leave the country, or fined according to the law.[34] All of this information was duly forwarded to the Exchequer, where it was recorded and certified in the Treasurer's remembrances and written into the great rolls.[35]

The sentences imposed on recusants at the Quarter Sessions varied considerably. Frequently the justices merely conducted brief enquiries of recusants and let them off with fines of less than a pound. There were some justices—especially in Northumberland—who were sympathetic, and it may well have been that several inclined to the Catholic faith themselves.[36] But the justices in districts of Yorkshire, for example, where Catholics predominated, were usually more harsh. Their fines for relatively minor violations of the recusancy laws ranged from £30 to £200. At Thirsk in October 1626, for instance, two justices fined Richard Pullen of Gillinge Parish £30 for harboring a recusant named Elizabeth Moore for three months. Thomas Crathorne paid £200 for similarly protecting four of his catholic servants, as did Appleton Wiske for housing five Catholic "sojourners." Justices John Wilson and Mathew Jobson of Richmond fined fifteen recusants a total of £1,300 for similar offenses in 1626. Two justices at Northallerton fined William Green, a gentleman recusant of Lanmouth, £100 for having his child baptized a Catholic and gave a third of the money to William Cawood, who had informed on Green.[37]

Doling out a sentence to suit the crime was not an easy job for any justice, and it was especially hard for those who had little formal legal training. Many of the justices of the peace had spent some time at the Inns of Court; others had picked up snatches of knowledge in private study and at the Assizes, where custom required their presence to hear learned judges interpret the statutes. Since the recusancy laws, and, indeed, all laws, required careful scrutiny to appreciate the subtleties involved, it is not surprising that the legal knowledge of justices sometimes proved inadequate. If they were uncertain about the procedure to be followed in cases involving recusants, justices could ask the advice of the itinerant magistrates at the Assizes. The frequency of such questions is indicated by a document of Charles's reign entitled, "The Resolucon of all the Judges of England upon severall questions against Popishe Recusants" in which the magistrates pose sample situations involving recusancy and render judgments. For example:

> QUEST: If he [a recusant] dwell in a place out of all parishes or in a decayed parrishe [what should be done?]
> ANS: In this case hee ought to resorte to the next parrishe or some other parrishe church, hee may bee indicted of anie parrishe within the countie.
>
> QUEST: If the officers of the prishe can not learne the christian name . . . of any Recusant what is to be done?
> ANS: If the master of the ffamilie will not discover the . . . Surname of those of . . . their ffamilie . . . the master or mistres should bee bound to their good behaviour, and it is

fitt the next Justice of Peace to the place suspected doe resorte thither, to knowe the true names, and they may bee
indicted by such names as they are knowne by; if other
names bee not found.

QUEST: If any bee indicted of Recusancy whether after
indictment or before committinge, the Justices of Assize or
Justices of the peace in their cessions can not take knowledge
of any conformitie, otherwise then upon their submission in
open court.

ANS: By the Stattute of 23 Eliz. a popishe Recusant may
submitt himselfe before the Bushopp before Indictment but
after Indictment there can bee noe knowledge taken of any
conformity, but by Submission in person in open court.

QUEST: Whether upon the traverse if it come to a triall,
it shalbe sufficient evidence to prove that the Recusant went
once or twice to churche or whether hee must not prove hee
hath gone to his parrishe church and hath gone every Sunday according to the Stattute of primo Eliz: all the latter
Stattuts referringe to that Stattute.

ANS: The comeinge to church must bee to the parrishe
churches and it must bee once in everie moneth to save the
twenty pound the moneth or two parts of the lands, But it
must bee everie Sunday to save the xiid the Sunday.

The questions and answers continue for several lengthy pages,
all about recusants' conforming and relapsing, the disposition
of their estates in the event of death, their failure to be present
for trial at the sessions, their arrears in fines, and so on.[38]

Questions of this sort undoubtedly interested the subordinate
officers of local government involved in enforcing the penal
laws, such as the churchwardens. These wardens, who were
usually of yeoman families, numbered about sixteen thousand
in 1625. Their duty concerned essentially the administration
of business in the parish—maintaining the church and its
grounds in good repair, receiving and expending money, and

keeping the peace. The Tudor revolution in government had made them in addition the police officers in religious affairs. Accordingly, the Canons of the Established Church (1604) required that the churchwardens report offenses by the clergy and laity in matters governed by the ecclesiastical courts,[39] and obliged them (and the constables) to present at the Quarter Sessions those within the parish who missed divine service for more than a month.

As we have noted earlier, few churchwardens fulfilled to the letter of the law their obligation to present recusants. In 1636, the Privy Council reminded the justices of the peace in Somerset of the "wilfull neglect and connivance of ministers, churchwardens and constables." No officers were more derelict in their duty, the councillors said, than the churchwardens, who ignored repeated instructions to report recusants,[40] and often presented only a handful of those living in their parishes. The Long Parliament had to threaten the churchwardens (1641) before presentments increased substantially.[41] It should also be kept in mind that, in so far as the Government relied on recusancy as a source of revenue during the 1630's, many Catholics of modest means were not worth the trouble of prosecution. Yet richer Catholic squires often escaped punishment, too. It was not unnatural that churchwardens should feel qualms about having to identify recusants who not only were socially their superiors but who also had formidable influence in local affairs.[42]

The petty constables, usually husbandmen and artisans, also could exercise police authority over recusants. Virtually every dispute and grievance in the parish required their attention.[43] Their duty to report recusants to the high constables of their hundred was clearly defined, yet despite a reward of forty shillings for every one so identified, and the risk of a twenty-shilling fine for concealing recusants, the constables as a rule did not present anywhere near their true number.[44] The constables of Hanley Castle, Worcester, reported in 1608 that recusants in the parish were increasing, yet few were presented at the Quarter Sessions until 1640, when 46 were tried. For all of Worcester the figures are even more revealing: 40 were cited in 1634, but 223 in 1642. It seems unlikely that in just nine years recusancy could have grown by 183 persons. Clearly, the constables must not have reported recusants until they were forced to.[45] Similarly, in Middlesex, the presentments were far fewer than one would expect. The churchwardens and constables of Cranford presented only two recusants in 1641, saying, "other visible and professed recusants we know none in our parish." In the same year Kensington Parish reported three recusants; a Harmondsworth constable, "after diligent enquirye," found six. The officials of Tuddington certified that "there be not any Popish Recusants inhabitinge in this . . . parish"; Hanwell and Illingedon also reported none. Not even the parishes within the shadow of Westminster Hall presented all of their recusants. This is specifically stated in a parliamentary notice to the constables of St. Martins-in-the-Fields (December 1640), which reads in part: "At the last sessions of the peace . . . in 4 Dec. you presented several recusants . . . [but] it is thought there are many more . . . within your parish." Appended was a list of about fifty recusants living in St. Martin's.[46] The Bishop of Bath and Wells, who relied on the constables for information about recusants, reported in 1636 that there were fewer in the diocese than there had been in 1635; yet in 1637 he complained to Laud of the sharp increase in recusancy. In the diocese of Norwich "above 40" were presented in 1637, but only "two or three" the year before. Since the figures for recusancy vary widely from year to year, it is reasonable to assume that presentments were irregular.[47]

Not all Catholics suspected of recusancy were presented by the constables or went before the Bench, but many were nevertheless questioned at length. Local peace officers like the petty and high constables ordinarily conducted such interrogations, but important cases were referred to their superiors, sometimes going all the way to the Privy Council. The questions put to Catholics followed a time-honored formula. Where were you born, or what place did you come from? Where have you lived overseas, and how long were you there? What was your business or employment? If you were a soldier, against whom did you bear arms? Have you any letters or verbal messages to give a particular man or woman in England? Of what religion are you? Are you a Jesuit or seminary priest? What is your reason for refusing the oath of allegiance? Who are your parents? Have you land and goods in England?[48]

Recusants were invariably questioned. Take the case of a priest named Johnson whom justices Sir Thomas Torringham and Sir Thomas Dentor interrogated in late October 1625. When the usual questions were put to Johnson he willingly confessed his priesthood but gave answers "full of neglect . . . [that] seemed to slighte or rather scorne the justices." Annoyed by his stubbornness, the justices sent Johnson to Lord Chief Justice Randolph Crewe, asking that he "take some pains in examining him, . . . his manner of life, his intendmentes for the future and his designes or purposes and that he knoweth to be practiced . . . by anie other."[49] Crewe managed to soften Johnson's obstinacy in three lengthy examinations between November 8 and 21, during which he admitted having lived in England for four years at the home of Mary Throckmorton in Weston, Buckinghamshire. Johnson thereby not only brought on his own imprisonment and later banishment, but also implicated his patroness, who was arrested.[50]

The interrogation of Thomas Walker, a close friend of Leonard Calvert, Lord Baltimore, and Stephen Baker, a mariner from Dorsetshire, by Mayor John Clungeon and three aldermen of Southampton was characteristic of the care taken to guard English ports against entry by recusants. Baker, just back from Newfoundland, testified before the board that he knew a priest there named Smith who was planning to return to England. Stephen Day, another witness, related that a ship captained by Calvert had recently docked at Southampton and that Walker, a passenger, had spent some time ashore with him. Day accused Walker, formerly an Anglican priest, of being a Catholic priest, saying: "in the voyage outwarde while the Companie of the said shipp were at prayers . . . Walker did whoope and make a noyes to the greate disturbance of the said Companie . . . And [that] he said [words] touching one named Smith a Semynarie Priest." Walker then testified that Smith had lately left Newfoundland, and vehemently denied that he himself was a priest. Clungeon imprisoned Walker but later released him on £100 bond, put up by Calvert on condition that the prisoner remain in St. Clement's Parish in London for one year.[51]

In the early seventeenth century there was little compassion for criminals, whether Protestant or Catholic, and the harsh treatment of recusants was neither unusual nor extraordinary. Men often spent months, even years, awaiting trial in foul, dilapidated, and vermin-ridden cells. A healthy person, imprisoned for a few months in a damp cell without adequate food or ventilation, frequently left it a victim of malnutrition, dysentery, pneumonia, or tuberculosis. Jail fever and the plague took dozens of lives. The sheriffs who nominally had custody of the common county prisons relegated their administration to jailers notorious for their brutal disregard of human suffering. Many jails, furthermore, were badly in need of repair, which the sheriffs seldom authorized because money spent for that purpose had to come from their own pockets, with the understanding that the Crown would reimburse them later. But sufficient money for the jails, or the prisoners in them, was rarely provided. The jails of London and its dependencies were generally quite as bad as those in the counties and were usually unfit to house prisoners in decent comfort.[52]

In all jails the physical well-being of the prisoners was a matter of their own concern, and they paid for both food and bedding. Their comfort thus depended on their relative wealth; with money, a criminal could live more or less comfortably in prison, perhaps lodging with the turnkey in the better rooms or in a separate apartment.[53] A man of small means fared worse. The jailer, who was without a regular salary from the state, made his living by selling straw, food, and drink to his charges at inflated prices. The complaints of prisoners in the Wood Street Compter, London, are typical; they paid 2d. the flagon for beer and ale, 12d. for sheets, and anything up to a shilling a pound for bread and salted meat—exorbitant prices for that day. Jailers exacted similarly high prices for tobacco, pipes, candles, and clean clothes. In addition, imprisonment for debt, a category into which some recusants fell, carried jailer fees for committal, release, and chamber rent. The fees varied widely, but they were often as much as the jailer could get. Rent ranged from 4d. a day to as much as a pound a week. If a prisoner was unable to pay, he slept on bare wooden planks.[54]

Those who had little or no money fared very badly. Since they often languished in prison for periods longer than they had anticipated,[55] their meager funds were soon expended. Thomas Metcalf, for instance, suffered from hunger for more than two years in a Lancaster jail while awaiting trial on suspicion of being a seminarian. Petitions to the King eventually won his transfer to a London prison, where he died. William Sturley was jailed on a similar charge in Newgate Prison, London, for eleven months before being released on bail in February 1627. In the event that a prisoner had no money at all to pay his keep, the Government, through a justice of the peace or a high constable, could appoint a committee composed of four of the inmate's neighbors to sell as much of his goods as was necessary to support him. If the offender had no goods, the petty constable and churchwardens of his home parish could tax the parishioners to pay jailer fees.[56] In any event, the prisoner often received no more than a penny a day with which to buy stale bread and perhaps some straw for a bed. If the money raised by a tax was too little to maintain all of the indigent prisoners of a particular parish, or if the price of food rose because of a bad harvest, indigent prisoners suffered accordingly.[57] In cases of extreme hardship, prisoners were allowed to beg food of passers-by at the prison gate.[58]

Recusants were sometimes incarcerated in castle prisons such as those at Chester, Gloucester, York, and Wisbech. The latter, a dilapidated property within the Bishopric of Ely, served as a recusant prison from 1580 to about 1633.[59] By 1625 it was no longer fit for human habitation, its lead roof, beams, iron, and glass having by then been removed.[60] Even so, it housed several priests, including John Southworth, for some time after September 1628.[61] Worcester Castle was little better. Recusants there were herded together in cramped cells and sometimes were put in irons.[62] Thomas Sammes, a priest imprisoned in Gloucester Castle in 1628, begged the Privy Council for a transfer to another jail because the castle was "a place altogether unfit for that purpose."[63] The jail at York Castle was among the worst in England. Its keeper, Samuel Hales, who had held the office since 1617, used it as a means of quick profit. He sold the posts of assistant keepers to retired pursuivants, old bailiffs, and soldiers of fortune, who frequently had as little compassion as he did. During the period of recusancy arrests, Hales introduced a new scale of charges: Catholic yeomen paid ten shillings for bedding, Catholic gentlemen twenty shillings, and Catholic peers forty shillings. Priests were charged as gentlemen and were often put in irons. The number of Catholics who died in York Castle is unrecorded, but crowded in cells without exercise or light, they were a prey to the plague and to jail fever which infested rooms partly under water because of the river's flooding.

They could neither receive charity from their friends nor practice their devotions. Sometimes they were led to church on
Sundays to listen to Protestant preachers.[64]

Conditions in the county jails, if Derby Prison was typical,
were little better. Built in 1588 over a ditch that served as the
town sewer, it was a place in which few prisoners could escape
the stench, periodic flooding, the plague or jail fever. Recusants,
covered with filth, were housed in cells open to public view.
Worse than this, they were thrown in with all types of scoundrels awaiting trial for murder and theft. The complaint of
George Fox, the founder of Quakerism, that he was confined for
six months among thirty felons in a "close stinking place" could
just as well have been made by a Catholic recusant. An undated
petition by a jailer named Henry Agard to the justices of the
peace in Derby (probably of the early 1640's) emphasized the
hunger among his charges. In thirteen weeks, he reported, only
£15 4s. 6d. was spent for bread, and 12s. for straw, apportioning
a penny a day for each prisoner.[65]

Several prisons in Middlesex County, some of them in London, also housed recusants. The Gatehouse, like the Tower,
was generally reserved for recusants of genteel birth; the Fleet,
Newgate, the Clink in Southwark, and the Wood Street Compter swallowed up every type of offender. The vile conditions in
the Fleet, largely a debtors' prison, defied comparison. The case
of Walter Fitzharris, an Irish Catholic, is an example of the
hardships that recusants underwent in prison. In 1639 seventeen of his coprisoners petitioned the Government for his release on the following grounds:

> [Fitzharris is] a closse prisoner in ye comon wards of ye
> ffleete, hee being a very poore man . . . And to our knowl-
> edges hee have had no mayntenance since his comeing
> heither . . . nor any Releife, nor food to live upon, but onely
> upon ye benevolences, & ye charities of good & well disposed
> people And beggin his bread at ye hole ye charitie is not

worth above two pence a weeke. whereby hee hath lived in greate want & misery both wth want of food, clothes & lodging.

In addition, Fitzharris endured corporal punishment at the hands of the jailer.[66]

The career of Father Henry Morse, who worked among the plague-stricken poor of London, is a biography of prison life. He spent at least nine years in three prisons—four years in York Castle, four more in the New Prison in London, and another year in Newgate. His description of life in Newgate is worth repeating. In March 1637 he was incarcerated with forty-seven criminals awaiting death on the gallows. Their stench made him ill on more than one occasion, as did their habit of slobbering their food like starving animals. Morse managed to obtain quarters in a third-story room, which proved somewhat better than the common wards below. The room had bars on the window as thick as a man's wrist, and stone walls on which prisoners had scribbled scriptural texts, verses, and obscenities. The only furnishings were board beds, a table, and chairs black with age and rot. The jailer sold sleeping holes in the walls at high rates, advertising them as free of vermin, and he charged exorbitant rates for an hour of fresh air in the prison yard.[67]

There were far fewer executions of Catholics under Charles I than there had been under either Elizabeth or James I. Between 1577 and 1603, Elizabeth's Government had put to death 183 Catholics, of whom 123 were priests, one an unordained friar, and 59 laymen.[68] The executions were resumed in 1607 under James I, and by 1618 some 23 Catholics had died for religious causes (excluding those connected with the Gunpowder Plot). Among them were 17 priests—three Benedictines, a Jesuit, and 13 seculars—and six lay folk.[69] But from 1625 to 1640 only three Catholics suffered the extreme penalty—Father Edmund

Arrowsmith and Richard Hirst at Lancaster in 1628, and Arthur Geoghegan, an Irish Dominican, at London in 1633. The circumstances leading to their deaths warrant some attention.

The Jesuit Edmund Arrowsmith, born in Winwick Parish, Lancashire, in 1585, was the son of stout recusants who themselves had been fined and imprisoned. Study at Douay prepared him for the priesthood, which he entered in 1612. Less than a year later he went to England, where he worked, principally in the north country of his birth, for the next fifteen years. Sometime during those years, perhaps in 1623, he became a Jesuit. Just how he came to be indicted in the late spring of 1628 is not clear, but it appears that a young man named Holden identified Arrowsmith as a priest and had him imprisoned in Lancaster Castle. At the summer assizes in Lancaster he came before Judge Henry Yelverton.

That Arrowsmith should have been tried by this man was a stroke of bad luck. Yelverton had had a stormy career in the law. As a serjeant-at-law he had been one of the prosecutors at the trial of the Earl of Essex in 1600, standing out in a rich green gown that ballooned around his rotund figure. He became solicitor-general in 1613, and attorney-general in 1617, for which he paid King James £4,000. Yelverton was an outspoken man. He aroused the anger of James in 1619 for attacking Buckingham,[70] and spent some time in the Tower for doing so. Charles nevertheless restored Yelverton to rank in 1625 as a fifth judge of the Common Pleas. According to John Cosin, a prebendary of Durham Cathedral, he was a strong Puritan.[71]

There is little doubt that during the trial Yelverton was motivated primarily by vindictiveness. Without allowing Arrowsmith to say anything in his defense, Yelverton judged him guilty of high treason for being a Jesuit, and sentenced him to be hanged, drawn, and quartered. Why Arrowsmith should have been executed when dozens of other priests got off with short imprisonments is difficult to understand; one may guess that Yelverton, faced with a large Catholic population in Lancashire and sympathetic to the parliamentary drive to enforce the recusancy laws, decided to make him an example. An interesting, if perhaps biased, description of Yelverton's conduct is contained in a letter written by a Catholic who was apparently at the trial and execution:

> the Judge in great rage protested he would not [go] out of towne, till he saw his [Arrowsmith's] 4 quartiers and head, and the prisoner himselfe should when he was alive see his owne bowells frie in the fire. . . . The Judge all the tyme of his execution stood in his chamber windowe, looking through a prospective glasse and when the prisoner was carried off the ladder he called for his dinner, and maid his word good for he had vowed hy would not dyne till he [Arrowsmith] was dead. . . . When the Judge departed from Lancaster seeing his head upon the castle, amongst the pinnacles thought it not high ynough for example sake, and therefore gave stricke command to his officers to see it sett six yards above the pinnacle.[72]

Richard Hirst, a yeoman of moderate means who farmed an estate near Preston, Lancashire, was also tried before Yelverton and died on the gallows a day or two after Arrowsmith. The Bishop of Chester sent a pursuivant, Christopher Norcross, and two assistants named Wilkinson and Dewhurst to arrest Hirst for recusancy. He resisted and was beaten, as were his wife and two servants. During the melee, Dewhurst tripped in a newly ploughed field and broke a leg; a fortnight later he died of infection. Hirst, though not directly responsible for the accident (Dewhurst admitted he had slipped), was indicted, tried, and convicted of murder. The testimony of several witnesses supported Hirst's innocence, but Yelverton, contrary to all precepts of justice, instructed the jury to return a verdict of guilty as a deterrent to recusancy. Hirst petitioned the King for a stay of execution, and it was granted, but Yelverton said he would honor the stay only on condition that Hirst renounce Catholicism and take the oath of allegiance. Hirst refused and was hanged on August 29, 1628.[73]

The quartering at Tyburn of Arthur Geoghegan, a Dominican friar from West Meath, Ireland, on November 27, 1633, gratified that portion of the London populace that still believed Catholics to be regicides. Geoghegan had only a few months earlier (April) joined the seven other members of his order then in England.[74] He had come to the English Mission from six years' work in Ireland and travels in several countries including Portugal, where the Spanish viceroy employed him to search foreign ships at Lisbon, Spain then being at war with Holland. Pursuing his duties, Geoghegan detained an Englishman, Captain Bust, whose ship was confiscated on suspicion that it was Dutch. Two years later Bust met Geoghegan in the street in London, and still bearing a grudge, had him imprisoned. Bust charged that Geoghegan had said at Lisbon that if he ever returned to England he would kill the King as a heretic. Geoghegan admitted under questioning that there was some slight foundation for the charge, but that his words had been misconstrued. What he had actually said, Geoghegan explained, was that if man did not have a free will, which he denied, then it would not be a sin to murder anyone, even the King. Few believed his story. Charles, hearing of the case, expressed the hope that the friar be excused, since he had uttered the words without real malice. Windebank and Henrietta also tried without success to save Geoghegan from conviction in the King's Bench on November 25 for speaking treasonable words. On the 27th he underwent the mutilation prescribed for treason. Contrary to custom, his members were not displayed upon the four gates of the city, but were either buried beneath the scaffold or carried off by friends to be respectfully interred abroad.[75]

Most of the Catholic squirearchy and peerage were able to ignore the laws affecting baptism, marriage, and burial. These

settled families, living on isolated rural estates where they at-
tracted little attention, customarily employed resident priests,
who administered the sacraments with only occasional interference from the Government. But few other Catholics had
such freedom. Some could conceal their Catholic baptisms and
marriages, but others had to pay heavily in the courts.

Those wishing to marry were faced with a dilemma: the
law required Catholics, like everyone else, to marry before par-
sons in parish churches; but Rome would not admit the validity
of such marriages. Moreover, the fact that priests were not
always close by when marriages were made led to all manner of
irregularities. The Court of High Commission at Durham
alone heard over a hundred cases of "clandestine marriages" between Catholics from 1628 to 1639.[76] Thomas Horsley, convicted of contracting marriage "in an open field," at first got off
with only an order to visit the vicar of Edlingham for instructions on what constituted a legal marriage. When he failed to
do so, and offered but feeble excuses, the court sentenced him (in
January 1637) to admit his "sinfull" marriage at the market
place of Alnwicke Village and to pay a £10 fine. A similar sentence was given to John Servant, who confessed on January 14,
1634, to having married Jane Pinckney in a ceremony before a
priest "who he thinketh hath noe lawfull authoritie to exercise
that functionn within the realme of England." He also had to
acknowledge the sin "in his penitentiall habit, at the markett
cross at Durham, on some Saturdaie, and paie 40 £ fine."[77]

The common-law marriages, adulteries, and divorces that
occurred within the Catholic community invariably created
scandal that was distressing to the clergy. Some of them seemed
to think that they were witnessing moral anarchy. The situation was hardly that serious, however, and many of the accusations of seculars that their regular brethren closed their eyes to
irregularities in marriage, or were a party to them, undoubtedly
stemmed from their quarrel over the bishop. In the "Abuses of
some Regulars & Lay Catholics concerning mariages & pious

legacies" a group of London seculars vividly portrayed how Catholic gentlemen such as Lord Morley, Sir William Tresham, Sir Charles Manners, and Sir Robert Huddleston had "divorced" their wives, and how "Lady Bainbery [was] living scandalously with Ld. Vaux."[78] Another secular charged that the Jesuits had ruled on the validity of marriages as though they were bishops and accused Father Blount of condoning the marriage of a lady already bound to another. The same correspondent chastized a Benedictine named Johnson who allegedly married a young boy to a woman old enough to be his mother. Father Edward Morgan, writing to Bishop Smith in 1632, reported that the Jesuits sanctioned Protestant baptisms of Catholic infants and had married young people under age without parental consent. Morgan was also critical of Sir George Calvert for "co-habitating" with Mary Winn, his late wife's maid and goddaughter, marrying her, and then putting her aside on grounds of affinity.[79]

There seem to have been fewer instances of governmental interference with Catholic baptisms than with clandestine marriages. One case was that of a simple recusant named Michael Urpeth. For allowing his friends Thomas Rames and Anne Thirway to christen their illegitimate child in his home, he paid a fine and went to jail. The High Commission questioned the efficacy of the baptism and instructed the parson of the parish where the child had been born "to examine if the said baptisme (if anie) be rightly and duely performed, and to do therein as by the rubricke is lymited."[80] The Government prosecuted even merchant strangers at Dover whose children had been christened by Catholic priests: "if anyone offends in this regard," the privy councillors warned, "he will be hailed before the Council and dealt with."[81]

Recusants could conceal the baptisms of their children much more easily than the burial of their dead. Few were laid to rest in consecrated ground, fewer still in Catholic cemeteries. In all of England there were no Catholic cemeteries except private family plots that went undiscovered or ignored, and the two cemeteries in London reserved for Henrietta's officers and servants; most Catholic dead were therefore buried in the graveyards of Protestant parish churches. Many undoubtedly had the benefit of priests in their last hours, however, and it was not uncommon for priests to place in coffins a clod of consecrated earth.[82] But today the tombstones of seventeenth-century Catholics cannot often be distinguished from those of their Protestant neighbors, for the Government allowed no symbols or script that would identify Catholic graves. For having inscribed "Catholick" upon her husband's tomb in 1633, Lady Wotton, a baroness of Kent, forfeited £500 and had to obliterate the word by order of the High Commission.[83]

No religious test such as the oath of allegiance was required of persons under sixteen years of age, but, even so, few Catholics seem to have taken advantage of the grammar schools, educating their children at home, or, if possible, abroad. Children of rich parents were frequently sent to Catholic seminaries in France, Spain, or Flanders, and whether they became priests or nuns or remained of the laity, they did much to keep alive the faith of their less educated coreligionists. The children of the squirearchy were usually educated by tutors, either clerical or lay.[84] The basis of such tutoring was usually a simple library of philosophical and devotional works and a volume or two of history and rhetoric.[85]

Here and there schools sprang up under the tutelage of local priests or lay schoolmasters forbidden to teach in the grammar schools because of recusancy. Father Blount founded a school in 1633, the College of the Immaculate Conception at Spink Hill, near Eckington in Derby. This institution served both as a clearinghouse for young Jesuits sent out to different stations in the area and as a day school for boys. At Stanley

Grange, Derbyshire, in the home of Anne, the sister of Lord Vaux, the Jesuits established a school in 1616 which was still educating sons of Catholic parents as late as October 1635, although soon after that, because of information provided by a former pupil, it was closed by pursuivants. Whether it ever reopened is not known. At the time of its dissolution the school had twelve or thirteen regular pupils, including Edward Wakeman, a grandson of the powerful Catholic Lord Abergavenny.[86] In the same year (1635) the Privy Council discovered a Catholic school near Wolverhampton. It had pupils from Staffordshire, Northamptonshire, and Worcestershire, and must therefore have enjoyed a wide reputation.[87] A school at Greenfield, near Holywell, known to Protestants and Catholics alike, had at least seven pupils from November 1626 to May 1627, when it had to close.[88] William Hill at Fareham taught about twenty pupils with the help of two Frenchmen, Nicholas Baillott and Amith Herbyn.[89] Others like Otho Polewheele, a Catholic music master,[90] and Richard Bradley, who was an usher for several years at Blackburn Grammar School,[91] managed for a while to conceal their recusancy.

Only those recusants who formally took the oaths of supremacy and allegiance had their change of religion recorded at the Quarter Sessions.[92] Yet many others, like the church papists, conformed to a point, attending Anglican service at sufficiently regular intervals to escape financial penalties. Uncertain though we are about the professed and practical converts to the Establishment, beyond doubt the pressure of persecution weakened the faith of many Catholics who were unwilling to sacrifice economic, social, or political advantages to continue in the old religion. There are numerous records of submission, like the following, of one Robert Hardwicke at Helmsley, Yorkshire, in January 1626:

> Conviction of Recusants presented and proclaimed at the last Oct.ʳ Sessions at Malton, except Rob. Hardwicke, who

at the present Sessions did very humbly on his knees, toke the Oath of Allegiance, and according to the certificate of the Minister and Wardens of the parish Church of Hovington, did there attend.[93]

What had been his crime in recusancy is not mentioned, nor can we know what events were responsible for his submission. One thing is striking, however: few of the clergy or the gentry submitted.[94] Rather, it was from the rank and file that converts were made to the State Church, and it was on them that the penal code had its greatest effect.

Chapter Seven

THE INFORMERS

I F SOME JUSTICES of the peace, constables, and churchwardens were lenient toward Catholics, the pursuivants and
common informers gave them no quarter. The pursuivants,
long-standing officers of justice, were messengers who did the
footwork of governmental councils and committees and of the
courts. As part of the enforcement of the penal laws, some pursuivants were assigned to guard recusants, or to conduct them
to trial, but on occasion they hunted them down under the authority of warrants issued usually by the Privy Council and the
Court of High Commission. The common informers, on the
other hand, motivated entirely by the prospect of pecuniary
profit, took it upon themselves to identify and arrest recusants
on their own authority, although they often attempted a pretense of legality by forging warrants. In 1640, Richard Holtby,
an elderly Jesuit living in the North, classified those who informed on Catholics into three groups: servants of the Privy
Council called King's messengers; bishops' officers, who usually
traveled in pairs to trap, arrest, and interrogate recusants sought
for trial in the ecclesiastical courts; and London ruffians who
worked together under a leader.[1] This chapter will deal with
the pursuivants and common informers who by commission or
self-appointment made or supplemented their living by taking
the statutory reward for the arrests of recusants.[2]

Pursuivants and common informers could make money at

the expense of recusants whom they reported by taking advantage of certain provisions of three penal laws. The first, 23 Eliz. I, c. 1, stipulated that one-third of the £20 monthly fines should go to anyone who would "sue for the same in any court of record, by action of debt, bill, plaint, or information." Under 3 Jac. I, c. 4, informers could take a half of the fines levied against recusants who refused the Anglican Communion. Other monetary rewards were assigned to informers under 3 Jac. I, c. 5. They could receive a third of the fines, up to £50, arising from the identification of persons who housed Catholic priests, said mass, or attended mass. One-half of the £100 fines imposed against recusants who came to Court, or to within ten miles of London without permission, or who were married by other than Anglican clergymen, or who practiced professions closed to them, were assigned to informers. A third of the fines paid by recusants whose children were baptized or whose dead were buried according to the Catholic rite went to informers.[3] In addition, the pursuivants and common informers sometimes extorted money from Catholics by threatening them with arrest.[4]

Although some of the pursuivants were no doubt motivated by a sense of duty, the common informers were generally shrewd and unscrupulous men of irregular occupation, who kept their identity a close secret so that few outside their circle knew them by name. A few of them were apostate Catholics who used their knowledge of the liturgy and theology of the Roman Church to good advantage, being admitted on occasion even into the homes of unsuspecting recusants. Catholics summoned before the Privy Council, High Commission, or Quarter Sessions by informers, who frequently fabricated charges to win a portion of their victims' fines, had little chance of acquittal or reprisal.

The Government knew that some of its pursuivants and most of the common informers were corrupt, and it sometimes punished them for exceeding the bounds of authority; but it felt that their work was useful not only as a means of curbing recusancy but also as a source of income through their collection of recusancy fines. Twice between 1629 and 1640 the Government questioned the wisdom of employing informers and the propriety of their methods, but it continued to rely on them at least until 1646.

The correspondence of Catholic priests and laymen clearly illustrates the fear with which informers were regarded. They were most numerous in London and in the northern counties, where Catholics made up a large proportion of the population. Father William Ward related to Thomas Rant, a colleague in Flanders, how "the Promouters and informers inst[antly] at our Queenes comminge [Henrietta Maria] began to be very busye, and so have continued since, and seased many with processe."[5] Rant, describing the persecution of Catholics in London to a Jesuit friend in Rome, said that the Lord Mayor "seased here uppon many mens goodes through pursuivants" and that "many a hundred [Catholics] have been utterly undonne, and many a more are in apparent danger [of arrest]."[6] News from the North was equally discouraging: "Matters for catholicks in England goe backward," Father Henry Clifford reported from Antwerp, for "informers and pursuivants are very busie, and shure many of our friends in yourkshire feele the smart of it in their meanes and p'sons by such caterpillars."[7]

The Government sometimes sent its pursuivants to expedite the collection of arrears in fines and rents arising from the practice of composition. It has already been pointed out that few Catholics could meet the heavy £20 monthly fines prescribed by the penal law of 1581, and that the penalties for nonpayment could be confiscation of as much as two-thirds of a recusant's land and all his goods. Then, in 1626 the Government reinstituted the practice of allowing recusants to compound for leases of the seized portions of their land. But if these practices mitigated the hardships of some Catholics they at the same time encouraged the activities of pursuivants. In July 1638, for instance, the Exchequer sent two pursuivants to Yorkshire to collect delinquent rents. Given the opportunity to be dishonest, the pursuivants took bribes rather than collect money owing to the Crown. Abuses by informers must not have been uncommon, for in 1635, Elizabeth, Countess of Anglesea, angry over their blackmailing innkeepers, petitioned the King to suppress the common informers. The petition went to Attorney-General Sir John Bankes, who denounced them as "scandalous to the Lawe & government."[8]

The priests, whose very presence in England was treasonous, were the most persecuted. In one instance the Privy Council empowered three pursuivants, Richard Wainwright, John Cox, and William Birkenhead, to find and arrest Father George Leyburn by any means they chose, and another pursuivant named John Wragg had an open warrant which he could use against any priest.[9] The councillors punished John Ayers, a Gloucestershire recusant, for beating an informer who had arrested him without cause.[10]

Informers could, of course, work most effectively when their identity was unknown, and they naturally shunned notoriety to avoid detection by Catholics, whose understandable caution made all strangers suspect. The pursuivants, also, perhaps out of fear that their blackmailing be found out, disclosed their activities to the Government only when pointedly questioned about them. Since there is no adequate record of the pursuivants, and since a number of common informers worked without governmental authorization, information about their activities and their personal lives is very difficult to uncover. The names of pursuivants appear sometimes in the Calendars of State Papers, in the minutes of the Privy Council, and in various court records. Less frequently, informers in general are mentioned in Catholic petitions for redress of abuses. In addition, one can find occasional references to informers in letters. However, Catholic correspondents made only fleeting comments about informers for fear their letters might fall into hostile hands.

The informers were not numerous. They were a closely knit

corps of men who worked alone, in pairs, and sometimes, as in the case of the London informers, in gangs, under leaders such as Humphrey Cross and Francis Newton, pursuivants who divided the profits of their vicious trade among their lesser brethren. Names such as John Wragg, Thomas Mayo, Richard Tomlins, John Gray, John Cook, William Birkenhead, and Richard Wainwright can be identified as those of informers, but little is known about any of them.

Although information is scanty, the careers of two pursuivants can be traced in broad scope. Perhaps the most notorious pursuivant was Cross, who in February 1627 was employed by the Privy Council to apprehend Charles Powell, a recusant suspected of possessing sacerdotal vestments. Three months later Cross journeyed to St. Edmondsbury in Suffolk to fetch Richard Walker for questioning about recusancy.[11] Soon thereafter he arrested the celebrated Frances Villiers, Viscountess Purbeck, daughter of Sir Edward Coke, formerly Chief Justice of Common Pleas. She had embraced Catholicism after a long period of unhappiness resulting from her unfortunate marriage to John Villiers, Viscount Purbeck, Buckingham's brother, who lost his mind about 1620.[12] Upon leaving her husband, she was convicted for adultery, publicly humiliated, and imprisoned.[13] Cross's connection with this trial brought him money and notoriety at Court. [14]

Thereafter, Cross figured prominently in many important cases concerning recusants, including the Clerkenwell incident. It was Cross and his gang of informers who were commissioned to watch the Talbot house in Clerkenwell and to make the arrests that put ten Jesuits in prison.[15] He and several others were also involved in the surveillance of Catholic foreign embassies in London, where large numbers of Catholics regularly attended mass. Of particular concern to the Privy Council was the residence in Durham House of the Marquis de Blainville, the French ambassador extraordinary, in whose private chapel about a hundred Catholics heard daily mass. On Sunday morning, February 26, 1627, a group of pursuivants and constables, including Cross, waited outside the embassy to arrest the Catholics as they left. But Blainville, forewarned of the plan, outwitted Cross by sending out armed servants, who rushed the guards and created a brawl that enabled the Catholics to escape. Several pursuivants were wounded in the melee, among them Francis Griffith, whose leg was badly slashed.[16] In March 1629, Cross was with two other parties of pursuivants and constables who arrested recusants leaving mass at the Spanish and Venetian embassies.[17]

What happened to Cross in the next few years is not known. He probably continued to work as a pursuivant, but there is no record of his activities. A letter written by Father Leyburn in May 1635 has a revealing note scribbled in the margin: "Crosse the pursevant is dead a Catholique."[18] Leyburn does not say exactly when he died, but he must have died at least five months earlier, for there is a memorandum among the records of the High Commission certifying that Faith Cross, "daughter of Humphrey Crosse, lately deceased," was paid £50 the previous December for her father's work.[19] Whether Cross became a Catholic is also uncertain. There is no good reason to doubt Leyburn's word, but it seems unlikely that the High Commission would have paid Faith Cross had her father actually become a Catholic.

The Apostate Catholic James Wadsworth (1604–56) began his career as a pursuivant at about the same time as Cross. It is indeed regrettable that a man like Wadsworth should have stooped to such work, for he had the advantages of a comfortable youth, a good education, and a talent for scholarship. Like many young Catholics of his generation, he studied abroad in the English seminaries at Seville and Madrid, where he showed promise as a historian. In 1618 he entered the novitiate of the Society of Jesus at the newly founded English College at Saint-

Omer, but he left after four years without taking Holy Orders.[20] He was captured by Moorish pirates and sold into slavery. After his release a year later, he served as interpreter to Prince Charles during the Prince's abortive effort to win a Spanish bride.[21]

Without positive employment in Spain, and hoping to find profitable work with the Crown on his return to London in 1625, Wadsworth became an Anglican convert. His conversion seems clearly to have been a matter of expediency, for he immediately offered his services to Laud, then Bishop of London, and to Buckingham. His knowledge of foreign languages won him a position representing the King in a minor capacity at Calais, Brussels, and Paris, but he was in prison for debt and spying during much of the two years he spent abroad. Once back in England, he was employed by the Privy Council as a pursuivant stationed in London.[22] Of his activities between 1627 and 1635 nothing can be said except that he and several other pursuivants were investigated for corrupt practices by the Court of High Commission in 1635.

The Court exonerated Wadsworth of this charge, but the business of hunting recusants had by that time become less appealing, and less profitable. Wadsworth managed to avoid investigation a second time in the spring of 1636 when a royal commission found a number of the pursuivants guilty of blackmail—though he seems to have been hard pressed for money, for he repeatedly petitioned the Privy Council for payment in "recompense for his bringing jesuits and papists to conviction."[23] Apparently he was still employed during the early years of the civil war, because he testified against Laud in 1643,[24] and he was present with Thomas Mayo on January 17, 1645, when the magistrates' court of St. Giles-in-the-Fields sentenced Father Henry Morse to death.[25] The disorder created by the rebellion ruined Wadsworth's career, and from 1648 until his death six years later he was "a common Hackney to the basest Catchpole Bayliff in Westminster."[26]

These brief accounts of the careers of Cross and Wadsworth suggest that, although the Government used the pursuivants to good advantage, employing them in a small way to curb recusancy and to augment the royal income, it took no particular pains to reward them properly and regularly. Cross, who claimed that he had caused the arrest and conviction of twenty-nine priests during his career, was paid only about 200 marks.[27] Another pursuivant received but 11s. for information acquainting the Lord Mayor of Leicester of a suspected Catholic plot.[28] In February 1636 the Court of High Commission, which regularly employed pursuivants, paid Wragg £70, Tomlins £80, Faith Cross £50, and William Flamstead £20 for services rendered during the previous three years.[29] When a royal commission in March 1636 charged John Gray with extortion, he attempted to justify his actions by pleading poverty.[30]

The pursuivants in their poverty not surprisingly turned to blackmail and even theft. Soon after Christmas 1636 the pursuivant Cook threatened to arrest the Jesuit Father Henry Morse,[31] who was then working among the plague-stricken parishioners of St. Giles's in Bloomsbury. Morse handed over the money that Cook demanded for his freedom,[32] only to be confronted again by Cook and another pursuivant named Francis Newton in February 1637. Morse challenged their authority to arrest him and scoffed at their threats, but he was arrested nonetheless and detained at a tavern in Fetter Lane, where Newton and Cook became intoxicated. The party then took a boat upriver to Westminster and lodged overnight at an inn on the Broad Sanctuary.[33] The following morning Morse managed somehow to escape, but two months later he was recaptured and imprisoned through the testimony of Principal Secretary John Coke, Newton's superior on the Council.[34]

The Crown had a strong case against Morse, for Newton had bribed several witnesses to sign a statement swearing that they knew Morse to have converted to Catholicism about twenty persons who had died of the plague.[35] Thirteen recusants, whom Morse had nursed through their sickness, then submitted affidavits stating that the alleged converts had long been Catholics. These witnesses were also jailed for recusancy as a result of information volunteered by William Haywood, the parson of St. Giles's. They next petitioned the King to stay legal action against Morse and to restrain the pursuivants, whose "misdeameanors and great oppressions" were going unpunished.[36] But Morse languished in Newgate Prison, arraigned but not convicted.[37]

These complaints by recusants and the intervention of Henrietta on behalf of Morse eventually drew Charles's attention to the devious methods employed by certain pursuivants. The King might not have taken much notice of the issue had not the papal envoy, George Conn,[38] whom Charles liked,[39] asked him to appoint a committee of privy councillors to review the behavior of the pursuivants. Conn hoped that such a committee would include Francis Windebank and Francis Cottington, whom he knew to be sympathetic toward Catholics, rather than councillors like Archbishop Laud and Henry Montagu, Earl of Manchester, who were outspoken enemies of Catholics. Conn intended the investigation to prove that some of the pursuivants had abused their authority, which might then convince Charles that the enforcement of the recusancy laws should be placed under the control of a more responsible agency such as the Star Chamber. In July 1638, Windebank and the Privy Seal investigated the criminal actions of several pursuivants against whom priests were called in to testify.[40]

This was not the first time that pursuivants and common informers had been called to task in King's Bench and Star Chamber. An Elizabethan informer, John Crapnell, who reputedly gave information against numerous recusants, was fined £10 and committed to the Fleet Prison in 1588 for causing "great trouble to the Courts" by giving false testimony. In 1610

Attorney-General Sir Henry Hobart brought charges in Star Chamber against ten pursuivants who accepted bribes from Jesuits and others and let them go free. Attorney-General Sir John Bankes[41] was involved in a Star Chamber case concerning an informer, John Sutton, during the Michaelmas Term of 1635. In that trial, which culminated in Sutton's being fined £1,000, Bankes delivered a lengthy diatribe against Sutton in particular and dishonest informers in general. "He . . . intermedles in matters of State, infumes in all courts . . . and pretends himself to bee a publique minister," Bankes said, and "in some causes [cases] he confesseth . . . that he received compensations [such as £14 from Henry Sandford] having no licenc to compound." Bankes went on to charge that the informers' unlawful behavior not only debased the law and defeated justice but also cheated the Crown of fines from recusants who were allowed to go free. Such practices encouraged Catholics to ignore the penal laws, Bankes concluded, and impugned the honor of the King, thereby raising public scandal.[42]

Among the manuscripts in Bundle 44 of the Bankes Papers in the Bodleian Library are a number of excerpts from various classical and medieval authors, collected perhaps by Bankes or his subordinates in preparation for Sutton's trial, which suggest that dishonest informers were generally looked on with contempt. One extract, drawn from an oration by Cicero, could not have been more to the point raised by Bankes:

Tis good there should be informers in a commonwealth, as in houses we keepe dogs to discover theeves. But if dogs for a peece of bread make a truce with the theeves, and so betray him whom they seeme to serve, their leggs shall be broken for that service.[43]

Such "caterpillars of a Republique," Bankes maintained, ought to be "rooted out of this kingdome."[44]

A general investigation of the behavior of pursuivants whose

work concerned recusants was conducted in March 1636 before
a committee composed of Sir Gregory Fenner, Sir Henry Spiller, Lawrence Whitaker, and Thomas Sheppard. They sub-
poenaed most of the pursuivants, but only Wragg, Newton,
Gray, Cook, and Griffin appeared for questioning.[45] This investigation was significant in that Catholics were called in to
testify. They were quick to submit statements. William Man,
of York, said that in 1625 Wragg and Tarbuck had searched his
home without a warrant, accused him on insufficient evidence
of being a priest, and taken him under close arrest to Lincoln,
where they blackmailed him for £260. Other witnesses added
that in the previous two years Wragg had accepted bribes totaling at least £75, and that Tomlins had collected £140 through
extortion. Newton was shown to have forced several Catholics
to pay £10 each. Elizabeth Ratcliffe told the investigating committee that Gray, Griffin, and Wainwright forced entry into her
home and stole £22 on the pretext that the money belonged to
a priest, even though she insisted that it was her own. Later,
she said, Mayo and Cross searched her home, struck down her
eighty-eight-year-old mother, and held her prisoner until she
paid what they asked.[46]

Such overwhelming evidence against the pursuivants left
little doubt about their guilt. Even so, they denied the charges.
A few of the pursuivants made statements. Gray's weak defense
was typical of them: he admitted his crimes at last, but tried to
justify them by pleading that the Government paid him so irreg-
ularly that he had to blackmail Catholics to earn a living. Then,
in a vain effort to elicit sympathy, he said that he had divided the
money with his friends and accomplices, Griffin and Wainwright.[47]

A report summarizing the findings of the committee was
submitted to Secretary Windebank on March 26, 1636. It recommended that the Government prosecute Wragg, Newton, Griffin, Gray, Wainwright, and Cook for blackmailing Catholics,

and for unjustifiably intruding upon their homes and stealing both money and goods. In short, the committee found that the pursuivants "abused the warrants committed to them for apprehension of particular persons," even in the streets, where they had "taken sundry priests, so it appears for bribes they have discharged them." In support of its recommendations, the committee appended to the report the affidavits of the Catholic witnesses.[48]

There is no evidence that the pursuivants were indicted or punished for their proved misdeeds. Presumably they got off with only a warning, and thereupon resumed their work as if an investigation had never taken place. Several circumstances worked to their advantage. A series of conversions to Catholicism among prominent Protestant courtiers created a scandal that soon brought the Catholic party into ill repute and abruptly ended the *entente cordiale* that Conn had established between London and Rome.[49] The Privy Council, spurred on by Laud, who repeatedly emphasized the dangers of Catholicism to the Established Church, issued three successive anti-Catholic proclamations within three months,[50] reinstituting suppression and thereby putting the pursuivants back to work.

The second proclamation of the Council (December 20, 1637) had scarcely been issued when John Gray captured the celebrated Dominican, Thomas Gage,[51] who had just returned to England from missionary work in Central America. His account of his meeting with Gray is so typical of the pursuivants' methods that it merits full quotation.

> At this time coming once from Surrey to London, I chanc'd to be discover'd and known to one of the State-Officers, a Pursevant . . . named John Gray, who meeting me one Day in Long-Acre, follow'd and dogg'd me as far as Lincoln-Inn Wall, where he clap'd me on the Shoulders, and told me, that he had a Commission against me, to apprehend me, and carry me to the Council Table, or to one of his Majesty's

Secretaries. To whom I spoke in Spanish (thinking thereby to free my self out of his Hands for a Spaniard:) but this would not do, for he reply'd he knew me to be an English man born, and by the Name of Gage. . . . He carr'd me to a Tavern, and there search'd my Pockets for Letters and Mony, which . . . was too little for him . . . and that I must go with him to answer before one of his Majesty's Secretaries. I told him, I would willingly go before the Archbishop of Canterbury, or before Sir Francis Windebanke at which he smil'd, saying, I knew well whom to make choice of to favour and protect me, but he would carry me to none of them, but to Secretary Cook [John Coke]. I fearing the Business might go hard with me, and knowing him to be greedy of Mony, told him that I would give him any thing that might content him, and so offer'd him twelve Shilling . . . and my Word to meet him in any place the next Day, with a better and fuller Purse. He accepted of my Mony for the present, and . . . appointed the Angel Tavern in Long-Acre . . . to be the Place of our Meeting, and so dismiss'd me. [52]

That evening Gage told his brother George, a secular priest who lived with Conn in Long Acre Street, what had happened. The next morning George Gage discussed the incident with Windebank, who quickly frightened off Gray.[53]

But Gray was not deterred for long. In June 1638 he arrested and caused to be imprisoned an eighty-year-old recusant named Francis Smith, who had testified against the pursuivants during the investigation of 1636. Smith had recently been released from Newgate Prison because of illness and age, and had gone to live with a friend at Cheam, in Surrey, where, the day following his arrival, Gray came to demand of him 35s., and £5 more later. When Smith could not raise the money, Gray put him under arrest on a charge of being a priest. What happened to Smith is not known, but there is a petition dated March 24, 1637, signed by him and other recusants, begging the King to take some action against pursuivants, at whose hands recusants suffered "great oppressions."[54]

That spring, 1638, Gray had himself been in serious trouble as a result of the complaints of several other Catholics blackmailed by him. Shortly after his encounter with Gage, Gray was imprisoned in the Compter in Southwark on evidence provided by a priest named Lawrence who accused him of stealing a trunk and some books. But the charge did not hold, and Gray was soon free.[55] A year and a half later (July 1639), the Privy Council again imprisoned him for taking "great fees . . . to the great oppression of his Majestie's subjects"—presumably blackmail—but he was released in September.[56] Gray continued to work on his own without official authorization for several years more. He was somehow involved with a Dominican, Thomas Middleton, late in 1640, only to be frightened off once more by Windebank, and in 1644 Gray took great delight in testifying for Parliament against Laud, who had caused his imprisonment in 1636.[57]

The employment of pursuivants to assist in the enforcement of the penal laws was a necessary, though unfortunate, expedient. Since there was no national or local police force, and since the churchwardens and constables often shirked their duty by not reporting recusants, there was probably no alternative but recourse to informers, if some order was to be introduced into the enforcement of the penal laws.[58] But the Government, out of a sense of responsibility if not out of justice, should have more closely supervised its informers, whose illegal actions contravened the spirit as well as the letter of the penal laws.

Chapter Eight

THE CALM BEFORE THE STORM

W HILE RECUSANTS in the country were bearing the
brunt of persecution imposed haphazardly by officers of the peace, the Catholics of London, chiefly those in the
Queen's circle, enjoyed a period of considerable religious freedom. Five years of relief from the demands of Parliament for
a stricter enforcement of the penal code did much to moderate
Charles's attitude toward his Catholic subjects. He himself
disapproved of religious persecution, and his theological beliefs
were in many ways not significantly different from those of
Catholics. Moreover, Henrietta skillfully induced Charles not
only to tolerate Catholic courtiers in her suite but even to accept
complacently the conversions to the old faith that robbed the
English Church of several of its most distinguished members.
Charles favored three privy councillors whose practical conformity to the Established Church shielded family connections
with Catholics and respect for Catholicism. Sparked by Henrietta, the Catholic revival drew vitality from two papal agents,
Panzani and Conn, whom Charles welcomed with surprising
cordiality. Capuchins in priestly garb walked openly about the
city, and Catholics flocked to mass in the Queen's new chapel
and in the chapels of the Catholic embassies without incident.

It is evident from the strength of the Catholic revival that
the Established Church did not have a rigid hold on all of its
congregations. It was one thing for the Government to decree

that all subjects conform to the Established Church; it was quite another thing to enforce the decree. How many Englishmen in the early seventeenth century still hovered between an old loyalty to Rome and the necessity of conforming to the Established Church cannot, of course, be determined. Just as the pressure of the penal laws broke down the faith of weak Catholics, so too did the authoritarianism of the Established Church fail to win the support of all Englishmen. There were undoubtedly persons who preferred Catholicism to Anglicanism but dared not publicly acknowledge their preference. Gordon Albion has suggested that three of Charles's chief ministers —Lord Treasurer Richard Weston, Chancellor of the Exchequer Francis, Lord Cottington, and Secretary of State Sir Francis Windebank—were "Catholics under the skin, . . . [who] construed to die in the Faith" of their ancestors at the eleventh hour.[1]

Lord Weston of Neyland, later Earl of Portland, who prudently directed England's financial affairs from 1628 to his death in 1635, remained an Anglican even though his wife and several of his children were acknowledged Catholics.[2] His eldest son married the Catholic second daughter of the Duchess of Lennox at Roehampton in 1632 in the presence of Henrietta and Charles, who gave the bride away.[3] Moreover, Weston permitted his wife to keep resident priests.[4] But despite Weston's close ties with Catholicism, he never lost favor with Charles or the Privy Council,[5] and he was at the height of his career when he died suddenly of what appears to have been diphtheria.[6] It was rumored that he had been converted to Catholicism on his deathbed.[7] Whether Weston actually was received into the Church by a priest summoned by Lady Weston is open to conjecture. The Venetian ambassador, who generally knew about such things, noted only the possibility of a conversion.[8]

Francis, Lord Cottington, who became Chancellor of the Exchequer in 1629, had definite leanings toward Catholicism, and had even been a temporary convert in 1623 during residence in Spain (though probably as a matter of convenience).[9] Cottington, a talented and pleasant fellow, was in great favor in Henrietta's court and was on close and friendly terms with a number of Catholic priests. He often exchanged informal visits with Father Thomas Rant,[10] and he defended a Jesuit who shared his opposition to a significant alteration in the oath of allegiance.[11] He frequently opposed proclamations by the Privy Council for the enforcement of recusancy laws.[12] When the councillors debated the advisability of putting the oath to all Catholics, Cottington spoke to the King against it, candidly suggesting that such a policy would question the loyalty of Catholics who had lived in peaceful obedience to the Crown. Cottington was also among the most outspoken of the courtiers who favored the reunion of the English and Roman Churches.[13]

Sir Francis Windebank, though a staunch Anglican of Laudian principles, was sympathetic to Catholicism and also favored the reunion of the churches. He was more deeply religious than either Weston or Cottington, and sought a theological compromise between Calvinism, which alarmed him, and Anglicanism, which did not entirely satisfy him. Catholicism appealed to him, though he frequently quarreled with the Jesuits over the questions of clerical celibacy and Communion, and both his official and his private actions indicate a sense of loyalty to Rome. According to the Venetian envoy, Windebank spoke "like a zealous Catholic." And he is reputed to have called Henry VIII "that pig" for instituting the break with Rome.[14] Although Windebank stood to suffer public reprobation when his daughter-in-law became a Catholic nun, he did nothing to prevent it; in fact, he told his son that her decision was an act of God.[15]

Windebank worked closely with Henrietta in the Catholic subscription for the Bishops' War, and he was forced to flee to France to escape an indictment by the Long Parliament for aiding dozens of imprisoned priests and recusants.[16] Parliament accused Windebank of issuing seventy-four letters of grace for over one hundred Catholics, who then allegedly caused twenty-one Anglican parishioners of St. Giles's in Holborn to renounce their religion.[17] Windebank, safe in Calais, flatly denied the charges against him in a long letter intended for Parliament: "For the other suspition of my being a favourer . . . of popery," he wrote, "I protest before the mighty God and as I shall answere on the last dreadfull daye that I know noe ground for the least suspition."[18] It would appear that Windebank wrote the letter partly to shield his family, whom he had left behind in London, and partly in the hope of salvaging something of his political career. There is little reason to question, on the one hand, his profession of devotion to Anglicanism in 1640, or, on the other hand, the statement of Père Cyprien de Gamaches, one of Henrietta's Capuchins, that he brought Windebank into the Catholic Church in September 1646.[19]

A fourth man of pro-Catholic sentiments who occupied a high place at Court was Sir Kenelm Digby. Although his father, Sir Everard Digby, had been executed for complicity in the Gunpowder Plot, Sir Kenelm nevertheless enjoyed the friendship of Laud, who tutored him at Oxford. He had a long career as naval commander, diplomat, courtier, and author that kept him closely associated with important affairs of state through three reigns. He followed Charles and Buckingham to Madrid in 1623, and led a victorious English fleet in the French war of 1627–29. In 1630, perhaps out of ambition, or perhaps out of a momentary conviction that there was no intellectual freedom within the Catholic Church, Digby shocked his coreligionists by taking the Anglican Communion at Whitehall. But he abandoned Anglicanism in 1635, to the peril of his political future and financial welfare. Two years earlier the Privy Council, unconvinced by his apparent conformity to the Establishment, charged him and his wife with supplying shot and armor for a recusant plot that was expected to erupt in the Midlands immediately after the departure of Charles for Scotland in 1633. Although the informers who had testified against Digby—Cornelius Simpkin, Christopher Coursey, and William Asby— paid for their perjury by public humiliation in Hanslup parish church and by doing penance before their victims, Digby's reputation nevertheless suffered.[20] He escaped incrimination a second time when he was accused of planning to have his two sons, Kenelm and John, educated in a French Catholic seminary.[21] Like Windebank, he worked with Henrietta to solicit Catholic funds for Charles's northern expedition against the Scots. Parliament tried to punish Digby for that in 1641, but he managed to reach the Continent, where he spent the next twenty years writing religious and political pamphlets, returning to England only on brief visits.[22]

These men of rank were not the only men of pro-Catholic sentiment in the Queen's circle at Somerset House. Leander Jones, Panzani, and Conn felt equally comfortable there. Dom Leander Jones,[23] president general of the English Benedictines, arrived in London in June 1634 from Flanders. Before setting out, he had written to Laud, an old acquaintance from St. John's College, Oxford, asking permission to enter England to see friends and relatives. Laud was cool to the idea, but he secured Charles's permission and assured Jones that he would not be subject to the penal laws so long as he conducted himself circumspectly. But Jones had more substantial reasons for being in England than simply to visit friends. In point of fact, he considered himself an unofficial intermediary between London and Rome (there is no evidence that Urban VIII had sent him). It is likely that Jones mainly wished to confer with several privy councillors, including Windebank, Cottington, and Weston, about their possible entry into the Catholic Church. Beyond that, he hoped to make some progress toward settling the two issues that had divided the Catholic community for most of the century—the oath of allegiance and the need for a Catholic bishop in England.

In these matters Jones held views that contradicted the convictions of many Catholics. He felt that neither English Catholics nor the Pope should object to the oath as it was, inasmuch as the King simply wanted his Catholic subjects to promise to recognize their duty of civil obedience. Jones also believed that Charles had no intention of forcing Catholics to deny the spiritual sovereignty of the Pope. On the question of a Catholic bishop for England, Jones insisted that since both Charles and his bishops were opposed to a bishop, none should be appointed. Any appointment, he maintained, would kill all chance of a reconciliation between the English and Roman churches. When Windebank and Cottington intimated that even Charles might be converted, Jones inadvertently became the spokesman of a small but influential group of Anglicans who wanted reunion with Rome and were convinced that Charles could be induced to accept the idea.[24] But Jones was sensible enough to realize that Charles would not consider reunion unless Rome allowed Catholics to take the oath of allegiance in an amended form that was acceptable to the Crown. He therefore asked Pope Urban to grant such permission, but the Pope refused to rescind the bull of May 30, 1626, which forbade Catholics to take the oath in any form under pain of serious sin and excommunication.[25] There was little hope of getting Charles's agreement after that. Nor, indeed, could the King or his ministers have altered the oath or the recusancy laws, which were statutory, without the consent of Parliament, a fact that Jones should have been aware of.

Although Jones failed in his ambitious plan of reconciliation, he did accomplish something worth while in clearing the air of controversy between the Benedictines and the seculars, who accused him of "double-dealing" in the question of the oath and in the dispute over the Bishop of Chalcedon.[26] Within three months he managed to resolve several disagreements in liturgical and jurisdictional matters.[27]

Jones stepped aside in December 1634 to make way for an accredited papal agent, Gregorio Panzani, who reached London on the 15th. Panzani had left Rome on August 28, carefully instructed by the Pope on what he ought and ought not to undertake. He was advised to make his primary concern the settlement of the dispute over the Bishop of Chalcedon, and he was cautioned not to discuss with non-Catholics either the reconciliation of England and Rome or the oath. Panzani took rooms by St. Martin's-in-the-Fields and was soon meeting with Windebank and Cottington, but several weeks passed before he had an audience with Charles. The King greeted him warmly, seemingly pleased at his coming, but told him bluntly that he was not to meddle in political affairs.[28] Panzani, forgetting his instructions, immediately broached the question of the oath and asked Charles whether he would be willing to delete certain passages objectionable to the Holy See. Charles replied that he could promise nothing, but would take the matter under consideration.[29] Panzani was heartened by such a sympathetic attitude, and he assumed that something would be done, but his optimism was unwarranted. He realized neither the strong opposition that would be encountered from both High Church and Puritan quarters, nor the meaninglessness of Charles's casual remarks.

The conferences between Panzani and Windebank were equally fruitless. They discussed the loyalty of Catholics, the jurisdiction of the Pope in England, and the possibility of altering the oath. Windebank told Panzani that nothing would be done about the oath unless the Pope agreed to tone down his briefs against it. Panzani promised vaguely to do everything he could to soften the Pope's opposition.[30] Panzani and Windebank also discussed the wisdom of permitting the return to England of the Bishop of Chalcedon. Windebank opposed his reinstatement on the ground that the Protestant bishops would not tolerate a Catholic bishop who would rival their own claims to episcopal jurisdiction. To that Panzani answered pedantically that a Catholic bishop had authority only over Catholics, and then merely in spiritual matters.[31]

By this time it was already apparent that Rome had chosen the wrong man to advance its interests in England. Panzani was sincere and industrious, but he was no match for the royal ministers, who knew better than to bring up controversial issues. Panzani spoke openly with Windebank about the quarrel among the clergy and defended the Jesuits, though he knew the Secretary's dislike of them. Windebank, in turn, told Panzani that the Jesuits should be banished altogether from England.[32] Thereafter they saw eye to eye on nothing.

When Pope Urban learned of these conferences, he wisely ordered Panzani to stop arguing about the oath and concentrate on settling the quarrel between the regulars and seculars. He also told him that he ought not to publicize his negotiations, for he might thereby give false hope to the Catholics, and spur them to spread propaganda for a modified oath, at the risk of renewed persecution. Finally, the Pope advised Panzani that he would soon be recalled to make way for a fully accredited papal representative who could negotiate directly with the King.[33]

In an attempt to pacify the clergy, Panzani first approached the Jesuits, but they balked at his support of Smith's episcopacy and refused to cooperate in settling the dispute. Thus vexed, Panzani changed his mind about the Jesuits. He complained about their stubbornness in a letter of April 11, 1635, to Francesco Barberini, the Cardinal Protector of England, charging that they refused to recognize his authority, advised Laud against allowing a Catholic bishop, and spread rumors that he, Panzani, had been sent by Richelieu to spy for France. In a letter dated June 13, Panzini added several further comments:

Every day I hear new complaints of them, and of their equiv-
ocations; and yet I have given them more encouragement
and tokens of confidence than to any others; which they
requite with spreading idle and personal reflections . . . to
all the particulars of my life. And of late, one father Roberts
of that order attacked me so briskly on account of partiality
in their disfavour, that I found myself obliged to make use
of the strongest asservations to silence him.[34]

Barberini offered no sympathy, and Panzani went on without
Jesuit support.

With the representatives of the secular clergy Panzani had
more success. Almost immediately he won the support of Leyburn, one of the important seculars of London,[35] and the rest of
the priests quickly fell into line. Panzani then made his primary
goal that of persuading the regular orders to assemble at a meeting and air their grievances. A conference between the leading
seculars and regulars, not including the Jesuits, was accordingly
held at his home on November 17, 1635. At least fourteen priests,
among them such noted ones as John Southcot and Christopher
Davenport, listened as Panzani read his proposed "Instrument
of Peace or Concord between the Secular Clergy and the Regulars." Point by point, they accepted the proposals, and then
signed the document in triplicate. While the meeting was in
process, according to Southcot, a Jesuit entered and exchanged
a few angry words with Panzani; he refused to sign the agreement in the name of his Society, and left in a huff over not having been invited to the meeting.[36]

In view of the bitter controversy that had been raging among
the clergy for so many years, it may appear surprising that the
priests came to such a quick and cordial compromise. In truth,
however, the agreement[37] was couched in such general terms
that the real points of dispute were not even mentioned. The
representatives of the seculars, Benedictines, Franciscans, Dominicans, and Carmelites promised to "bury their animosities,

and to abstain from all recrimination" while "leaving their respective rights and privileges untouched." They also promised to work together to reconquer England for the Catholic Church, to protect the Holy See against "false representations," and to respect the English Government. Finally, the agreement provided that the clergy meet four times a year, or as often as the need arose, to settle their differences. In short, the "Instrument of Peace or Concord" settled nothing of consequence. The very wording of the document admitted of evasion in that the signatories merely pledged to continue what they already had been doing; there was no mention of their views about the oath, the need for an English Catholic bishop, or the privileges of their orders.[38]

Panzani spent the next few weeks arranging for the exchange of diplomatic agents between London and Rome. Arthur Brett, the English representative, left London with Charles's promise to allow a Catholic bishop for England if the Pope would permit a more lenient oath and two other political concessions.[39] But Brett died en route, and Count Cartegna, the papal agent, was detained at Ravenna. Two others replaced them. William Hamilton, a zealous, competent, and dashing young Catholic, went to Rome, and George Conn, the taciturn, affable, and extremely able canon of St. John Lateran, set out for England. They had much in common: both were Scots, both enjoyed excellent reputations as diplomats, and both were handsome men trained to smile their way past opposition.[40] For the purposes of this study, only Conn's activities are of interest.

He landed at Rye on July 26, 1636, after more than a month's journey across the Continent, and proceeded to London, where Charles received him warmly and introduced him to the courtiers.[41] Within a month, however, an outbreak of the plague forced the Court to leave London. Conn and Panzani traveled to Oxford with the royal entourage, which was greeted by a cheering crowd of townspeople, dons, and students. Conn took

lodging in Christ Church College and ate a lavish dinner at
St. John's in the company of the royal couple and Laud. That
evening there was a performance of a new comedy, *The Pas-
sions Calm'd,* which was a timely portrayal of a King, an agent,
and a wise man. The next morning Charles left for New For-
est, Henrietta proceeded to Oatlands, and Conn and Panzani
went on to Richmond, where they waited for the cold winds of
December to drive the plague from London.[42]

Back in London, with Panzani on his way to Rome, Conn
soon became an inseparable companion of the King, who ad-
mired Conn's knowledge of politics and theology and delighted
in his well-phrased flattery. On one occasion an assembly of the
Knights of the Garter waited while the King showed his new
favorite around his gallery. Conn accompanied the King to
meetings of the Privy Council, where he sat on a level with the
Queen, an honor ordinarily given only to the chief ministers.
The placid Venetian envoy observed that even the most ada-
mant Protestant courtiers visited Conn at home.[43] Moreover, to
the consternation of the Puritans[44] and the delight of the seculars, Conn preached frequently, traveled in state through the
streets of London,[45] and said daily mass for hundreds of Catholics.[46]

But Conn was not misled by Charles's conspicuous favor.
He was too sophisticated a man not to realize that favors quickly
given might also be quickly withdrawn. Nor did he expect Laud
and the Puritans to stand idly by while Charles flirted with
Rome, contemplated religious freedom for Catholics, and made
loose promises to alter the oath. He continued to act the part of
a credulous servant while he set about gaining the more stable
support of Henrietta.[47] Conn aroused the Queen from her com-
placent attitude toward the welfare of her coreligionists, and
succeeded for a time, at least, in making her, as well as one of
her favorites, Walter Montagu, an active agent in the propaga-
tion of the faith.[48]

Conn had largely abandoned any hope of converting Charles to Catholicism, although Rome still believed it possible. In October 1633, Henrietta had sent a Scottish Catholic, Sir Robert Douglas, to Rome to tell the Pope of Charles's earnest desire to enter into permanent relations with the Holy See. Thereafter, prelates such as Barberini and Cardinal Gianfrancesco del Bagno, an adviser to the Pope on English affairs, believed that the conversion of Charles was only a matter of time, and that the right papal agent might finally succeed in bringing him into the Catholic Church. Pope Urban also felt that whatever leanings Charles might have toward the Catholic Church would be strengthened by bestowing a cardinalate on one of his subjects, presumably Conn. The choice of an agent was all-important. Unfortunately, Urban's first choice was Panzani, who so antagonized most Protestants that even Conn, with all his skill, could not alter Charles's firm conviction that a man would be saved so long as he accepted Christ, whatever the precise form of religion.[49]

During the years of the missions of Panzani and Conn several important Anglican courtiers became converts to Catholicism. Early conversions, like that of the first Lord Baltimore, had been discreetly made so as not to arouse the Anglican community. But Henrietta boasted openly about the proselytes whom the Capuchins won from the Established Church, thereby, of course, provoking further animosity from the Anglicans.

The wife of Endymion Porter, Olivia, herself a convert, was one of the most important and devout of the lay apostolates at Court. When she learned that her father, John, Lord Boteler, lay dying at his country house near Hatfield, she had him taken to London, where the Capuchins secured his last-minute conversion to Catholicism. She was also largely responsible for the conversion of Mary, Marchioness of Hamilton, Buckingham's niece, whose youthful beauty had withered under the strain of malignant disease. Mary's staunchly Puritan father, Lord Denbigh, called in the Bishop of Carlisle to be at her side during the last hours. The Bishop vowed that he would stake his own salvation upon her death as a Protestant, but she nevertheless died a Catholic.[50] The conversion of Olivia's sister, Lady Frances Newport, who was a friend of Walter Montagu and Tobie Mathew, also converts, startled the Anglican courtiers even more. Neither the sensitive temperament nor the formidable theological knowledge of Lady Frances could withstand the persistence of the Capuchins, who successfully refuted point by point her arguments against Catholicism until the foundation of her faith sank in the quicksand of her own uncertainty.[51]

Lady Elizabeth Falkland, the wife of the former Lord Deputy of Ireland, became a Catholic soon after Charles's coronation, but unlike others she suffered a good deal because of it. Following an argument over religion[52] her husband drove her from their home in November 1626. Thereafter she was ostracized by her Protestant friends and was refused admission to Court.[53] She was cheated of a share in her father's will, and lacked the money even to pay the rent on her modest dwelling in Drury Lane, but she managed nevertheless to raise a family of ten children, four of whom became Benedictines.[54] Then Laud intervened. Hearing that she had led two of her daughters into the Roman Church, he had the High Commission take them as wards of the state.[55] The Privy Council then indicted her for refusing to acknowledge that she had sent two of her sons to a Continental seminary.[56] She escaped punishment, however, and thereafter was left in peace.

The activities of the converts centered around Henrietta Maria's court and her chapel on the grounds of Somerset House, which was completed in 1635. The chapel, designed by Inigo Jones, the Surveyor-General (who was himself a Catholic),[57] was a small but magnificently embellished structure. Beneath a dome forty feet high stood the altar, raised on three broad tiers of steps and marked off with balustrades; on either side of a columned arch were niches containing statues of the prophets. There were rich tapestries, silver gilt chandeliers, and dozens of costly vases.[58]

The solemn consecration of the chapel on December 8 inaugurated three days of pageantry.[59] The Abbé du Perron (who had recently been made Bishop of Angoulême), the Queen's Almoner, sang the pontifical high mass, which Henrietta attended with a "concourse of people . . . so great that it seemed as if all the inhabitants of London had concerted to attend this noble ceremony."[60] Thereafter the chapel never closed until the Long Parliament forced Henrietta to take refuge in France; even when the ambassadors locked their doors in fear of the plague, or to comply with a governmental order restricting the attendance at mass by English Catholics, the services continued at Somerset House.[61]

The French Capuchins who served the chapel labored tirelessly among the Catholics of London. Each Saturday the monks recited the Litany of the Blessed Virgin and made Benediction. Catholic fraternal orders, such as the Confraternity of the Rosary, gathered on the first Sunday of every month to confess their sins and to receive Communion. The Capuchins also taught catechism classes in French and English on Wednesdays, Thursdays, and Saturdays to remedy the hazy religious knowledge of Catholics who had forgotten the axioms of their faith, and to instruct converts. Even Catholics in prison or in sick beds had Communion brought to them.[62]

The religious freedom of the Catholics of London at this time was in such sharp contrast to the persecution of earlier years that the Venetian ambassador marveled at it. "The priests have never had so much liberty," he wrote to the Doge; "whereas in the past Catholics could only hear mass at the embassies, with great risk of being arrested when they came out,

. . . [now] anyone who wishes a celebration [of mass] in his own house can avoid the danger of the penalty with slight circumspection."[63]

But such freedom would not be enjoyed much longer, for Laud was quietly preparing to cement the cracks that resurgent Catholicism had made in the structure of the English Church. Laud had, of course, long opposed the extension of religious toleration to Catholics. He devoted much of his episcopacy to defending the liturgy of the Established Church against Puritan inroads, and he felt compelled to stifle Catholicism as well, not only to satisfy his own rigid sense of duty and to meet the letter of the law, but also to silence persistent charges that he secretly sympathized with Rome.[64] Although thoughtful men could not honestly question his devotion to the English Church, he was nevertheless distrusted by the Puritans, who bombarded him with passionate diatribes full of biblical quotations. For that matter, few contemporaries of Laud understood him. He was neither a profound theologian nor a sentimental ritualist, but a superb administrator who supervised his church directly, if perhaps too closely. He may have been too concerned with external forms of ceremony rather than with fundamental spiritual values, but only a man completely devoted to his church could have been so afraid of surrendering to Catholicism in an unguarded moment. In March 1626, Laud tells us in his diary, he awoke in a cold sweat from a dream that he had been converted to Rome. Should that ever happen, he wrote, he would be "aggrieved" more by the scandal to the Anglican cause than by his own heresy.[65]

Many of the proclamations by the Privy Council against recusancy can be traced directly to Laud's influence.[66] He would have had Walter Montagu prosecuted for apostasy had not Henrietta intervened,[67] and he convinced the Council to destroy the devotional articles at St. Winifred's Well, a popular shrine in the Diocese of St. Asaph, which was frequented alike by Catholics and Anglicans.[68] Laud also did his best to prevent the publication of Catholic literature. In one case among many he stopped the circulation of St. Francis de Sales's *Introduction to a Devout Life,* had the printer arrested and the translator searched for, and all available copies of it burned.[69] Laud wrote to Bishop Joseph Hall (Exeter) during the war with Scotland in 1639 that the enemies of episcopacy were not only the Scots, but also "the subtiler factions of . . . Rome [that sought to bring about] . . . a monarchical government of the Pope" in England.[70]

Two aspects of the Catholic revival, a lenient oath of allegiance and freedom of worship for the Queen and her courtiers, particularly angered Laud. He would not listen to proposals by Panzani and Conn to alter the oath, and he supported the position of Catholics like Father Thomas Preston who accepted the oath as it was.[71] In May 1635, Laud reminded the Council and the King of the heresy being daily practiced at Somerset House, and he would not permit the Council to forget it until a proclamation forbidding the attendance at mass there by English Catholics was issued in 1637.[72] Of all the royal ministers, Laud was least sympathetic to religious freedom for Catholics and most eager to force their submission to the Established Church. Puritan charges of his complicity with Rome were entirely without justification. "The Papists are the most dangerous Subjects of the Kingdom," Laud wrote to Viscount Wentworth, and, given the opportunity, they would "grind Protestants to Powder."[73]

Most English Protestants, indeed would no sooner have accepted the idea of union with Rome or of religious toleration of Catholics than they would have admitted the error of their own religious beliefs. No more devoted a disciple of this rigid attitude can be found than Laud, whose revisionist program in the Established Church, extended to Scotland, was a significant element in the outbreak of rebellion among the Scots.

Chapter Nine

THE SCOTTISH WAR

O N SUNDAY MORNING, July 23, 1637, in Edinburgh's St. Giles's Cathedral, an irate Presbyterian Scotswoman raised her voice to protest the introduction of the new Anglican Prayer Book and canons that Charles had prescribed for use in every Scottish parish. The congregation, as if by plan, began to shout and move about restlessly. A stool hurled at Patrick Lindsay, Bishop of Edinburgh, went wide of the mark and barely missed the Dean's head, and Archbishop John Spottiswoode ordered the magistrates to drive the rioters into the street. While the service continued, the throng outside shattered the stained glass windows and tried to force open the great doors of the church. With this outburst of resistance to religious innovations in Scotland began a rebellion that was long overdue.

The Presbyterian clergy governed the Kirk by presbytery and synod. Although King James had forced episcopacy upon the Scots, by the time of Charles's ascendancy the Anglican bishops permitted the Calvinist ministers to preach and practice Presbyterianism without legal restraint. Charles and Laud visited Edinburgh in 1633, and after only a casual appraisal of the state of the Anglican Church, became convinced that immediate steps should be taken to revitalize it. Among other matters, Charles ordered that uniformity of worship should be enforced to discipline ministers who ignored the Anglican liturgy. In 1634, Charles instructed the Scottish bishops to draft a new Prayer Book and canons. These were authorized in 1636 by Charles, Laud, Juxon, and others without the advice or consent of the General Assembly, the Presbyterian clergy, or any other ecclesiastical body. The Scots ministers, who had previously enjoyed virtual autonomy in parochial affairs, were not unnaturally annoyed at not having been consulted; nor did they like the tinge of papism so introduced into Scottish clerical matters by the foreign English. The Scottish nobility, always independent and authoritarian, were indignant at their apparent subordination to the Anglican bishops. So it can be seen that thousands of Scottish nobility, gentry, clergy, and general populace were more than willing to sign a Covenant, in which they swore to withstand, to death if necessary, the religious reforms that Charles imposed. When the Assembly in Glasgow repudiated bishops, talk of insurrection filled the air, and military preparations commenced on both banks of the Tweed.[1]

Charles, confronted with the reality of armed insurrection in Scotland, at first proposed an unrealistic plan to raise about 21,000 men to guard England's northern frontier, even though there was no money in the Exchequer to support an army.[2] Risking further hostility from a nation already burdened with extraordinary levies, Charles nevertheless tried once more to raise money, without recourse to Parliament, to pay for the troops that were to rendezvous with him at York by April 1. Most of the measures to raise funds failed. The Corporation of London refused to pay a forced loan of £200,000 despite pressure put upon the Lord Mayor and aldermen by the Privy Council. The peers of the realm, especially those in the King's service, at first made excuses to avoid paying their share of the loan, but then grudgingly advanced a considerable sum.[3] By May 1639, however, Charles had despaired of raising an additional £6,000 a month to pay the 4,300 newly mustered troops at Newcastle.[4] In the end, having no money to maintain a regular army, Charles had to marshal the nobility to serve at their own expense at the head of the trainbands (militia).

But the trainbands, undisciplined and inexperienced, were

generally unwilling to fight. On the eve of the march onto Scottish soil, officers refused to call out their men, and rioting spread among the troops.[5] Desertions became commonplace, and there was serious question that a sufficient number of men could be enlisted long enough to constitute an army. Colonel George Gage suggested that Charles bring over 10,000 Catholic Flemings on condition that the penal laws be rescinded; such an army, he thought, could be supported at first by English Catholic money, and for at least six months more by a papal subsidy.[6] Though the suggestion was enticing, Charles could not act on it, for only Parliament could put aside the laws, and he was unwilling to convene it. Faced, then, with the problem of finding troops at home, he raised them chiefly in the North, which was heavily Catholic. Thus, in the financial and military crises then confronting the Crown, Charles counted on substantial support from the Catholics, and their clergy worked hard to help him.

The corporate loyalty of the Catholic community appeared certain even before the Scottish hostility to the ecclesiastical reforms erupted into armed conflict. Father Anthony Champney, the dean of the secular clergy, wrote two letters in December 1638 exhorting his subordinates to pray for peace in Europe, then in the throes of the Thirty Years' War, and for the pacification of the Scots' "discontented humors."[7] He advised the priests to warn their parishioners of the danger to the Crown and to the Catholics in England that the Scottish insurrection augured, and to be ready to serve the King in whatever service he might ask. In addition, Champney reminded the clergy and faithful that St. Paul had strictly commanded all men to be subject to their legally constituted superiors, and he pointed out that Charles, Henrietta, and Windebank were deeply impressed by the willingness of Catholics to serve the Crown. But above all else, Champney wanted it clearly understood that the welfare of the English Catholics was contingent upon the preservation of the existing government: "For if the faction of those rebellious spiritts should prvaile (which God forbid)," he wrote, "the Catholickes doubtlesse will feele the ill effects of it more than others."[8]

While the clergy traveled through their districts encouraging Catholic support for the Crown, Queen Henrietta, Conn, and the superiors of four of the regular orders made plans to solicit Catholic financial aid. Henrietta, for once in her relations with the Catholics, pleased Charles in a wholehearted effort to marshal the full strength of English Catholicism behind him. She had circulated under her signature a letter to the leading Catholic gentry, peers, and clergy, asking their help in a nationwide collection of money, not only to help finance the war but also to manifest the loyalty of the Catholic body. The letter, written April 17, 1639,[9] by a committee composed of Kenelm Digby, Basil Brooke, John Winter, and Walter Montagu,[10] implored Catholics to donate "some considerable sum of money freely and cheerfully" to prove their gratitude to the King, who had "so often interested himself in the solicitation of their benefits." As an added incentive, Henrietta promised every benefit and protection against the penal laws to those who would work for the success of the subscription.[11]

The formidable organizational problems of such an undertaking were ironed out during a number of meetings held at Conn's home from the middle of March to early June.[12] That the papal agent should have led the drive was only fitting, for he had the respect not only of Charles but of the Catholic laity and clergy as well. Conn immediately set to work to raise at least £12,500.[13] Although he was already suffering from the painful internal ailment that would take his life at Rome the following January,[14] he composed a lengthy statement, which was countersigned by leading Catholic gentlemen in London, denouncing the Covenant of the Scots and pledging Catholic military and financial support against the insurrection.[15] He also tried, though unsuccessfully, to prevent the enforcement of

a royal proclamation, issued the preceding January at the insistence of the Privy Council, authorizing the reinforcement of the
penal laws.[16]

That the Catholic subscription should even have got under
way is remarkable. For the first time since the eruption of the
archpriest controversy in the 1590's, the seculars and regulars
truly put aside their doctrinal and administrative differences for
the sake of harmony in a critical moment. Five superiors—
Anthony Champney of the seculars, William Price of the Benedictines, Thomas Middleton of the Dominicans, Christopher
Davenport of the Franciscans, and Henry More of the Jesuits—
circulated copies of a letter,[17] dated April 4, 1639, ordering
priests throughout the country to implore their parishioners to
contribute money bountifully.[18] Enclosed with every letter was
a copy of a seventeen-point set of instructions, entitled "Advices
and Motives," which was designed to help the lay coadjutors in
their collections.[19]

"Advices and Motives" is a fascinating document in the psy-
chology of fund-raising. Collectors were to point out first of all
that King Charles depended on Catholic funds for the financial
success of the Scottish expedition and the consequent security of
England. Second, prospective benefactors were to be reminded
that Henrietta personally had endorsed the subscription. Third,
no one could refuse to contribute on the grounds that their expenses, such as composition rents, were too heavy. Such persons
were to be told that "In London . . . even those who are much
weighed down in debts . . . have borrowed money to give . . .
as if their estates were free." Finally, Catholics in the southern
counties were to be instructed to donate no later than the end
of Easter Term; those in the Midlands and in the North were
to be given until the close of Midsummer Term. How much
each person should give would depend on their means, but an
eighth, ninth, or tenth of their annual incomes was to be considered a minimum.[20]

While Henrietta attended daily mass in her new chapel, and Catholic courtiers fasted on Saturdays to ensure Charles's safety in battle,[21] the collection began in every hundred where Catholics resided. Overseers for each county were chosen from among influential gentry, and they were assisted by coadjutors in every parish. The clergy, however, soon assumed the task of actually gathering the money—perhaps because, as Champney suggested to his archdeacons in a letter of June 1, 1639, the gentry could not so easily elicit the support of "the servants and poorer sort of Catholics" as could their trusted confessors.[22]

There is, unfortunately, no complete list of the collectors, but the more important ones are known. Oddly enough, we must go for them to Prynne, the Puritan pamphleteer, who took the trouble to name many of them in a publication meant to discredit Laud.[23] A list of the collectors for both England and Wales was compiled by an anonymous chronicler in 1641.[24] Among the many unimportant names are a number of those of prominent Catholic peers and gentry, such as Sir Robert Charnock of Bedfordshire, Sir Francis Howard of Cumberland, George Arundell of Dorsetshire, Sir John Winter of Gloucestershire, Sir Henry Beddingfield of Norfolk, and Lord Baltimore of Wiltshire. The anonymous chronicler of 1641 named 120 collectors, but there must surely have been two or even three times that many in order to carry out the canvassing, which was so widespread as to include even Protestant families in which one or more members were Catholic.

The subscription raised £14,000,[25] a creditable sum, but much less than one might have expected. That amount of money would support the English army in the field for only a month and a half. A few gentlemen gave generously:[26] the Marquis of Worcester, for instance, gave £1,500, and the Marquis of Winchester donated £1,000.[27] A few friends of Henrietta, including Lady Denbigh and Lady Killigrew, each gave £100.[28] In addition, from May 1 to November 15, 1639, the recusants of several southern counties paid fines totaling £2,436 which the Crown probably used to help finance the war.[29] If each Catholic family—70,000, let us assume (taking 360,000 as the number of Catholics at this time)—contributed but one pound, at least £70,000 should have been raised. Most families must therefore have given only a few pennies, or a shilling or two at the most. From this point of view, the subscription was a failure.

One can suggest several reasons why Catholics did not contribute more. Certainly the renewal of persecution by royal proclamation in 1638 must have dampened enthusiasm for the subscription. That Catholics were being harried as usual is proved by the fact that they petitioned Charles in August 1639 to restrain the sheriffs of Norfolk, Lancashire, and Yorkshire, and the bishops of several northern dioceses, from enforcing the penal laws; unless Charles stopped such rigorous persecution, the petitioners warned, the subsidy would "come to nothing."[30] Also, of course, Catholics, like most other Englishmen, wanted neither to go to war nor to be taxed to support a war,[31] and, Catholics of humble means understandably resented the pressure put on them by their own collectors—some were even threatened with public humiliation if they did not contribute, or if they contributed too little.[32] Still other Catholics, perhaps fearing that the Government might learn their true financial status and fine them accordingly, would not divulge their income, as required by the eighth point of the "Advices and Motives."

But the most important reason for the failure of the Catholic subscription was a forged letter, purportedly sent by Pope Urban VIII to Conn, which advised Catholics not to support the King, either financially or militarily. The real author of the letter is not known, but copies of it were widely circulated and generally accepted by Catholics as authentic.[33] The Pope supposedly ordered Conn to remind Catholics to consider their existing financial burdens before surrendering more money too freely: they should "be not so forward with their money more than what laws and duty force them to pay without any innovation at all" in their security against the penal laws. Conn was noticeably upset by the letter, and he expended much effort convincing prominent Catholics that they should ignore it.[84]

Despite their unwillingness to give financial support, however, many Catholics readily joined the trainbands. Numerous Catholics marched into Scotland on June 1 with Thomas Howard, Earl of Arundel, England's aging marshal whom Charles put in nominal command of the army. The Catholic militia were among the most ill-equipped troops comprising the twelve regiments mustered in Yorkshire. In January 1639, Sir Jacob Astley, a diplomat and soldier, reported to Windebank that recusants were sending their Catholic servants to the rendezvous point unarmed and untrained.[85] An anonymous priest, writing after the Peace of Berwick, complained that Catholic soldiers went to the quarter musters in their counties with only such weapons as they could hurriedly purchase at their own expense.[86] Most of the Protestant troops were also undisciplined and ill-equipped, but they at least had some weapons at home to use in battle. Not so the Catholics. The general confiscations of recusants' arms in 1610, 1625,[87] and 1638 had deprived them of all their weapons except those that were "convenient for the guard of their houses."[88] And now, it seemed, there were no records of the disposition that had been made of the confiscated weapons. The Privy Council, hearing complaints of the scarcity of pikes, halberds, and the like, frantically ordered the clerks of the Council to find out what had been done with them. The clerks reported that the confiscated weapons had been lost, stolen, or allowed to rust.[89]

Catholic soldiers, in addition to the handicap of going to battle poorly armed, were humiliated, accused of treason, and even, in at least a few instances, put to death on account of their religion. Two days after crossing the Tweed, the English army sighted an approaching column of Alexander Leslie's infantry, numbering about 8,000 men. The Earl of Holland, commander of the English cavalry, afraid to meet the Scots in open battle, ordered his men to retreat. To save face he accused a scout, a local man who was a Catholic, of knowingly leading the troops into a trap. Although it was illogical to suspect a Catholic of betraying them to the Presbyterians, it was as good an excuse as any for cowardice.[40] Catholics were also blamed for starting the war. The Scots attempted to demoralize the English troops by circulating pamphlets charging that the unpopular war had been undertaken at the advice of pro-Catholic ministers who hoped thereby to revive the Roman liturgy in England.[41] Such propaganda bred riots in English ranks, including one in a company of trainbands at Warminster in Wiltshire. Suspecting that their commanding officer, Captain Drury, was a Catholic, they mutinied and deserted.[42] On June 18 a company of 600 pressed men from Dorsetshire stationed at Faringdon, Berkshire, murdered one of their Catholic officers named Lieutenant Moore, deserted, and pillaged the town. Another officer, Francis Windebank, the Catholic son of the Secretary, hearing that his company would murder Popish officers, dissimulated his religion by having his men sing psalms, listen to a reading of prayers, and take rounds of "drink and stinking tobacco of six pence a pound."[43]

It was indeed fortunate in view of the lack of funds and the reluctance of the troops that the Scots permitted King Charles to make a truce at Berwick on June 18. The whole expedition had been a farce: the navy, under James, Marquis of Hamilton, failed to take Leith, and Holland's cavalry would not fight. The Scots could easily have crossed the Tweed, but Leslie wisely held back rather than risk arousing English nationalism by an invasion. Instead, he forced Charles to sign a treaty that gave the Scots what they wanted. Both sides agreed to disband their forces, and the English commissioners surrendered to the demand that the Scottish General Assembly be permitted to resolve the disputed ecclesiastical questions for themselves. The Assembly promptly replaced the Episcopal system of church government with the Presbyterian system, and then went ahead in June 1640 to resume the war with England.

Renewed war with the Scots created another crisis in England. Charles recalled Viscount Wentworth from Ireland, made him Earl of Strafford and chief adviser, and took his suggestion to summon Parliament. Once convened, the Commons showed Charles that they intended to follow the same course they had plotted during the Parliament of 1628–29 in refusing him money to put down the Scots, and in resuming debate on parliamentary privileges and religious reform. When Charles learned that the Commons were negotiating independently with the Scots, he ordered a dissolution of the Short Parliament, which had been in session for only three weeks.

Charles then joined his discontented troops at York, but he was unable to stem the advance of the Scottish army, which by September 1640 had moved as far as Morpeth, just north of Newcastle. Leslie, whose troops were occupying Northumberland and the Bishopric of Durham, declared that the Scots only wished to protect their rights and had no intention of conquering England, thereby accentuating rumors that the Catholics had brought on the invasion. Indeed, before a Scotsman set foot on English soil the word had been spread that only Catholic homes and chapels would be pillaged.[44] The English rural population in the North as a whole suffered as a result of the Scottish occupation, but few felt the sting of it more than the Catholics, many of whose homes were burned, reputedly because they refused to supply the invading armies with food.[45]

The situation was hopeless. Charles called his peers to assemble in council at York in early October, and at Ripon opened negotiations with the Scots for a military truce. The English commissioners, among them three Catholics, signed the thirteen articles of peace that confirmed the Scots' occupation of Durham and Northumberland, at a cost to the English of £850 a day until a treaty could be concluded. One condition insisted upon by the English commissioners was that the invaders promise to molest neither "Papists, Prelates nor their adherents," and to cease plundering and taxing them.[46]

Charles had no recourse but to summon Parliament again. As the Members journeyed to Westminster, charges of Catholic responsibility for the catastrophe of Scottish victory swept the city. Pamphleteers conveniently forgot the Government's intention to revitalize the ecclesiastical system in Scotland, and remembered Presbyterian charges that the Catholics had provoked church reform. At least one observer, an alderman of Newcastle, where fear of the Scots was particularly strong, rightly recognized the absurdity of such talk and admitted that religious innovations were hardly worth a war.[47] Most Englishmen, however, probably believed the allegation that Catholics were to blame for all of England's misfortunes. Angry Londoners murmured against "doggish friars" and "popish masses" as the newly elected Parliament prepared to suppress the Catholics.[48] If they were apprehensive about what lay ahead, the Venetian ambassador knew what to expect. Once Parliament convened, he prophesied, there would be a "desolation of the Catholic Faith in this country, with a notable diminution of the King's authority."[49] He could not have been more accurate.

NOTES

(Full titles and publication information will be found in the Bibliography.)

CHAPTER ONE

1. Read, *Mr. Secretary Cecil and Queen Elizabeth*, p. 19.

2. There are no good histories of the penal laws. Old accounts are incomplete and difficult to obtain. Two nineteenth-century accounts are those of Christopher Anstey and Richard Madden; the earliest history of the laws, Henry Care's *Diaconica*, is still useful. General histories of Catholicism in England during the sixteenth and seventeenth centuries touch upon the implementation of the laws without really discussing them in any detail. Of these, Charles Dodd's *Church History of England* and Joseph Gillow's *A Literary and Biographical History* are valuable, although the latter is in some ways unreliable. For Catholicism under Elizabeth, see Meyer's *England and the Catholic Church under Queen Elizabeth*, Neale's *Queen Elizabeth*, and Hughes's *The Reformation in England*. One of the finest surveys of the penal laws can be found in Anthony H. Forbes's unpublished U.C.L.A. dissertation, "Faith and True Allegiance," chaps. 1–4. I read Forbes's study after this chapter was finished, but I relied on his fine piece of scholarship to clarify certain points of law.

3. The term recusant, from the Latin *recusare*, to refuse, although applicable to all religious dissenters, Catholics and Protestants alike, was ordinarily used to describe a dissenter who had been tried for violating the penal laws, specifically those governing church attendance. To avoid repetition of the word "popish" to identify Roman Catholic recusants, I have used the term recusant as applicable only to Catholics. Where I make reference to Protestant recusants, I use these words.

4. *Statutes of the Realm*, 1 Eliz. I, c. 1 & 2 (1559).

5. Neale, *Elizabeth I and Her Parliaments, 1559–1581*, pp. 116–21.

6. *Statutes of the Realm*, 1 Eliz. I, c. 1 (1559).

7. Hughes, *The Reformation in England*, III, 32–34.

8. *Statutes of the Realm*, 5 Eliz. I, c. 1 (1563): "An Act for the assur-

ance of the Queen's royal person over all estates and subjects within her dominions."

9. *Ibid.*, 16 Richard II, c. 5 (1392): "Praemunire for purchasing bulls from Rome, the Crown of England subject to none." The penalties under this Act included loss of property, goods and chattels, and possible imprisonment—in short, all the penalties imposed for treason, except death.

10. Von Pastor, XVIII, 201–2. Catholics were imprisoned in ever increasing numbers; by February 1569 "the prisons were filled with Catholics, and at the end of May the persecution was more violent than ever."

11. *Ibid.*, XVIII, 195–223. In May 1566, Pope Pius V questioned Elizabeth's right to the throne as one "who pretended to be Queen of England."

12. *Statutes of the Realm*, 13 Eliz. I, c. 1 (1571): "An act whereby certain offenses be made treason"; 13 Eliz. I, c. 2 (1571): "An Act against the bringing in, and putting in execution of bulls, writings, or instruments and other superstitious things from the see of Rome."

13. *Ibid.*, 13 Eliz. I, c. 3 (1571): "Fugitives."

14. Guilday, p. xvii.

15. *Ibid.*, p. 111 n. Before 1570 only one or two Continental seminaries were supported by English Catholics. But in 1597, the Jesuit Henry Tichborne stated that English money maintained 70 scholars at Douay, 120 at Saint-Omer, 80 at Valladolid, 60 at Seville, 60 at San Lucar, and 90 at Lisbon.

16. Pollen, "The Accession of James I," pp. 572–86.

17. Guilday, pp. xvii–xviii.

18. *Statutes of the Realm*, 23 Eliz. I, c. 1 (1581).

19. *Ibid.*, sects. 4, 5, 10, 11. The Act also provided for the punishment of persons who kept a Catholic teacher, the penalty being £10 a month. The teacher himself could be imprisoned for a year.

20. *Ibid.*, 27 Eliz. I, c. 2 (1585): "An act against jesuits, seminary priests, and other such like disobedient persons."

21. Hughes, *The Reformation in England,* III, 248; Read, *Mr. Secretary Walsingham and the Policy of Queen Elizabeth,* II, 310.

22. *Statutes of the Realm*, 27 Eliz. I, c. 2, sects. 2–7.

23. *Ibid.*, sects. 13, 16.

24. Hughes, *The Reformation in England,* III, 363–64. See also Gerson, pp. 589–94.

25. *Statutes of the Realm*, 29 Eliz. I, c. 6 (1587): "An act for the more speedy and due execution of certain branches of the statute made in the twenty-third year of the Queen's majesty's reign, intituled, An act to retain the Queen's majesty's subjects in their due obedience."

26. *Ibid.*, 35 Eliz. I, c. 1 (1593): "An Act to retain the Queen's

majesty's subjects in their due obedience." Sects. vii and ix, on the harboring of recusants, were repealed by 3 Jac. I, c. 4 (1606), and for the most part 35 Eliz. I, c. 1 was revived by 3 Car. I, c. 4 (1628) and 16 Car. I, c. 4 (1641).

27. *Ibid.*, 35 Eliz. I, c. 2 (1593): "An act for restraining popish recusants to some certain places of abode."

28. This paragraph and a half is summarized from Willson, pp. 24, 99, 111, 217–19; see chap. 13 for James's relations with the English Catholics, and chaps. 7 and 8 on James and the Catholics in Scotland before 1603. See also Vol. III of Bellesheim's *History of the Catholic Church of Scotland*.

29. *Statutes of the Realm*, 1 Jac. I, c. 4 (1603): "An act for the due execution of the statutes against Jesuits, seminary priests, recusants, etc."

30. The Government perpetuated the practice of confiscating two-thirds of recusants' land.

31. There are many accounts of the Gunpowder Plot, yet none has added much of consequence since Samuel R. Gardiner's *What Gunpowder Plot Was*, published in 1897 in answer to John Gerard's *What Was the Gunpowder Plot?* of the previous year. See Willson, pp. 223–27, for an excellent summary of the plot, and James's reaction to it. The impossibility of Father John Gerard's complicity in the plot, a matter of dispute for some time, is proved brilliantly by A. F. Allison in his article, "John Gerard and the Gunpowder Plot," *Recusant History*, V (1959), 43–63.

32. *Statutes of the Realm*, 3 Jac. I, c. 4 (1606): "An act for the better discovery and repressing of popish recusants."

33. Willson, p. 228.

34. Meyer, *England and the Catholic Church under Queen Elizabeth*, pp. 269–72.

35. Ryan, pp. 177, 183.

36. *Statutes of the Realm*, 3 Jac. I, c. 5 (1606): "An act to prevent and avoid dangers which grow by popish recusants."

37. *Ibid.*, 7 Jac. I, c. 6 (1610).

CHAPTER TWO

1. The preceding paragraphs are based partly on Willson, pp. 425–31.

2. For the negotiations and terms of the Spanish treaties see B.M. Sloane MSS, 826, ff. 9–19b, 1623.

3. Gardiner, *History of England*, V, 1–9, 17–19, 27–29.

4. *Dodd's Church History*, V, Appendix pp. cccxxxviii–ix.

5. Bishop of Lincoln to Buckingham, 30 August 1623, B.M. Add. MSS, 34727, ff. 47–48.

6. Carlyle, p. 38.

7. Willson, pp. 434-44.

8. Hippeau, pp. 244-48.

9. Albion, pp. 49-55.

10. Rushworth, I, 168-69; Albion, pp. 56-60.

11. Thomas D. Hardy, II, 858.

12. *A Rebuke to the High-Church Priests*, pp. 24-25. This pamphlet, in the British Museum, contains a thorough but biased analysis of the French treaty.

13. *Dodd's Church History*, V, 168, and Appendix pp. cccxlvi-vii.

14. "Immunities . . . to Recusants in . . . Leases upon Composition," W.C.A. MSS, A Series, XIX, f. 119, January 1625; "G. M." to Thomas More, 6 January 1625, *ibid*.

15. Henry Ellis, 2d ser., III, 183 n.

16. Gardiner, *History of England*, V, 313; Willson, pp. 445-46.

17. Historical Manuscripts Commission, *The Manuscripts of Henry Duncan Skrine*, Part I, p. 4.

18. *Calendar of State Papers, Venetian*, 1625-26, p. 4.

19. *Ibid.*, p. 30.

20. *H.M.C. Skrine*, p. 14; *Acts of the Privy Council of England*, 1625-26, pp. 195-96.

21. Green, p. 7; Albion, pp. 68-72.

22. Green, pp. 8-10; Henry Ellis, 2d ser., III, 190-92.

23. Henry Ellis, 2d ser., III, 177-78.

24. *C.S.P. Venetian*, 1625-26, pp. 34-52; *H.M.C. Skrine*, p. 11.

25. *Calendar of State Papers, Domestic Series, of the Reign of Charles I*, 1625-26, pp. 43-45; Rushworth, I, 170.

26. William Ward to Thomas Rant, June 1625, W.C.A. MSS, A Series, XIX, f. 166.

27. *Ibid.*, f. 211, 22 August 1625.

28. *H.M.C. Skrine*, p. 12.

29. Rushworth, I, 58-60.

30. Hippeau, pp. 241-44.

31. Thomas D. Hardy, II, 859.

32. Henry Ellis, 2d ser., III, 201-2.

33. William Farrar to a friend, 5 October 1624, W.C.A. MSS, Roman Letters, f. 9.

34. *Ibid.*, f. 24, 1 October 1624.

35. Henry Clifford to Thomas More, 4 October 1624, *ibid.*, ff. 8-8b.

36. Thomas Rant to More, 8 and 17 October 1624, *ibid.*, ff. 10, 20.

37. Clifford to [?], 1 November 1624, *ibid.*, f. 33.

38. George Muskett to More, 4 November 1624, *ibid.*, f. 34.

39. *Ibid.*, f. 43, 12 November 1624.

40. Rant to [?], 23 November 1624, *ibid.*, f. 58.

41. J. K. to [?], January 1625, W.C.A. MSS, A Series, XIX, ff. 9-12.

42. *Acts of the Privy Council, 1625–26,* pp. 201–5.

43. Historical Manuscripts Commission, *The Manuscripts of the Earl Cowper,* I, 42, 229.

44. Stocks and Stevenson, III, 259.

45. *C.S.P. Domestic, 1625–26,* pp. 193, 487.

46. *Acts of the Privy Council, 1625–26,* pp. 188–89. On October 30 the Council ordered the confiscation of arms held by Catholic peers, and a few of them, like Lord Vaux of Harrowden, resisted and were imprisoned.

47. See Matthews, ed., "Records Relating to Catholicism in the South Wales Marches in the 17th and 18th Centuries."

48. *H.M.C. Cowper,* I, 227, 242.

49. *C.S.P. Domestic, 1625–26,* p. 165.

50. Willson, p. 95.

51. Meyer, "Charles I and Rome," pp. 13–20.

52. *H.M.C. Skrine,* p. 5.

53. *Journals of the House of Commons,* I, 800–804 (hereafter cited as *C.J.*); S. R. Gardiner, ed., *Debates in the House of Commons in 1625,* pp. 12, 14, 18 (hereafter cited as *C.D. 1625*); Gardiner, *History of England,* V, 341–44.

54. *C.J.,* I, 805, 813; *C.D. 1625,* pp. 18–25.

55. *C.J.,* I, 809; *C.D. 1625,* p. 67.

56. *C.D. 1625,* p. 68; *C.J.,* I, 809; Gardiner, *History of England,* V, 397–98.

57. Relf, pp. 57–58, 61–62.

58. *C.J.,* I, 802, 805–6; *C.D. 1625,* pp. 47–53; Gardiner, *History of England,* V, 351–54; Rushworth, I, 209.

59. *C.J.,* I, 810–11; *C.D. 1625,* pp. 69, 73–91, 93–102; Rushworth, I, 173–76.

60. *C.J.,* I, 815; *C.D. 1625,* pp. 118–19, 124, 127; Gardiner, *History of England,* V, 431–32.

61. Rushworth, I, 191–92; *H.M.C. Skrine,* p. 31; *C.S.P. Domestic,* 1625–26, p. 84.

62. Gardiner, *History of England,* VI, 3–4.

63. *C.S.P. Venetian, 1625–26,* p. 129.

64. *H.M.C. Skrine,* p. 25.

65. Gardiner, *History of England,* V, 4 n., explains that the appointments contravened the spirit, not the law, of the treaty. Article 2 stipulated that vacancies in the household be filled by Catholics. Louis made no provision for the appointment of Protestants when there were no vacancies.

66. *Acts of the Privy Council, 1625–26,* p. 166; *H.M.C. Skrine,* p. 27.

67. Gardiner, *History of England,* VI, 5; *C.S.P. Venetian, 1625–26,* p. 178 n.

68. B.M. Stowe MSS, 132, f. 213, 1626. These are notes on the conference between the French committee and Holland and Carlisle at Paris.

69. Houssaye, pp. 187–89; *Acts of the Privy Council, 1625–26*, pp. 171, 216.

70. Gardiner, *History of England*, VI, 27.

71. Houssaye, pp. 187–91.

CHAPTER THREE

1. Gardiner, *History of England*, VI, 1–8, 10–21, 24–33, 37–47.

2. Henry Clifford to Rant, 22 August 1625, W.C.A. MSS, A Series, XIX, f. 211.

3. *C.S.P. Domestic, 1625–26*, p. 57.

4. *Ibid.*, pp. 66, 417, 480.

5. *Ibid.*, 1627–28, pp. 267, 361. Henrietta was given Pontefract Castle, Oatlands Manor, Nonsuch Palace, Hanslop House, and Somerset House. These properties returned handsome profits: manors, £4,111 8s. 1d; farm rents, £14,055 0s. 3d; total revenue, £18,166 8s. 4d.

6. *H.M.C. Skrine*, p. 122.

7. Gardiner, *History of England*, VI, 48.

8. *C.S.P. Domestic, 1625–26*, p. 225.

9. *C.S.P. Venetian, 1625–26*, p. 311.

10. Strickland, IV, 30.

11. *C.S.P. Domestic, 1625–26*, p. 246. Sir Benjamin Rudyerd wrote that Henrietta "stood in a window at Sir Abraham Williams' to see the show."

12. Gardiner, *History of England*, VI, 48.

13. *H.M.C. Skrine*, p. 44.

14. Historical Manuscripts Commission, *The Montagu Papers*, III, 265; Henry Ellis, 2d ser., III, 212–13.

15. Rous, pp. 1–2.

16. Gardiner, *History of England*, VI, 56; Albion, p. 83.

17. Houssaye, pp. 193–96.

18. *H.M.C. Skrine*, pp. 46–48; Henry Ellis, 2d ser., III, 223.

19. Historical Manuscripts Commission, *The Manuscripts of the Duke of Rutland*, I, 476.

20. *C.S.P. Venetian, 1625–26*, pp. 388, 398.

21. B.M. Add. MSS, 39288, f. 6, 26 June 1626. This is a transcript (temp. Charles II) of a contemporary account of Henrietta's walk to Tyburn. The details differ somewhat from Gardiner, *History of England*, VI, 135–36.

22. *D.N.B.*, XVI, 201–2.

23. Henry Ellis, 2d ser., III, 241.

24. King Charles to Buckingham, 20 November 1625, B.M. Harleian MSS, 6988, ff. 1–1b.

25. Gardiner, *History of England*, VI, 38.

26. Charles to Buckingham, January 1626, B.M. Harl. MSS, 6988, f. 5.

27. Bishop of Mende to M. d'Herbault, 24 July 1626, P.R.O., Baschet's Paris Transcripts, 31/3/64, ff. 111, 115b.

28. *C.S.P. Domestic,* 1625–26, p. 390.

29. Henry Ellis, 2d ser., III, 237.

30. Verney, pp. 14–15.

31. Charles to Buckingham, 7 August 1626, B.M. Harl. MSS, 6988, f. 11.

32. Bishop of Mende to Louis XIII, 12 August 1626, P.R.O., Baschet's Paris Transcripts, 31/3/64, f. 138.

33. *C.S.P. Domestic,* 1625–26, p. 403; Henry Ellis, 2d ser., III, 245–47.

34. *C.S.P. Domestic,* 1625–26, pp. 398, 546.

35. *Ibid.,* p. 396; Henry Ellis, 2d ser., III, 242–43, 247–48.

36. Bishop of Mende to d'Herbault, July 1626, P.R.O., Baschet's Paris Transcripts, 31/3/64, f. 122.

37. Henrietta Maria to Bishop of Mende, 2 August 1626, *ibid.,* f. 126.

38. Bishop of Mende to d'Herbault, 18 August 1626, *ibid.,* ff. 148b–49.

39. *C.S.P. Domestic,* 1625–26, p. 400.

40. Michaud, III, 238–40.

41. Albion, p. 88.

42. P.R.O., Baschet's Paris Transcripts, 31/3/64, 23 August 1626: "Instruction au Sr. Marechal de Bassompierre Ambassadeur Extraordinaire en Angleterre."

43. Strickland, IV, 37.

44. *H.M.C. Skrine,* pp. 85–86.

45. The commissioners were Lord Keeper Coventry, President of the Council the Earl of Manchester, Lord High Treasurer Weston, Principal Secretary Conway, Buckingham, Carleton, and the Earls of Pembroke, Dorset, Carlisle, and Holland. *Ibid.,* p. 88 n.

46. B.M. Stowe MSS, 132, ff. 196–276, November 1626: Negotiations of Blainville and Bassompierre in England.

47. *H.M.C. Skrine,* p. 91.

48. B.M. Stowe MSS, 132, f. 212b; for a list of Henrietta's household see the B.M. Egerton MSS, 1048, ff. 186–87, 1626.

49. *H.M.C. Skrine,* p. 94; *C.S.P. Domestic,* 1625–26, p. 469.

50. *C.S.P. Venetian,* 1625–26, p. 616.

51. *Ibid.,* 1626–28, pp. 20–21, 30–32.

52. *H.M.C. Skrine,* p. 101.

53. *Ibid.,* pp. 98, 104–10; *C.S.P. Venetian,* 1626–28, p. 97; Albion, pp. 91–92.

54. Rous, p. 8.

55. *H.M.C. Skrine,* p. 138.

56. Charles to Buckingham, 13 August 1627, B.M. Harl. MSS, 6988, ff. 33–34.

57. *Ibid.*, f. 220, 1626: births of royal children; Strickland, IV, 43–45.

58. See *D.N.B.*, IV, 1189–96.

59. Gardiner, *History of England*, VII, 10–12.

60. In the British Museum, "Prynne's Tracts," Vol. 1.

61. *Ibid.*, pp. 3–4. Prynne made a good case for the similarity between doctrine as outlined by Cosin and Roman Catholic doctrine. Witness, for example, the comparison of Anglican and Catholic laws on the times when marriage is permitted, as given on p. 55.

62. *C.S.P. Venetian,* 1628–29, pp. 540–41, 600; *C.S.P. Domestic,* 1629–31, pp. 233, 289.

63. Bishop of Mende to d'Herbault, 6 August 1629, P.R.O., Baschet's Paris Transcripts, 31/3/66, f. 131.

64. *Ibid.*, ff. 115–18, 20 May 1629: "Instruction baille a Monsieur de Chasteauneuf s'on allant Ambassadeur Extraordinaire en Angleterre."

65. Châteauneuf to Cardinal Richelieu, 10 July 1629, *ibid.*, ff. 121–24.

66. Châteauneuf to Père de Bérulle, 23 July 1629, *ibid.*, ff. 125–30; same to same, 27 August 1629, *ibid.*, f. 143.

67. Same to same, 10 July 1629, *ibid.*, ff. 126–27.

68. Châteauneuf to Richelieu, 28 October 1629, *ibid.*, f. 179.

69. Same to same, 7 November 1629, *ibid.*, ff. 184–85.

70. Their names were Fathers Leonard of Paris (superior), Cherubin of Amiens, Esmé of Beauvais, Ange of Soissons, Lambert of Fliscour, Jean Louis of Avaney, Joseph of Paris, Cyprian of Gamaches, Blaise of Paris (replaced by Brother Marin a year later), Sebastian of Bar-sur-Seine, Basile of Rheims, and Seraphin of Compiègne. All served in the Queen's chapel except Basile and Seraphin, who were assigned to the French embassy.

71. Birch, II, 300–301.

72. Lomas, p. 106.

73. On Leighton see Gardiner, *History of England,* VII, 143–52.

74. B.M. Harl. MSS, 6988, f. 220 (n.d.): births of royal children.

75. Châteauneuf to Richelieu, 2 June 1630, P.R.O., Baschet's Paris Transcripts, 31/3/66, f. 267; M. Fontenay-Mareuil to M. Bouthillier, August 1630, *ibid.*, f. 276b.

76 *C.S.P. Venetian,* 1629–32, pp. 361, 368–69, 372.

77. Bodl. Rawlinson MSS, B 258, ff. 1b–2: Account of the Christening of Charles II in St. James's, 27 June 1630.

78. Fontenay-Mareuil to Bouthillier, August 1630, P.R.O., Baschet's Paris Transcripts, 31/3/66, f. 276b.

79. Strickland, IV, 47.

80. *C.S.P. Venetian,* 1629–32, p. 298. About the same time, Laud undertook to remodel St. Paul's Cathedral. A subscription to raise funds

for the work was made among important, presumably rich lords and ladies. Charles asked Henrietta how much she would contribute. She replied that she would donate £10,000 if Laud would promise that two daily masses could be said in the church. Otherwise she would give not a penny.

81. Rushworth, I, 171.

82. *Les royales ceremonies faites en l'édification d'une chapelle de Capuchins à Londres en Angleterre, dans le Palais de La Royne.*

83. John Southcot to Peter Fitton, 14 June 1633, W.C.A. MSS, A Series, XXVII, ff. 173–75.

84. Strickland, IV, 50.

85. *C.S.P. Venetian,* 1632–36, pp. 157, 163.

86. Southcot to Fitton, 13 December 1633, W.C.A. MSS, Anglia A, VII, f. 68.

CHAPTER FOUR

1. See Notestein, *The Winning of the Initiative by the House of Commons, passim.*

2. *H.M.C. Skrine,* p. 49.

3. *C.S.P. Venetian,* 1625–26, p. 351.

4. *C.J.,* I, 826–38.

5. *Ibid.,* pp. 853–54.

6. *Ibid.,* p. 857. The committee on religion during this Parliament included John Pym (chairman), Sir Thomas Hobby, Sir George Moore, Robert Harley, Sir Thomas Denton, Edward Peyton, Sir Dudley Digges, and Edward Spencer. From time to time others were added.

7. *Ibid.,* p. 851.

8. Rushworth, I, 240–41.

9. *Ibid.,* pp. 242–43.

10. *C.J.,* I, 865–67. From February to May, 1626, Parliament was more concerned with Buckingham, naval mismanagement in the French war, privilege cases, and the subsidy, than with the issue of religion. However, accusations against John Digby, Earl of Bristol, were brought before the Lords. Bristol was accused of attempting to convert Charles to Catholicism during his Spanish trip in 1623.

11. The list of Catholics in public office and the charges against them are in Rushworth, I, 392–96. Similar lists of Catholics were prepared and presented to the King by the Commons in 1624 and 1628. The following is a breakdown of the major offices held by Catholics during those years:

Lords Lieutenant of Shires............ 4
Deputy Lieutenants.................. 16
Justices of the Peace................. 61

High Sheriffs........................ 2
Commissioners of Sewers............ 5
Commissioners of Oyer and Terminer. 2
Custos Rotulorum................... 1
Coroner 1
Colonel of Footbands............... 1
Captains of Footbands.............. 4
                                    ——
                        Total 97

This list is the work of Brian Magee in his *The English Recusants*, pp. 56–57. Many of the gentry and peers of the nation were Catholics. At least 58 of the 782 knights created by Charles I, as well as about one out of every five peers, were Catholics. Soden, p. 153.

12. *H.M.C. Rutland*, I, 477.

13. Rushworth, I, 207.

14. See Gardiner, *History of England*, VI, chap. 58.

15. Mitchell, pp. 114–17.

16. *H.M.C. Skrine*, p. 141.

17. Gardiner, *History of England*, VI, 132–33.

18. For detailed studies of this Parliament, see *ibid.*, chaps. 62–64, and VII, chap. 67; Notestein and Relf; and Hulme, chaps. 10, 11, 13.

19. *C.J.*, I, 873.

20. Relf, pp. 64–65.

21. *C.S.P. Domestic*, 1628–29, pp. 20, 53, 86. Humphrey Cross, Justinian Povey, and Long put the value of the goods taken at £164. They also confiscated £7 13s. 9d. in cash.

22. Gardiner, *History of England*, VI, 238–39.

23. Nichols, p. 5; *C.S.P. Venetian*, 1628–29, p. 46.

24. The feast of St. Joseph today falls on March 19; in the seventeenth century it was on the 17th.

25. *C.J.*, I, 876.

26. Heath's "Discovery" is printed fully in Nichols, pp. 21–30.

27. The forged letter is in Rushworth, I, 474–76.

28. Nichols, pp. 8–12.

29. Relf, p. 69.

30. *C.S.P. Venetian*, 1628–29, p. 46.

31. *C.J.*, I, 880; *C.S.P. Venetian*, 1628–29, p. 47; *H.M.C. Skrine*, p. 144.

32. *C.J.*, I, 911.

33. *Ibid.*, pp. 914–15.

34. Relf, pp. 228–29.

35. *Statutes of the Realm*, 3 Charles I, c. 2 (1628); *C.J.*, I, 915.

36. Gardiner, *History of England*, VI, 318–25.

37. For an account of the popular reaction to Buckingham's death, see Henry Ellis, 2d ser., III, 264–65.

38. *C.J.*, I, 920.

39. Gardiner, *History of England*, VII, 21–22; *C.J.*, I, 922.

40. Notestein and Relf, pp. 18, 20–21, 24–28; Gardiner, *History of England*, VII, 34–42.

41. Notestein and Relf, pp. 28–29; *C.J.*, I, 922, 924.

42. Gardiner, *History of England*, VI, 312–15; VII, 44–47.

43. The Commons' debates on the pardons, too lengthy for full discussion here, are in Notestein and Relf, pp. 33–60; *C.J.*, I, 926–30; Gardiner, *History of England*, VII, 49–50.

44. Notestein and Relf, pp. 64–83; Gardiner, *History of England*, VII, 57; Nichols, pp. 12–20.

45. Notestein and Relf, pp. 95–101.

46. For the events in the Commons on March 2, 1629, see *ibid.*, pp. 101–6; Rushworth, I, 660; Gardiner, *History of England*, VII, 65–76; and Hulme, pp. 307–15.

CHAPTER FIVE

1. *C.S.P. Domestic, 1625–26*, p. 215.

2. *Ibid.*, p. 258.

3. *Ibid.*, pp. 320, 381.

4. *H.M.C. Cowper*, I, 393.

5. *Acts of the Privy Council, 1625–26*, p. 491.

6. Berkshire Record Office, William Trumbull MSS, Miscellaneous, XXXVI: "Certificate touchinge the Jesuits at Bruxelles," 14 August 1625.

7. *C.S.P. Domestic, 1625–26*, pp. 180–81.

8. *Ibid.*, 1627–28, p. 367.

9. *H.M.C. Cowper*, I, 407.

10. There is a letter in the W.C.A. MSS, A Series, XXIII, ff. 73–74, dated 1628, written by Richard Smith, Bishop of Chalcedon, which lists some of these Catholic clergy and peers.

11. W.C.A. MSS, A Series, XXIV, ff. 115–18: "Points to be Consulted in the next Consultation of the Chapter," 16 October 1630.

12. Thomas Greene to Southcot, 1635, *ibid.*, XXVIII, ff. 239–41.

13. George Leyburn to Fitton, 5 July 1633, *ibid.*, f. 187.

14. Leyburn to Bishop of Chalcedon, 24 November 1636, *ibid.*, ff. 613–15.

15. Southcot to Edward Hope, 26 August 1636, *ibid.*, ff. 515–17.

16. William Price to Mr. Benson, 5 September 1628, *ibid.*, XXII, ff. 379–80.

17. *Ibid.*, XXVIII, f. 33: Certification of Loan by Secular Clergy, 17 February 1635.

18. Richard Worthington to Fitton, 4 January 1638, *ibid.*, XXIX, f. 149.

19. *Ibid.*, XXVI, ff. 255–56: Deed by Thomas Roper and George Skinner, 9 July 1632.

20. Bodl. Bankes MSS, 51/23, 2 December 1637; 17/41, July 1635; and 17/49, 8 November 1637.

21. Farrer and Brownhill, II, 93.

22. Jordan, II, 189 n.

23. Southcot to Fitton, 29 March 1633, W.C.A. MSS, Anglia A, VII, f. 64.

24. According to Caraman, p. 70, between the time of the Gunpowder Plot (1605) and 1625, the center of gravity of strong Catholic practice and sentiment shifted from London to the isolated gentry families in the North. Nevertheless, London and its environs still contained the heaviest concentration of Catholics in the country. They lived in the more densely populated streets in Holborn, Bloomsbury, and St. Giles-in-the-Fields, along the northern perimeter of the city, and in the eastern boroughs of Shoreditch and Wapping.

25. Various letters, 15 June to 8 November 1631, W.C.A. MSS, A Series, XXIV, ff. 447, 605, 611, 613, 617, 619, 621, 627–33, 639, 643, 649, 659, 661, 665, 667, 679, 737.

26. Southcot to Fitton, 8 February 1633, *ibid.,* XXVII, ff. 17–19.

27. *Ibid.,* ff. 533–34.

28. *Ibid.,* XXVI, ff. 307–9, 13 August 1632.

29. *Ibid.,* ff. 495–97, 1632.

30. Caraman, p. 72.

31. W.C.A. MSS, XX, ff. 83–85, 29 August 1626: "Examination of John Trumble, priest, before John Coke and R. Heath."

32. Magee, pp. 23–26, 42–43, 104, 156.

33. Population figures differ widely. I have taken those of Davies, p. 261.

34. Magee, p. 103.

35. Stanfield, ed., "The Archpriest Controversy"; Penelope Renold, ed., *The Wisbech Stirs (1595–1598),* Publications of the Catholic Record Society, LI (London, 1958); T. G. Law, ed., *A Historical Sketch of the Conflicts Between Jesuits and Seculars in the Reign of Queen Elizabeth* . . . (London, 1889).

36. Mr. A. F. Allison, co-editor of *Recusant History* and librarian to the Catholic Record Society, is preparing for publication in *Recusant History* a series of studies on the conflict between the Jesuits and Bishop Smith in the 1620's and early 1630's.

37. William Allen (1532–94), of Rossall in Lancashire, took a B.A. in Oriel College, Oxford, despite his Catholicism and became principal of St. Mary's Hall. His staunch defense of the old religion forced his resignation in 1560 and his exile to Flanders the following year. He returned to Lancashire for reasons of health in 1562 and escaped arrest for three years even though he repeatedly attacked the Established Church, thereby arousing the civil authorities. Although he left his homeland for the last time in 1565, few played so vital a role as Allen

in shaping the Catholic counter-reformation in England. It was he who directed the English Colleges at Douay and Rome (which he had helped to found), he who undertook the preparation of the Douay Bible, and he who sent hundreds of English seculars and Jesuits to rejuvenate their disheartened coreligionists. He actively supported Philip II's claim as England's rightful monarch after the execution of Mary Stuart, and he was made a cardinal in 1587 so that he might follow the Spanish Armada as Rome's legate after the conquest. On Allen see Gillow, I, 14–20; *D.N.B.*, I, 314–22; and Garrett Mattingly, *The Armada* (Boston, 1959), pp. 53–68.

38. Mathew, *Catholicism in England*, p. 78.

39. Stanfield, pp. 140–41.

40. *Ibid.*, p. 132; *Dodd's Church History*, II, 362.

41. Bishop (1553–1624) was educated at Oxford and Douay. He was in England from 1581 to 1585, and again during 1591–93, before being made Vicar General.

42. Nichols, p. 4 n.; Albion, pp. 109–10.

43. A list of Smith's archdeacons is in W.C.A. MSS, XIX, ff. 171–72, 24 June 1625; Nichols, pp. 58–59.

44. *C.S.P. Venetian*, 1626–28, pp. 408, 622–23; *C.S.P. Domestic*, 1628–29, p. 55; *Dodd's Church History*, III, 76–79.

45. Bishop of Chalcedon to Richard Blount, 15 May 1628, and Blount to Bishop of Chalcedon, 7 June 1628, W.C.A. MSS, A Series, XXII, ff. 261–62.

46. Fitton to Bishop of Chalcedon, 26 January 1628, *ibid.*, f. 19.

47. *Ibid.*, f. 111: Chalcedon's general approbation of the regulars, 17 February 1628.

48. *Ibid.*, f. 465: Memorandum of William Cape, 24 July 1628.

49. A list of these writings from 1625 to 1628 is given in *ibid.*, XXIII, ff. 7–9, *c.* 1628.

50. *Ibid.*, XXIV, ff. 287–88: "Protestation Against the Bishop's Authority," 1631.

51. *Ibid.*, XXII, f. 383, 24 June 1628.

52. Leyburn to Bishop of Chalcedon, *c.* 1628, *ibid.*, XXIII, ff. 127–28.

53. Lord Arundel of Wardour to Bishop of Chalcedon, 29 November 1627, *ibid.*, XX, ff. 667–68.

54. Southcot to Fitton, 10 August 1632, *ibid.*, XXVI, ff. 301–3.

55. *C.S.P. Domestic*, 1628–29, pp. 58, 407, 527; *C.S.P. Venetian*, 1628–29, p. 459 n.; Rushworth, II, 13–14.

56. W.C.A. MSS, A Series, XXIII, ff. 323, 449, 20 February and 28 July 1629.

57. Bishop of Chalcedon to Fitton, 12 July 1631, *ibid.*, XXIV, f. 535.

58. *Ibid.*, ff. 765, 771, 9 and 18 December 1631.

59. *Ibid.*, f. 519; Bishop of Chalcedon's Patent, 10 July 1631.

60. The Westminster Archives, A Series, Vols. XXIV (1630–31)

through XXIX (1640), are full of letters between the seculars and regulars. Vol. XXIV, particularly, contains a wealth of information dealing with Smith's resignation, and comments pro and con on episcopal jurisdiction in England.

61. In a book such as this, references to the individual regular orders must necessarily be few and more or less general. Some good detailed studies exist. On the Jesuits see Ethelred L. Taunton, *The History of the Jesuits in England, 1580–1773* (London, 1901), which, though partly unreliable, is still useful; and H. Foley, ed., *Records of the English Province of the Society of Jesus,* 7 vols. (London, 1882). Caraman's biography of Henry Morse is especially good on the Jesuit community in the 1630's and 1640's. On the Franciscans see Father Thaddeus, *The Franciscans in England, 1600–1850, Being an Authentic Account of the Second English Province of Friars Minor* (London, 1898), and J. B. Dockery, *Christopher Davenport, Friar and Diplomat* (London, 1960), especially for the Franciscans under Charles I. For the Carmelites, one might look at B. Zimmerman, *Carmel in England: A History of the English Mission of the Discalced Carmelites 1615 to 1849* (London, 1899), which is particularly full for the seventeenth century. Godfrey Anstruther, *A Hundred Homeless Years,* has provided a long-overdue evaluation of the work of the Dominicans in the English mission. Numerous lengthy articles, too many to single out here, on particular missionaries of several orders have appeared in *Recusant History.*

CHAPTER SIX

1. The "price revolution" of *c.* 1540 to *c.* 1640 was characterized by a gradual inflation in prices and a fall in the real value of money. A good indication of how this revolution affected wages may be seen in the increase in fees paid to government officers at all levels during the early seventeenth century. This is brilliantly surveyed in Aylmer, "Charles I's Commission on Fees," pp. 58–67.

2. The proclamation is in *H.M.C. Skrine,* pp. 108–9; *C.S.P. Domestic,* 1627–28, pp. 57, 166, 230; *C.S.P. Venetian,* 1626–28, p. 154.

3. Bowler, "Some Notes on the Recusant Rolls of the Exchequer," p. 183.

4. Bodl. Bankes MSS, 16/66, 10 June 1637: Extract concerning compositions for recusancy.

5. *C.S.P. Domestic,* 1627–28, p. 449. For a full discussion of the operations of the commission for compounding in the North see Talbot, pp. 295–303.

6. *C.S.P. Domestic,* 1629–31, pp. 35–36. Talbot, pp. 307–64, has numerous examples of compositions.

7. Strafford, I, 49–50.

8. *D.N.B.,* III, 721–24.

9. Strafford, I, 52–53. Examples of these harsh compositions are in Talbot, p. 303, and *C.S.P. Domestic,* 1629–31, p. 318.

10. Bodl. Bankes MSS, 71/1–3: "Particulars of the Suffolk lands of Henry Foster, recusant . . . ," November and December 1634.

11. *Ibid.,* 71/4–5: "Particulars of the Dorset lands of Francis Mathews, recusant . . . ," 25 February 1638/39.

12. *Ibid.,* 29/5: Memoranda by Thomas Wentworth, Francis Cottington and others, 8 June 1640. For other histories of composition see 29/1–6, 1632–40.

13. *Ibid.,* 29/3: Memoranda by John Bankes and others, 20 July 1640.

14. Peter Fitton to [?], June 1633, W.C.A. MSS, Roman Letters, f. 120.

15. *C.S.P. Domestic,* 1633–34, pp. 348, 443–44.

16. *H.M.C. Cowper,* II, 80.

17. Atkinson, III, 311.

18. *C.S.P. Domestic,* 1631–32, p. 494; 1639, p. 542.

19. Stocks and Stevenson, III, 249.

20. Aylmer, "Charles I's Commission on Fees," pp. 61, 65; Magee, p. 156.

21. *C.S.P. Domestic,* 1627–28, p. 450; 1629–31, p. 218.

22. Aylmer, "Charles I's Commission on Fees," p. 65.

23. *C.S.P. Venetian,* 1625–26, p. 499.

24. Bodl. Bankes MSS 55/99 and 55/112, 2 August 1639.

25. *C.S.P. Domestic,* 1625–26, p. 514.

26. Thomas Coventry to Justices Jones and Whitlock, 6 July 1629, B.M. Add. MSS, 32093, f. 24.

27. Petition by Exchequer Officers to the King, November 1640, B.M. Add. MSS, 6176, f. 16; Talbot, p. 296; Aylmer, *The King's Servants,* p. 139.

28. Dietz, pp. 117–71.

29. *Ibid.,* pp. 143–52. The yearly totals were as follows: 1635, £12,-807 13s.; 1636, £8,280 16s. 1d.; 1637, £11,662 9s. 1d.; 1638, £19,673 8s. 1d.; 1639, £7,858 10s. 4d.; 1640, £32,287 19s. 11d.

30. Jordan, II, 184.

31. Justices of the quorum were especially capable because of long magisterial experience or considerable formal legal training.

32. Sheppard, pp. 124–37.

33. *Ibid.,* p. 127.

34. Ratcliff and Johnson, VI, xxiv–xxvii.

35. B.M. Add. MSS, 32093, f. 24: "Exemptions to the Bill on Recusants," n.d.

36. Ross, pp. 259, 270, 276.

37. Atkinson, III, 191, 259, 270, 276.

38. B.M. Add. MSS, 26651, ff. 21–30 [temp. Chas. I]. See also the reports of Sir William Jones (1566–1640), justice of the Court of Com-

mon Pleas, on cases involving recusants in the 1620's and 1630's in the B.M. Hargrave MSS, 317 [temp. Chas. I].

39. Makower, pp. 345–46.

40. Bates-Harbin, II, 262–63.

41. See, for example, the large number of presentments made by the churchwardens of Chester in Bennett and Dewhurst, pp. 104–6 (documents 20 to 70).

42. Notestein, *The English People on the Eve of Colonization,* p. 249.

43. *Ibid.,* pp. 228–39.

44. Dodds, pp. 103–5.

45. Bund, ed., *Worcestershire Quarter Sessions Papers,* I, Part 1, ccxvi–ccxviii.

46. This and other notices to the several parishes of Middlesex are in the B.M. Add. MSS, 38856, ff. 19–58, December and January 1640–41.

47. *An Introduction to the Following History Containing the Diary of . . . William Laud,* pp. 525, 540, 542, 548, 559.

48. B.M. Add. MSS, 38856, ff. 9–15: "Original Interrogations and Examinations addressed to the D. of Buckingham," 1626.

49. *Acts of the Privy Council, 1625–26,* p. 226.

50. *Ibid.,* pp. 225–26, 246; *C.S.P. Domestic, 1625–26,* 153.

51. Anderson, II, 20, 38–39, 40–42.

52. Peyton, I, xxiii.

53. Rushworth, I, 240–41.

54. British Museum Thomason Tracts, No. 50: "The poor Prisoners Petition for Charity . . . To . . . the Parliament . . . ," December 1654.

55. A year or more in prison awaiting trial was not uncommon. A prison roster of 1638 for Worcestershire lists one recusant as having been imprisoned in July 1637, two in August, two in September, four in October, three in November, and six in December. These recusants could have been brought to trial in either of two Quarter Sessions— Michaelmas and Epiphany. Bund, *Worcestershire Quarter Sessions Papers,* I, Part 1, xlii–xliii.

56. *C.S.P. Domestic, 1625–26,* p. 269; *1627–28,* pp. 45–46, 405, 556.

57. Sheppard, pp. 45–47.

58. Cox, II, 5.

59. *The History of Wisbech,* pp. 88–128. An account of the Elizabethan priests imprisoned at Wisbech is given in Penelope Renold's *The Wisbech Stirs (1595–1598).*

60. John Morris, *The Troubles of Our Catholic Forefathers* (London, 1877), pp. 223–39.

61. P.R.O., P.C. 38/497: "Wisbeach Castle to be made ready for . . . priests . . . ," 30 September 1628.

62. Bund, *Worcestershire Quarter Sessions Papers,* I, Part 1, clvi.

63. *Acts of the Pricy Council, 1627–28*, p. 337.

64. Caraman, pp. 53–55.

65. Cox, II, 4–5, 265, 340.

66. Bodl. Bankes MSS, 51/48, 1 December 1639, and 51/46, 2 January 1638/39: Petitions by Fitzharris and others to the King.

67. Caraman, pp. 125–28.

68. Hughes, *The Reformation in England*, III, 338.

69. Mathew, *Catholicism in England*, pp. 72–73.

70. Willson, 386, 419.

71. Ornsby, ed., *The Correspondence of John Cosin*, Part I, xxiii.

72. W.C.A. MSS, A Series, XXII, ff. 573–75, 27 August 1628. Compare this description with Father William Hart's account of Arrowsmith's execution in *ibid.*, ff. 671–75, 27 December 1628.

73. Gillow, III, 487–89.

74. There were few Dominicans in England during Charles's reign. In 1625 only Thomas Middleton, Vicar General of the Dominicans in England, William Fowler, and [?] Watson were on the English Mission. Five more had arrived by 1635: Reginald Michaelis, Vincent Craft (alias Peter Martyr), George Popham, Lewis of St. Ildefonse, and Robert Armstrong. Of these, only Middleton and Popham played major roles. Anstruther, *A Hundred Homeless Years*, pp. 123, 129, 131–32, 150.

75. *Ibid.*, pp. 143–46; Caraman, p. 73; *C.S.P. Domestic, 1633–34*, pp. 220, 260.

76. Longstaffe, *passim*.

77. *Ibid.*, pp. 74, 122–23. For other good examples see pp. 14, 70–72, 141, 186.

78. W.C.A. MSS, A Series, XXII, ff. 535–37 [1632?].

79. John Nelson to Fitton, 22 March 1632, *ibid.*, f. 133. See also the arguments over the validity of civil marriage before justices of the peace, and the permissibility of clandestine marriages in XXX, f. 599, 1653.

80. Longstaffe, p. 186.

81. P.R.O., P.C. 2/47, pp. 9–11: Order forbidding merchant strangers to christen their children as Catholics, 18 December 1636.

82. Birch, II, 342.

83. W.C.A. MSS, A Series, XXVIII, ff. 17–19, 8 February 1633.

84. Mathew, *The Social Structure in Caroline England*, p. 54. The case of the Arundels of Naworth is typical. Lord William Howard (1563–1640) as a boy was tutored by a Catholic, Gregory Martin, and a priest came regularly to the house to teach the family French. Ornsby, *Selections from the Household Books of the Lord William Howard of Naworth Castle*, pp. lxi–lxii.

85. Mathew, *The Age of Charles I*, pp. 135–36.

86. Cox, I, 285–88.

87. Mathew, *The Social Structure in Caroline England*, p. 54 n.

88. W.C.A. MSS, A Series, XX, ff. 291, 295, 325, 391, 27 January and 23 June 1627.

89. Mathew, *The Social Structure in Caroline England,* p. 130 n.

90. P.R.O., P.C. 2/47, pp. 160, 165, 23 and 28 April 1637.

91. Mathew, *The Age of Charles I,* p. 147 n.

92. See, for example, the conversions of Catholics to Anglicanism in Atkinson, III, 258–64; Ratcliff and Johnson, I, 252–55; Jeaffreson, *passim;* Longstaffe, pp. 134–35, 140–42, 172–86.

93. Atkinson, III, 254.

94. One example of a priest who officially conformed is a Father Jukes (alias Symonds), described as "long bred in the College of Jesuits at Rome." He took the oaths "among many Popish recusants whom . . . Bishop [Thornborough of Worcester] had converted" (*C.S.P. Domestic,* 1627–28, p. 289). Of course, there were others, like the Dominican Thomas Gage, who went over to the Church of England without a formalized submission.

CHAPTER SEVEN

1. Caraman, p. 42.

2. *Ibid.,* pp. 41–42.

3. *Statutes of the Realm,* 23 Eliz. I, c. 1, sect. 11; 3 Jac. I, c. 4, sect. 3; 3 Jac. I, c. 5, sects. 2–4, 8, 9, 13–16, 25. Forbes, pp. 89–90.

4. William Ward to Rant, June 1625, W.C.A. MSS, A Series, XIX, f. 166.

5. Rant to Thomas Mayo, 29 October 1624, *ibid.,* Roman Letters, f. 32.

6. Henry Clifford to [?], 18 October 1624, *ibid.,* f. 21.

7. Clifford to More, 15 November 1624, *ibid.,* f. 47.

8. Bodl. Bankes MSS, 9/8, 31 July 1635.

9. P.R.O., P.C. 2/43, p. 241, 15 September 1633.

10. *Ibid.,* 2/44, pp. 420–21, 22 February 1634.

11. *Acts of the Privy Council, 1627–28,* p. 192.

12. *C.S.P. Domestic,* 1619–23, p. 405.

13. P.R.O., P.C. 2/44, p. 228 (date?).

14. *Acts of the Privy Council, 1627–28,* p. 192.

15. P.R.O., P.C. 2/38, p. 84, 18 April 1628; *C.S.P. Domestic* 1628–29, pp. 20, 53.

16. Pollen, "The Note-Book of John Southcote," p. 94.

17. P.R.O., P.C. 2/39, pp. 690–92, 13 March 1629. A later MS shows Cross's diligence in this work: "This day [14 February 1631] Cutbert Prescott, John Cusack, George Matchett, Simon Price, John Browne & Margaret Clacke [were] taken by Humphrey Cross one of the Mes-

sengers of his Majte's Chamber comming frome masse from the Spanish Agentt." *Ibid.*, 2/41, p. 194 (1628?)

18. Leyburn to Bishop of Chalcedon, 8 May 1635, W.C.A. MSS, A Series, XXVIII, f. 81. John Southcot also noted Cross's conversion to Catholicism in his diary: "Crosse the famous pursevant died Catholick." Pollen, "The Note-Book of John Southcote," p. 109.

19. *C.S.P. Domestic*, 1635-36, p. 498.

20. Wadsworth wrote *The English Spanish Pilgrim* (1629), in which he described his student life at Saint-Omer College. See A. F. Allison, "John Heigham of S. Omer (*c.* 1568-*c.* 1632)," *Recusant History*, IV (October 1958), 228.

21. *D.N.B.*, XX, 425-26; *Dodd's Church History*, II, 429.

22. *D.N.B.*, XX, 426.

23. *C.S.P. Domestic*, 1633-34, p. 319.

24. *Ibid.*, 1643-44, p. 232.

25. Caraman, p. 173.

26. *D.N.B.*, XX, 426.

27. P.R.O., P.C. 2/49, p. 208, 16 September 1638. See also *C.S.P. Domestic*, 1637-38, pp. 75-76, 451.

28. Stocks and Stevenson, III, 322.

29. *C.S.P. Domestic*, 1635-36, p. 498. The court defined the duties of its pursuivants as "discovering and apprehending priests, jesuits, and schismatical recusants, seizing popish and seditious books, and apprehending delinquents questioned for incest, adultery, and other great crimes punishable by ecclesiastical authority."

30. *Ibid.*, p. 329.

31. *D.N.B.*, XIII, 1010-11; see Morse's diary in the "Papers relating to the English Jesuits," B.M. Add. MSS, 21203.

32. Caraman, pp. 113-14.

33. *C.S.P. Domestic*, 1636-37, p. 555.

34. Caraman, pp. 137-38.

35. The petitioners drew attention to the alarming spread of Catholicism in St. Giles's Parish. The papists, they said, "are so exceedingly multiplied that in that part of the parish called Bloomsbury there are as many or more than Protestants." *C.S.P. Domestic*, 1636-37, p. 499.

36. *Ibid.*, pp. 8, 499, 519. The witnesses specified the crimes committed by Newton, Mayo, Gray, and Wadsworth.

37. Leyburn to Bishop of Chalcedon, 26 May 1637, W.C.A. MSS, A Series, XXIX, ff. 51-53.

38. P.R.O., Roman Transcripts, Conn Correspondence, Series I, 31/9/124, 12 March 1637. The transcripts of Conn's letters are also in the B.M. Add. MSS, 15389-92.

39. *C.S.P. Venetian*, 1632-36, pp. 217-18, 274.

40. Albion, p. 165.

41. *D.N.B.*, I, 1041-43. Sir John Bankes (1589-1644), born in Cum-

berland, was educated at Queen's College, Oxford, but he left in 1607 without taking a degree to read law at Gray's Inn. He practiced law from 1614 to 1634, except for brief terms in the Commons in 1624 and 1628. He became Attorney-General in 1634 and carried on his duties with moderation, caution, and brilliance.

42. Bodl. Bankes MSS, 44/56–57, 1588–95, and 44/7–9, November 1635.

43. *Ibid.*, 44/7, Michaelmas Term, 1635.

44. *Ibid.*, 44/8, 1635.

45. *C.S.P. Domestic*, 1635–36, p. 326.

46. *Ibid.*, pp. 327–28.

47. *Ibid.*, p. 329.

48. *Ibid.*, p. 326.

49. *Laud's Diary*, p. 55. Cf. Rushworth, II, 380; Gardiner, *History of England*, VIII, 238.

50. *C.S.P. Venetian*, 1636–39, pp. 324, 254–55; Rushworth, II, 453; Thomas D. Hardy, II, 895. These decrees threatened the severest penalties against anyone who heard mass in the Queen's chapel (5 November 1637); forbade proselytization by Catholic priests and laymen (20 December); and extended the penalties to loss of property and possible execution for those who administered the sacraments according to the Roman rite (January 1638).

51. Thomas Gage (d. 1656), called Thomas de Sancta Maria, studied abroad at English Jesuit seminaries before becoming a Dominican at Vallodolid about 1612. While at Loreto, Italy, in 1641, according to his own statement, he renounced his vows and left the Catholic Church after becoming skeptical over the miracles attributed to the picture of the Virgin Mary at the shrine in Loreto. Gage's fame lies in the publication in 1648 of a book remarkable for his century, *The English-American: . . . or, A New Survey of the West Indies* (*D.N.B.*, VII, 793–95). An interesting sidelight on Gage's career is that after he left the Catholic Church he himself became an informer and sent some of his former colleagues to the gallows. See the Introduction by Thompson to his edition of *Thomas Gage's Travels in the New World*.

52. Gage, *Some Remarkable Passages Relating to Archbishop Laud*, pp. 3–4.

53. Thomas Gage later related the incident to Windebank, who told him that "John Gray was a knave."

54. *C.S.P. Domestic*, 1637–38, pp. 511–12, 519.

55. P.R.O., P.C. 2/48, p. 271, 26 January 1637. Gray was first imprisoned in January 1634 for "misbehaving him selfe in a certaine search." W.C.A. MSS, Anglia A, VIII, f. 69, 10 January 1634.

56. P.R.O., P.C. 2/49, p. 47, 30 March 1638; P.C. 2/50, p. 277, 31 July 1639, and p. 319, 29 September 1639. Two months earlier, the pursuivant John Wragg was jailed in the Fleet for two days (P.C. 2/50, p.

102, 3 May 1639). A Jesuit named John Browne, who was arrested in 1640, described Wragg as "the greatest Knave in the Countrey, for mony he would doe any thing, he carried in his pouch a number of Citations, and when he pleased for mony dismissed any one." Browne, *A Discovery of the Notorious Proceedings of William Laud.*

57. *London's Intelligencer,* 17 July 1644 (British Museum King's Pamphlets, No. 167), p. 242.

58. Forbes, p. 88.

CHAPTER EIGHT

1. Albion, p. 198. I have relied greatly in portions of this chapter on the work of Gardiner and Albion.

2. Gardiner, *History of England,* VI, 361.

3. W.C.A. MSS, A Series, XXVI, ff. 235–38, 22 June 1632.

4. Leyburn to Bishop of Chalcedon, 8 April 1634, *ibid.,* XXVII, ff. 425–28.

5. *Ibid.,* XXVI, ff. 235–38, 22 June 1632.

6. *C.S.P. Venetian,* 1632–36, p. 350.

7. Strafford, I, 389.

8. *C.S.P. Venetian,* 1632–36, pp. 350, 355.

9. Mathew, *Catholicism in England,* p. 83; Albion, p. 43.

10. Rant to Thomas Mayo, 16 October 1626, W.C.A. MSS, Roman Letters, f. 15.

11. Southcot to Bishop of Chalcedon, 11 April 1632, *ibid.,* A Series, XXVI, f. 162.

12. P.R.O., P.C. 2/42 (1632) and 2/51 (1640), *passim.*

13. Leyburn to Bishop of Chalcedon, 22 May 1636, *ibid.,* XXVIII, ff. 405–6; Gardiner, *History of England,* VIII, 140.

14. *D.N.B.,* XXI, 633–37; *Dodd's Church History,* III, 59.

15. *C.S.P. Domestic,* 1639, p. 291.

16. MS Diary of Henry Townshend, 1640–63 (copy), B.M. Add. MSS, 38490, f. 19.

17. B.M. Harleian MSS, 1219, f. 99, 1640: Charges against Windebank.

18. *Ibid.,* ff. 353–62: Contemporary copy of letter by Windebank to the Lord Chamberlain, February 1640.

19. Birch, II, 400–401.

20. P.R.O., P.C. 2/43, p. 59, 28 June 1633; Albion, pp. 200–201.

21. P.R.O., P.C. 2/46, p. 96, 25 May 1636, and p. 118, 1 June 1636.

22. Digby wrote, among other works, *A Conference with a Lady about Choice of Religion* (1638), and *Of the Immortality of Man's Soul* (1644).

23. Jones (alias Scudamore and Skidmore), born about 1575 in Llan-

winach, Brecknock, Wales, joined the Benedictines of St. Martin's, and after a brilliant D.D. at Salamanca and special studies at various monasteries, held important posts at Douay and Cismar. Thereafter he served as president general of the restored Anglo-Benedictine congregation (1619–21), prior at Douay (1621–25, 1629–33), and again as president general from 1633 until his death in 1635. Henrietta had him interred in her chapel at Somerset House.

24. Sitwell, pp. 133–66.

25. *C.S.P. Domestic*, 1628–29, p. 55; *C.S.P. Venetian*, 1626–28, pp. 85–86.

26. W.C.A. MSS, A Series, XXVII, f. 428, 8 April 1634.

27. *Ibid.*, ff. 495–96, 30 September 1634: Agreement between Edward Bennett and Leander Jones.

28. Albion, p. 149.

29. *C.S.P. Venetian*, 1636–39, pp. 302–3.

30. Berington, ed., *The Memoirs of Gregorio Panzani*, pp. 142–45.

31. *Ibid.*, pp. 146–47.

32. *Ibid.*, pp. 168–69. Windebank suggested that the English Church might unite with the Roman Church if three concessions were made by the Pope: (1) Communion should be given in both kinds; (2) mass and other offices should be said in English; (3) the English clergy should be allowed to marry.

33. *Ibid.*, pp. 171–72.

34. *Ibid.*, pp. 174–75.

35. Leyburn to Bishop of Chalcedon, 21 January 1635, W.C.A. MSS, A Series, XXVIII, f. 5.

36. Southcot to Fitton, 20 November 1635, *ibid.*, ff. 175–76; M. Pougny to Bouthillier, 12 December 1635, P.R.O., Baschet's Paris Transcripts, 31/3/68, ff. 263a–b.

37. Copies are in the B.M. Add. MSS, 36448, ff. 41–42, and in W.C.A. MSS, A Series, XXVIII, ff. 163–68, 17 November 1635.

38. See the Venetian ambassador's analysis of the agreement in *C.S.P. Venetian*, 1636–39, pp. 68–69.

39. Charles wanted the restoration of his brother-in-law, Frederick, to the Palatinate, and dispensation for a marriage between one of Frederick's daughters and the King of Poland. Berington, *Memoirs of Panzani*, p. 206.

40. *C.S.P. Venetian*, 1636–39, pp. 302–3; Guilday, pp. 247–49.

41. Albion, p. 159.

42. Leyburn to Edward Bennett, 3 September 1636, W.C.A. MSS, A Series, XXVIII, ff. 523–26.

43. *C.S.P. Venetian*, 1636–39, pp. 217–18.

44. *Ibid.*, p. 120. "The Puritans . . . carefully observe Coneo's proceedings and artfully try to make his Majesty jealous of him . . . saying

that [he] . . . may form conventicles and plots against . . . the general quiet of the realm."

45. Birch, II, 330.

46. Conn to Cardinal Barberini, 9 April 1637, P.R.O., Roman Transcripts, 31/9/124.

47. *C.S.P. Venetian*, 1636–39, pp. 148–49.

48. *D.N.B.*, IV, 945–46; Clarendon, I, 232.

49. Hughes, "The Conversion of Charles I," pp. 113–25.

50. Gardiner, *History of England*, VIII, 238.

51. *Ibid.*, p. 239.

52. Birch, II, 170; Gillow, III, 666.

53. Weber, pp. 24–25, 30, 272–74.

54. Albion, p. 99.

55. *C.S.P. Domestic*, 1634–35, pp. 159–60.

56. P.R.O., P.C. 2/46, pp. 95–96, 25 May 1636.

57. James Lees-Milne, *The Age of Inigo Jones* (London, 1953), pp. 86–89; J. Alfred Gotch, *Inigo Jones* (London, 1928), p. 163; *D.N.B.*, X, 1004. It is not clear just how much of the design was actually by Jones. There are sketches by him of an altarpiece, a niche, and a screen, but these were perhaps done for an earlier chapel at Somerset House, designed for the Infanta and later renovated for Henrietta Maria. The old Somerset House was demolished in 1775.

58. Isaac D'Israeli, *Commentaries on the Life and Reign of Charles the First, King of England*, 5 vols. (London, 1828), II, 234–35; Birch, II, 306–8.

59. W.C.A. MSS, A Series, XXVIII, ff. 195–96, 9 December 1635; Strafford, II, 505.

60. P.R.O., Baschet's Paris Transcripts, 31/3/68, f. 269b, 19 December 1635.

61. *C.S.P. Venetian*, 1636–39, pp. 120–21.

62. Birch, II, 310–16.

63. *C.S.P. Venetian*, 1636–39, pp. 69–71.

64. William Laud to Oxford University, 28 June 1641, B.M. Add. MSS, 11056, f. 80. In this letter Laud says: "my name [is] disperse, and grosly abused, by the multiplicitie of Libellious pamphlets, and my selfe bad from my . . . accesse to the . . . [Catholics] . . . And 'tis vox populi that I am popishly affected."

65. *Laud's Diary*, p. 39.

66. *C.S.P. Venetian*, 1636–39, pp. 358–59.

67. Gardiner, *History of England*, VIII, 239.

68. Father William West described St. Winifred's Well as a "place . . . famous to all this Kingdome, as well Protestants as Catholicks, and whither Catholicks of all degrees flock dayly in great multitude, and now more than ever" (W.C.A. MSS, A Series, VIII, f. 85, 12 July 1632).

The following year the Bishop of St. Asaph complained in his annual report to Laud that "the Number and Boldness of some Romish Recusants increaseth much in many Places and is encouraged by the Superstitious and frequent Concourse to Winifred's Well," *Laud's Diary*, p. 524.

69. Albion, p. 217.

70. *C.S.P. Domestic,* 1639–40, p. 88.

71. *Ibid.,* 1633–34, pp. 577–79.

72. P.R.O., P.C. 2/48, p. 163, 29 October 1637; *C.S.P. Venetian,* 1636–39, pp. 358–59. The Venetian ambassador gave four reasons for the Council's proclamation of December 20, 1637: (1) the Catholic liturgy was exercised with excessive liberty in Catholic homes; (2) the people were annoyed at the Court conversions to Catholicism, particularly Lady Newport's; (3) Laud wished to offset Scottish charges that he sought to convert England to Roman Catholicism; (4) it was suspected that Conn had promised Laud a Cardinal's hat if he would support a modified oath of allegiance.

73. Strafford, I, 426.

CHAPTER NINE

1. Gardiner, *History of England,* VII, 304–15, 373.

2. P.R.O., Baschet's Paris Transcripts, 31/3/71, f. 23, 3 March 1639. A list by Windebank of the original muster of foot and horse, 20,942 men in all, is given by county in the Bodl. Clarendon MSS, XV, f. 80 (1638?).

3. P.R.O., P.C. 2/51, pp. 34–36, 26 November 1639. This is a list of approximately 120 peers and gentry, Catholics and non-Catholics, who contributed money in the summer of 1639.

4. King Charles to Windebank, 17 May 1639, Bodl. Clarendon MSS, XVI, f. 112. For other comments on the state of the treasury, see Windebank to King Charles, 24 May 1639, *ibid.,* ff. 126a–b.

5. Bruce, p. ix.

6. George Gage to Windebank (1639?), Bodl. Clarendon MSS, XV, ff. 76–77.

7. Champney to the English Catholic Clergy (copy), 12 December 1638, *ibid.,* ff. 54a–b.

8. Champney to English Catholics (copy), 2 January 1639, W.C.A. MSS, A Series, XXIX, ff. 145–46.

9. Henrietta Maria to English Catholics (copy), 17 April 1639, *ibid.,* f. 257. Another copy is in the B.M. Sloane MSS, 1470, ff. 37a–38b. It is also printed in the anonymous pamphlet, *A Coppy of . . . the letter*

sent by the Queenes Majestie concerning the collection of the Recusants Mony for the Scottish Warre, Apr. 17. 1639. I am indebted to Dr. D. Rogers for allowing me to see this pamphlet from his personal library.

10. Bruce, p. x.

11. B.M. Sloane MSS, 1470, f. 38a.

12. *C.S.P. Venetian,* 1636–39, pp. 535, 545; *C.S.P. Domestic,* 1639, p. 189.

13. *C.S.P. Venetian,* 1636–39, p. 535.

14. Conn to Cardinal Ferragalli, 22 July 1639, P.R.O., Roman Transcripts, 31/9/124, ff. 243–44.

15. Same to same, 18 March 1639, *ibid.,* f. 233.

16. *C.S.P. Venetian,* 1636–39, pp. 358–59, 545.

17. Albion, pp. 421–22.

18. Anstruther, "Lancashire Clergy in 1639," pp. 38–39.

19. A contemporary copy of this document, dated simply 1639, is in the B.M. Sloane MSS, 1470, ff. 41–53. Another copy, worded somewhat differently, is in the Bodl. Rawlinson MSS, D. 720, pp. 27–34, 1639.

20. B.M. Sloane MSS, 1470, ff. 41–53.

21. *C.S.P. Domestic,* 1638–39, p. 623.

22. Anstruther, "Lancashire Clergy in 1639," p. 39.

23. *Hidden Workes of Darkenes Brought to Publike Light,* pp. 191–93.

24. *A Coppy of . . . the letter sent by the Queens Majestie,* n.p.

25. Anstruther, "Lancashire Clergy in 1639," p. 38.

26. P.R.O., P.C. 2/51, pp. 34–36, 26 November 1639.

27. Wedgwood, p. 250.

28. *C.S.P. Domestic,* 1639, pp. 73–74.

29. *Ibid.,* 1639–40, p. 99.

30. Bodl. Clarendon MSS, XVII, ff. 80–81: Petition by Recusants to King Charles, August 1639.

31. P.R.O., Roman Transcripts, 31/9/124, f. 239, 13 May 1639.

32. B.M. Sloane MSS, 1470, ff. 41–53, 1639, point 14.

33. Contemporary copies of the letter are in the B.M. Add. MSS 37157, f. 33, 1639, and in the P.R.O., Roman Transcripts, 31/9/124, ff. 242–43, 15 July 1639.

34. Conn to [?], *ibid.,* 31/9/124, ff. 238–40, 13 May and 7 June 1639.

35. *C.S.P. Domestic,* 1638–39, pp. 291–92.

36. W.C.A. MSS, A Series, XXIX, ff. 289–90, 19 February 1640.

37. Historical Manuscripts Commission, *The Manuscripts of Rye and Hereford Corporations,* p. 175.

38. *C.S.P. Domestic,* 1638–39, pp. 229–30. This is a note of measures taken for the defense of the country.

39. P.R.O., P.C. 2/49, p. 301, 16 December 1638.

40. Wedgwood, p. 272.

41. *C.S.P. Venetian,* 1636–39, p. 536.

42. Bruce, p. xv.

43. Gardiner, *History of England,* IX, 173; Champney to Bishop of Chalcedon, 6 August 1640, W.C.A. MSS, A Series, XXIX, f. 340.

44. Bruce, pp. xxi–xxiii.

45. *C.S.P. Venetian,* 1640–42, 75.

46. William Trumbull MSS, Miscellaneous, XLI, No. 120: Articles of Cessation between England and Scotland at Ripon, 1640.

47. Letter of an Alderman of Newcastle to a Friend, 8 September 1640, *ibid.,* XX, f. 48.

48. Christie, p. 33; *C.S.P. Domestic,* 1639–40, pp. 42, 246.

49. *C.S.P. Venetian,* 1640–42, pp. 78–79.

BIBLIOGRAPHY

MANUSCRIPTS

Berkshire Record Office, Reading, Berkshire:
    William Trumbull MSS
Bodleian Library, Oxford University, Oxford:
    Clarendon MSS
    Rawlinson MSS
    Sir John Bankes MSS
British Museum, London:
    Additional MSS
    Egerton MSS
    Hargrave MSS
    Sloane MSS
    Stowe MSS
Public Record Office, London:
    Baschet's Paris Transcripts
    Privy Council Registers
    Roman Transcripts, Panzani and Conn
Westminster Cathedral Archives, Archbishop's House,
       Westminster Cathedral, London:
    A Series
    Roman Letters

PRINTED SOURCES

Acts of the Privy Council of England. Vols. XL–XLII (1625–28).
    London: Stationery Office, 1934, 1940.
Albion, Gordon. *Charles I and the Court of Rome, A Study in 17th
    Century Diplomacy.* London: Burns, Oates, and Washbourne,
    1935.

Allison, Antony F., and Rogers, David M. *A Catalogue of Catholic Books in English Printed Abroad or Secretly in England, 1558–1640.* 2 parts. Bognor Regis: The Arundel Press, 1956.

Anderson, R. C., ed. *The Book of Examinations and Depositions, 1622–1644.* 3 vols. Southampton: Southampton Record Society, 1929–34.

Anstey, Christopher. *A Guide to the Laws of England affecting Roman Catholics.* London, 1819.

Anstruther, Godfrey. *A Hundred Homeless Years. English Dominicans, 1558–1658.* London: Blackfriars Publications, 1958.

———. "Lancashire Clergy in 1639. A Recently Discovered List among the Towneley Papers," *Recusant History,* IV (January 1957), 38–46.

———. *Vaux of Harrowden, a Recusant Family.* Newport: R. H. Johns, 1953.

Atkinson, J. C., ed. *The North Riding Record Society. Quarter Sessions Records.* 9 vols. London: For the Society, 1884–92.

Aylmer, G. E. "Charles I's Commission on Fees, 1627–40," *Bulletin of the Institute of Historical Research,* XXXI, No. 83 (May 1958), 58–67.

———. *The King's Servants. The Civil Service of Charles I, 1625–1642.* New York: Columbia University Press, 1961.

Bassompierre, François de. *Memoirs of the Embassy of François de Bassompierre.* Translated by G. W. Croker. London, 1819.

Bastide, Charles. *The Anglo-French Entente in the Seventeenth Century.* London: John Lane, 1914.

Bates-Harbin, E. H., (ed.). *Quarter Sessions Records for the County of Somerset.* 3 vols. Somerset Record Society, Vols. XXIII–XXV. London: Harrison and Sons, 1907–12.

Bellesheim, Alphons. *History of the Catholic Church of Scotland from the Introduction of Christianity to the Present Day.* Translated from the German by D. Oswald Hunter Blair. 4 vols. Edinburgh: Blackwood and Sons, 1887–90.

Bennett, J. H. E., and Dewhurst, J. C., eds. *Quarter Sessions Records with Other Records of the Justices of the Peace for the County Palatine of Chester, 1559–1750.* Record Society of Lancashire and Cheshire, Vol. XCIV. Chester: Record Society of Lancashire and Cheshire, 1940.

Berington, Joseph, ed. *The Memoirs of Gregorio Panzani: Giving an Account of His Agency in England, in the Years 1634, 1635, 1636.* Birmingham: Swinney and Walker, 1793.

————. *The State and Behaviour of English Catholics from the Reformation to the Year 1780.* London: R. Faulder, 1780.

Birch, Thomas. *The Court and Times of Charles the First.* 2 vols. Edited by R. F. Williams. London: Colburn, 1848.

Bone, Quentin B. "Henrietta Maria and the English Rebellion, 1609–1669." Unpublished Ph.D. dissertation, University of Illinois, 1954.

Bowler, Dom Hugh, ed. *London Sessions Records 1605–1685.* Publications of the Catholic Record Society, Vol. XXXIV. London: John Whitehead and Son, 1934.

————. "Some Notes on the Recusant Rolls of the Exchequer," *Recusant History,* IV (April 1958), 182–98.

Boyan, P. A., and Lamb, G. R. *Francis Tregian: Cornish Recusant.* London: Sheed & Ward, 1955.

Browne, John. *A Discovery of the Notorious Proceedings of William Laud, . . . Confessed by John Browne.* London, 1641.

Bruce, John, ed. *Notes on the Treaty Carried on at Ripon Between King Charles I and the Covenanters of Scotland, A.D. 1640, Taken by Sir John Borough, Garter King of Arms.* Publications of the Camden Society, Vol. XCI. London, 1869.

Bund, J. W. W., ed. *Calendar of the Quarter Sessions Papers: Worcestershire.* Vol. I (1591–1643). Worcester: Baylis and Son, 1900.

————. ed. *Diary of Henry Townshend of Elmley Lovett. 1640–1663.* 2 vols. in 4 parts. Worcester Historical Society, Vol. XXXIV. London: Michell Hughes and Clarke, 1915–20.

Calendar of State Papers and Manuscripts to English Affairs Existing in the Archives and Collections of Venice and in other Libraries of Northern Italy. Vols. XIX–XXV (1625–42). Edited by A. B. Hinds. London: Stationery Office, 1913–24.

Calendar of State Papers, Domestic Series, of the Reign of Charles I, 1625–1649. 23 vols. Edited by J. Bruce and W. D. Hamilton. London: Stationery Office, 1858–97.

Calendar of the Clarendon State Papers Preserved in the Bodleian Library. 4 vols. Edited by O. Ogle, W. H. Bliss, F. J. Routledge, and W. Dunn Macray. Oxford: The Clarendon Press, 1872–1932.

Caraman, Philip. *Henry Morse: Priest of the Plague.* London: Longmans, Green, 1957.

Care, Henry. *Diaconica: or An Abstract of All the Penal Laws Touching Matters of Religion.* London: G. Larkin, 1687.

Carlyle, Thomas, ed. *Oliver Cromwell's Letters and Speeches with Elucidations*. 3 vols. in one. London: Ward, 1846.

Challoner, Richard. *Memoirs of Missionary Priests, as Well Secular as Regular; And of Other Catholics of Both Sexes, That Have suffered Death in England on Religious Accounts from the Year of Our Lord 1577 to 1684*. London: Burns, Oates, and Washbourne, 1924.

Christie, William Dougall, ed. *Memoirs, Letters, and Speeches of Anthony Ashley Cooper, First Earl of Shaftesbury*. London: John Murray, 1859.

A Coppy of . . . the letter sent by the Queens Majestie concerning the collection of the Recusants Mony for the Scottish Warre, Apr. 17. 1639. London, 1641.

Cox, The Reverend J. Charles, ed. *Three Centuries of Derbyshire Annals, as Illustrated by the Records of the Quarter Sessions of the County of Derby, from Queen Elizabeth to Queen Victoria*. 2 vols. London: Bemrose and Sons, 1890.

Darnell, W. N., ed. *The Correspondence of Isaac Basire, D.D., Archdeacon of Northumberland and Prebendary of Durham, in the Reigns of Charles I and Charles II with a Memoir of His Life*. London: John Murray, 1831.

Davies, Godfrey. *The Early Stuarts, 1603–1660*. 2d ed. Oxford: The Clarendon Press, 1959.

The Dictionary of National Biography. Edited by Sir Leslie Stephen and Sir Sidney Lee. 22 vols. London: Oxford University Press, 1921–22.

Dietz, F. C. "Receipts and Issues of the Exchequer during the Reigns of James I and Charles I," *Smith College Studies in History*, XIII (1927–28), 117–71.

Digby, Sir Kenelm. *Private Memoirs of Sir Kenelm Digby, Gentleman of the Bedchamber to King Charles the First*. London: Saunders and Otley, 1827.

Dodd, Charles (pseud. for Hugh Tootel). *Church History of England from the Commencement of the Sixteenth Century to the Revolution of 1688*. Edited by M. A. Tierney, 5 vols. London, 1839–43.

Dodds, George E. "The Rural Constable in Early Seventeenth Century England." Unpublished Ph.D. dissertation, Yale University, 1939.

Ellis, Henry, ed. *Original Letters, Illustrative of English History . . . from Autographs in the B.M. and . . . Other Collections*.

11 vols. in 3 series. London: Harding, Triphook, and Lepard, 1824–46.

Ellis, T. P. *The Catholic Martyrs of Wales, 1535–1680.* London: Burns, Oates, and Washbourne, 1933.

Farrer, William, and Brownhill, J., eds. *The Victoria History of the County of Lancaster.* 8 vols. London: James Street, and Constable and Company, 1906–14.

Foley, Henry, ed. *Records of the English Province of the Society of Jesus.* 7 vols. London: Burns and Oates, 1882.

Forbes, Anthony H. "Faith and True Allegiance: The Law and the Internal Security of England, 1559–1714." Unpublished Ph.D. dissertation, University of California at Los Angeles, 1960.

Gage, Thomas. *Some Remarkable Passages Relating to Archbishop Laud, Particularly of his Affection to the Church of Rome. Being the Twenty-Second Chapter of Gage's Survey of the West Indies,* . . . London: S. Popping, 1712.

Gardiner, Samuel R., ed. *Debates in the House of Commons in 1625.* Camden Society Publications, 2d series, Vol. VI. London, 1873.

———. *History of England from the Accession of James I to the Outbreak of the Civil War, 1603–1642.* 10 vols. London: Longmans, 1883–84.

———. *What Gunpowder Plot Was.* London: Longmans, 1897.

Gerard, John. *What Was the Gunpowder Plot? The Traditional Story Tested by Original Evidence.* London: Harper, 1896.

Gerson, A. J. "English Recusants and the Spanish Armada," *The American Historical Review,* XXII (1917), 589–94.

Gillow, Joseph. *A Literary and Biographical History, or Bibliographical Dictionary, of the English Catholics from the Breach with Rome to the Present Time.* 5 vols. London: Burns and Oates, 1885–1902.

Green, M. A. E., ed. *Letters of Queen Henrietta Maria including her Private Correspondence with Charles the First.* London: Richard Bentley, 1857.

Guilday, Peter. *The English Catholic Refugees on the Continent, 1558–1795.* London: Longmans, Green and Co., 1914.

Hardy, Thomas Duffers, ed. *Syllabus of Rymer's Foedera.* 3 vols. London: Longmans, 1869–85.

Hardy, William L., ed. *Calendar to the Sessions Books and Sessions Minute Books and Other Sessions Records of the County of*

Hertford, 1619 to 1657. Hertfordshire County Records, Vol. V. Hertford: Charles Longmore, 1928.

The Harleian Miscellany, a Collection of Scarce, Curious, and Entertaining Pamphlets and Tracts, as well in Manuscript as in Print Selected from the Library of Edward Harley, Second Earl of Oxford. 10 vols. London: White, Murray, and Harding, 1808–13.

Haynes, Henrietta. *Henrietta Maria.* London: Metheun, 1912.

Hippeau, M. C., ed. *Mémoires inédits du Comte Leveneur de Tillières Ambassadeur en Angleterre sur la cour de Charles 1er et son mariage avec Henriette de France.* Paris: Poulet-Malassis, 1863.

Historical Manuscripts Commission. *The Manuscripts of Henry Duncan Skrine, Esquire, of Claverton Manor, Somerset.* London: Stationery Office, 1887.

———. *The Manuscripts of His Grace the Duke of Rutland, Preserved at Belvoir Castle.* 4 vols. London: Stationery Office, 1888–1905.

———. *The Manuscripts of Rye and Hereford Corporations; Captain Loder-Symonds, Mr. E. R. Wodehouse, M.P., and Others.* London: Stationery Office, 1892.

———. *The Manuscripts of the Earl Cowper, K.G., Preserved at Melbourne Hall, Derbyshire.* 3 vols. London: Stationery Office, 1888–89.

———. *The Montagu Papers, Second Series, Preserved at Montagu House, Whitehall.* 3 vols. London: Stationery Office, 1926.

———. *Report on the Manuscripts of the Family of Gawdy . . . Formerly of Norfolk.* London: Stationery Office, 1885.

The History of Wisbech [Wisbeach] with an Historical Sketch of the Fens and Their Former and Present Aspect. Wisbech: William Watts, 1833.

Houssaye, L'Abbé M., ed. "L'Ambassade de M. de Blainville à la cour de Charles 1er, roi d'Angleterre," *Revue des questions historiques,* Vol. XXII (January 1878).

Hughes, Philip. "The Conversion of Charles I," *The Clergy Review,* VIII (August 1934), 113–25.

———. *The Reformation in England.* 3 vols. New York: Macmillan Company, 1954.

Hulme, Harold. *The Life of Sir John Eliot, 1592 to 1632.* New York: New York University Press, 1957.

Hutchinson, Julius, ed. *Memoirs of the Life of Colonel Hutchinson*

Governor of Nottingham by His Widow Lucy. Revised by C. H. Firth. 2 vols. London: John Nimmo, 1885.

Huxley, Gervas. *Endymion Porter: The Life of a Courtier, 1587–1649.* London: Chatto and Windus, 1959.

Hyde, Edward, Earl of Clarendon. *The History of the Rebellion and Civil Wars in England.* 6 vols. Oxford: The Clarendon Press, 1847.

Hyland, St. George K. *A Century of Persecution Under Tudor and Stuart Sovereigns from Contemporary Records.* London: Kegan Paul, 1920.

An Introduction to the Following History Containing the Diary of the Most Reverend Father in God William Laud, Lord Archbishop of Canterbury: Extending from His Birth to the Middle of the Year, MDCXLIII. London, 1694.

Jeaffreson, John Cordy, ed. *Middlesex County Records.* 3 vols. London: The Middlesex County Records Society, 1888.

Jordan, Wilbur K. *The Development of Religious Toleration in England.* 4 vols. London: Allen and Unwin, 1932–40.

Journals of the House of Commons. Vol. I (1547–1628). [London], 1803.

Law, T. G., ed. *The Archpriest Controversy.* 2 vols. Camden Society Publications, Vols. LVI and LVIII. London: Longmans, 1896–98.

A Life of Archbishop Laud. By "A Romish Recusant." London: Kegan Paul, 1894.

Lomas, S. C., ed. *The Memoirs of Sir George Courthop, 1616–1685.* The Camden Society Miscellany, Vol. XI. London: The Royal Historical Society, 1907.

London's Intelligencer, 17 July 1644 (British Museum King's Pamphlets, No. 167).

Longstaffe, W. Hylton Dyer, ed. *The Acts of the High Commission Court within the Diocese of Durham.* Publications of the Surtees Society, Vol. XXXIV. Durham: George Andrews, 1858.

Madden, Richard. *The History of the Penal Laws Enacted Against Roman Catholics.* London: Thomas Richardson, 1847.

Magee, Brian. *The English Recusants: A Study of the Post-Reformation Catholic Survival and the Operation of the Recusancy Laws.* London: Burns, Oates, and Washbourne, 1938.

Makower, Felix. *The Constitutional History and Constitution of the Church of England.* London: S. Sonneschein, 1895.

Mathew, David. *The Age of Charles I.* London: Eyre & Spottis-woode, 1951.

———. *Catholicism in England, 1535–1935. Portrait of a Minority: Its Culture and Tradition.* London: Longmans, 1936.

———. *Sir Tobie Mathew.* London: Max Parish, 1950.

———. *The Social Structure in Caroline England. The Ford Lectures Delivered in the University of Oxford in Michaelmas Term 1945.* Oxford: The Clarendon Press, 1948.

Matthews, John Hobson, ed. "Records Relating to Catholicism in the South Wales Marches in the 17th and 18th Centuries," in *Miscellanea,* Publications of the Catholic Record Society, Vol. II. London: Catholic Record Society, 1906.

Meyer, Arnold Oskar. "Charles I and Rome," *The American Historical Review,* XIX (October 1913), 13–26.

———. *England and the Catholic Church under Queen Elizabeth.* Translated from the German by J. R. McKee. London: Kegan Paul, 1916.

Michaud, M., ed. *Biographie universelle ancienne et moderne.* 45 vols. 2d ed. Paris: Thoisnier Desplaces, 1843.

Mitchell, Williams M. *The Rise of the Revolutionary Party in the English House of Commons, 1603–1629.* New York: Columbia University Press, 1957.

Montague, Richard. *Appello Caesarem, or An Appeal to Caesar.* London: 1625.

———. *A Gag for the New Gospel? No: A New Gag for an Old Goose* . . . London, 1624.

Neale, J. E. *Elizabeth I and Her Parliaments.* 2 vols. New York: St. Martin's Press, 1958.

———. *Queen Elizabeth.* London: Jonathan Cape, 1934.

Nédoncelle, Maurice. *Trois aspects du problème Anglo-Catholique au XVIIe siècle avec une analyse des XXXIX articles d'apres Chr. Davenport et J. H. Newman.* Strasbourg: Bloud and Gay, 1951.

Nichols, John G., ed. *The Discovery of the Jesuits' College at Clerkenwell in March 1627–8.* The Camden Society Miscellany, Vol. II. London: The Camden Society, 1853.

Noake, John. *Worcester Sects; or a History of the Roman Catholics and Dissenters of Worcester.* London: Longmans, 1861.

Notestein, Wallace. *The English People on the Eve of Colonization.* New York: Harper & Brothers, 1954.

————. *The Winning of the Initiative by the House of Commons.* London: Oxford University Press, 1924.

Notestein, Wallace, and Relf, Frances Helen, eds. *Commons Debates for 1629.* Minneapolis: University of Minnesota Press, 1921.

Oman, Carola. *Henrietta Maria.* London: Hodder and Stoughton, 1936.

Ornsby, The Reverend George. *The Correspondence of John Cosin, D.D. Lord Bishop of Durham: Together with Other Papers Illustrative of His Life and Times.* 2 parts. Publications of the Surtees Society, Vol. LII. Durham: Andrews and Company, 1869–72.

————. ed. *Selections from the Household Books of the Lord William Howard of Naworth Castle: With an Appendix Containing Some of His Papers and Letters, and Other Documents, Illustrative of His Life and Times.* Publications of the Surtees Society, Vol. LV. Durham: Andrews and Company, 1878.

Page, William, ed. *The Victoria History of the County of Durham.* 3 vols. London: James Street, and the St. Catherine Press, 1905–28.

Pastor, Ludwig von. *The History of the Popes.* English ed. edited by Ralph Francis Kerr. Vols. XVIII and XIX. London: Kegan Paul, 1929.

Peyton, S. A., ed. *Minutes of Proceedings in the Quarter Sessions Held for the Parts of Kesteven in the County of Lincoln, 1674–1694.* Vol. I. Publications of the Lincoln Record Society, Vol. XXV. Lincoln: Ruddock and Sons, 1931.

Pollen, J. H. "The Accession of James I," *The Month,* CI (1903), 572–86.

————. *The English Catholics in the Reign of Queen Elizabeth, 1558–1580.* New York: Longmans, 1920.

———— ed. "The Note-Book of John Southcote from 1623 to 1647," in *Miscellanea,* Publications of the Catholic Record Society, Vol. I. London: Catholic Record Society, 1905.

Prynne, William. *A Brief Survay and Censure of Mr. Cozens His Couzening Devotions.* . . . London, 1628.

————. *Hidden Works of Darkenes Brought to Publike Light, or A Necessary Introduction to the History of the Archbishop of Canterburie's Triall.* London, 1645.

————. *The Unlovelinesse of Love-Lockes* . . . London, 1628.

Ratcliff, S. C., and Johnson, H. C., eds. *Warwick County Records.* 8 vols. Warwick: L. Edgar Stephens, 1935–47.

Read, Conyers. *Mr. Secretary Cecil and Queen Elizabeth.* New York: Alfred A. Knopf, 1955.

———. *Mr. Secretary Walsingham and the Policy of Queen Elizabeth.* 3 vols. Oxford: Oxford University Press, 1925.

A Rebuke to the High-Church Priests, for turning the 30th of January into a Madding-Day, by Their Railing Discourses Against the Revolution . . . London: S. Popping, 1717.

Relf, Frances Helen, ed. *Notes of the Debates in the House of Lords Officially Taken by Robert Bowyer and Henry Elsing, Clerks of the Parliaments, A.D. 1621, 1625, 1628.* Publications of the Camden Society, 2d series, Vol. XLII. London: Royal Historical Society, 1929.

Ross, Dorothy Jean. "The Country Justice in English Local Government During the First Half of the Seventeenth Century," Unpublished Ph.D. dissertation, McGill University, 1939.

Rous, John. *Diary of John Rous, Incumbent of Santon Downham, Suffolk, from 1625 to 1642.* Edited by M. A. E. Green. Publications of the Camden Society, Vol. LXVI. London: The Camden Society, 1856.

Les royales ceremonies faites en l'édification d'une chapelle de Capuchins à Londres en Angleterre, dans le Palais de La Royne. Rheims: Nicholas Constant, 1633. (British Museum pamphlet, North Library.)

Rushworth, John. *Historical Collections of Private Passages of State, Weighty Matters in Law, Remarkable Proceedings in Five Parliaments. . . . 1618 . . . 1629.* 7 vols. London, 1721.

Ryan, Clarence J. "The Jacobean Oath of Allegiance," *The Catholic Historical Review,* XXVIII (1942), 159–83.

Sheppard, William. *A New Survey of the Justice of the Peace His Office.* London: Printed by J. S., Fleet Street, 1659. In the British Museum, Collection of Pamphlets, 1659–60.

Sitwell, Gerard. "Leander Jones's Mission to England, 1634–5," *Recusant History,* V (January 1960), 133–66.

Smith, Alice Kimball. "The English Country Clergy in the Early Seventeenth Century." Unpublished Ph.D. dissertation, Yale University, 1936.

Soden, Geoffrey. *Godfrey Goodman, Bishop of Gloucester, 1583–1656.* London: S.P.C.K., 1953.

Stanfield, Raymond, ed. "The Archpriest Controversy," in *Mis-*

cellanea, Publications of the Catholic Record Society, Vol. XXII. London: Catholic Record Society, 1921.

The Statutes, from the Twentieth Year of the Reign of Henry III . . . to the Second Session of the Sixty-fourth Year of Queen Victoria. 20 vols. London, 1888–1909.

Stocks, Helen, and Stevenson, W. H., eds. *Records of the Borough of Leicester, Being a Series of Extracts from the Archives of the Corporation of Leicester, 1603–1688.* 3 vols. Cambridge: The University Press, 1923.

Strafford, Thomas Wentworth, Earl of. *The Earl of Strafforde's Letters and Despatches with an Essay Towards his Life by Sir George Radcliffe . . .* Edited by William Knowler. 2 vols. London: William Bowyer, 1739.

Strickland, Agnes. *Lives of the Queens of England from the Norman Conquest.* 6 vols. London: Bohn Library, 1901.

Sutcliffe, M. *The Unmasking of a Masse-monger. Who in the Counterfeit Habit of S. Augustine hath cunningly crept into the Closets of many English Ladies . . .* London: Nicholas Bourne, 1626.

Talbot, Clare, ed. *Miscellanea, Recusant Records.* Publications of the Catholic Record Society, Vol. LIII. London: The Catholic Record Society, 1961.

Thomason Tracts. No. 50. British Museum (December 1654).

Thompson, J. Eric S., ed. *Thomas Gage's Travels in the New World.* Norman: University of Oklahoma Press, 1958.

Trevor-Roper, H. R. *Archbishop Laud, 1573–1645.* London: Macmillan, 1940.

Verney, John. *The Life and Death of that Matchless Mirrour of Magnanimity and Heroick Vertues Henrietta Maria de Bourbon . . .* London, 1669.

Weber, Kurt. *Lucius Cary Second Viscount Falkland.* New York: Columbia University Press, 1940.

Wedgwood, C. V. *The King's Peace, 1637–1641.* London: Collins, 1955.

Willson, David Harris. *King James VI and I.* London: Jonathan Cape, 1959.

Index

INDEX

Abbot, Archbishop George, 41, 63, 94, 98
Abergavenny, Henry, Lord, 64, 87
Advice of a Catholic to his Fellow-Catholics in England, The, 31
Agard, Henry (jailer of Derby Prison), 110
Albion, Gordon, 135, 181
Allegiance, oath of, 13–15, 25, 84, 136, 139–40, 144, 149
Allen, Captain George, 46
Allen, Cardinal William, 84, 172–73
Ambassador, Tuscan, *see* Salvetti, Amerigo
Ambassadors, French, *see* Bassompierre, François de; Blainville, Marquis de; Châteauneuf, Claude de; Chevreuse, Duc de; d'Effiat, Marquis; Fontenay-Mareuil, Marquis de
Ambassadors, Spanish, 8, 83, 125. *See also* Gondomar, Count
Ambassadors, Venetian, 49, 83, 98, 125, 135ff, 144, 147, 160. *See also* Pesaro, Signor; Rosso, Andrea
Ange of Soissons (Capuchin), 168
Anglesea, Elizabeth, Countess of, 123
Anne of Denmark, 11, 31
Apostles' Creed, 52
Archpriest controversy, 84–85. *See also* Blackwell, George; Jesuits
Armada, Spanish, 2
Arminianism, 34, 71ff. *See also* Commons, House of; Laud, William; Montague, Richard; Parliament
Armstrong, Robert (Dominican), 177
Arrowsmith, Edmund, trial and execution of, 112–13
Arundell, George (Dorset recusant), 155
Arundells of Wardour, 78, 88
Asby, William (informer), 138
Astley, Sir Jacob, 157

Babington Plot, 2, 8
Bacon, Sir Edmond, 96
Bagno, Cardinal Gianfrancesco del, 145
Baillot, Nicholas (recusant teacher), 118
Baker, Stephen, 106f
Baltimore, Lord, 87, 155. *See also* Calvert, George; Calvert, Leonard
Bankes, Sir John, 123, 129, 179–80
Baptisms, Catholic clandestine, 91, 97, 102, 115–16
Barberini, Cardinal Francesco, 141f, 145
Barrault, Jean, Bishop of Bazas, 54
Basile of Rheims (Capuchin), 168
Bassompierre, François de, 47–50 *passim*
Beaulieu, residence of Charles I at, 37
Beddingfield, Sir Henry, 155
Benedictines, 55, 81, 116, 142, 146, 154; strength of, 68; financial welfare of, 79–80; and archpriest controversy, 84
Bérulle, Père de, confessor to Henrietta, 25, 27
Berwick, Peace of, 157–59
Birkenhead, William (pursuivant), 123
Birkhead, George, 84
Bishop, Dr. William, 85, 173
Bishops, Anglican, 12, 34
Bishops' War, 150–60 *passim. See also* Catholics; Scotland
Blackwell, George, Archpriest, 15, 84
Blainville, Marquis de, 37–42, 124–25
Blaise of Paris (Capuchin), 168
Blount, Richard, Provincial of English Jesuits, 85–86, 116f
Boteler, John, Lord, 145
Bradley, Richard (recusant teacher), 118
Brett, Arthur, 143